STRIPPED AND SCRIPT

STRIPPED AND SCRIPT

Loyalist Women Writers of the American Revolution

KACY DOWD TILLMAN

University of Massachusetts Press

AMHERST AND BOSTON

ISBN 978-1-62534-432-8 (paper); 431-1 (hardcover)

Designed by Sally Nichols
Set in Minion Pro and Baskerville
Printed and bound by Maple Press, Inc.

Cover design by Milenda Nan Ok Lee
Cover art by Marcus Stone, *The Letter, 1877* (oil on panel). Private Collection.
Photo © Christie's Images / Bridgeman Images

Library of Congress Cataloging-in-Publication Data
Names: Tillman, Kacy Dowd, 1980– author.
Title: Stripped and script : loyalist women writers of the American
Revolution / Kacy Tillman.
Description: Amherst : University of Massachusetts Press, 2019. | Includes
bibliographical references and index. |
Identifiers: LCCN 2018051831 (print) | LCCN 2019009624 (ebook) | ISBN
9781613766828 (ebook) | ISBN 9781613766835 (ebook) | ISBN 9781625344311
(hardcover) | ISBN 9781625344328 (pbk.)
Subjects: LCSH: United States—History—Revolution,
1775–1783—Women—Biography. | American women loyalists—Biography. |
American loyalists—Biography. | American prose literature—Women
authors—History and criticism.
Classification: LCC E277 (ebook) | LCC E277 .T55 2019 (print) | DDC
810.9/9287—dc23
LC record available at https://lccn.loc.gov/2018051831

British Library Cataloguing-in-Publication Data
A catalog record for this book is available from the British Library.

An earlier version of chapter 2 was published in *Women's Narratives of the Early Americas and the Formation of Empire,* edited by Mary MacAleer Balkun and Susan C. Imbarrato (New York: Palgrave, 2016) and is used with permission by Palgrave. Selections from chapter 3 appeared in *The Consequences of Loyalism: Essays in Honor of Robert M. Calhoon,* edited by Rebecca Brannon and Joseph S. Moore (Columbia: University of South Carolina Press, 2019), but have here been revised; these are published with permission from the University of South Carolina Press.

For Jackson, Andrew, Mom, and Dad

CONTENTS

vii

PREFACE

This book began with an ellipsis. The first time I ever read a published collection of letters—Flannery O'Connor's *The Habit of Being*—I was nineteen years old in an undergraduate course on "Religion and Literature." I noticed that the book was dotted with [. . .], suggesting the editor had excised portions of certain missives. When I asked my professor what the editor had removed and why, he told me if I was willing to drive 925 miles to Milledgeville, Georgia, to the O'Connor Special Collection Archive, I could find the answer for myself. I didn't know what he meant, as I had never even heard of special collections, much less archives. But I was curious, so I went. What I discovered there changed the trajectory of my career. Whole passages of O'Connor's letters had been strip-mined, the editor (at the family's request) cutting and pruning out chunks of racist ideology in an effort to groom the writer's public persona as a lovable, if not curmudgeonly, devout Catholic intellectual. I quickly became interested in the ways in which people develop their identities—and had their identities formed for them—through letters.

I learned a lot of hard lessons on my first pilgrimage to an archive. It's difficult to publish controversial scholarship about people whose relatives are still living. Holding old letters up to the light is taboo. Knowing when to use a cradle or a weighted string takes practice. And research (like labor, I would later learn) is tedium peppered with moments of trepidation and elation. This reflection on ellipses—on edited and amended political opinions and carefully crafted public personae—taught me to read for the stories that are not told behind the stories that are. To answer my questions about the art of epistolarity and journal-keeping, and the origins of such manuscript-based artistic performances, I looked to the golden age of letter-writing in America:

the eighteenth century. And that led me to look to the loyalists, who wrote the original elided narratives of the American Revolution.

This book tells the story of loyalist women writers who lost everything and used letters and journals to resist, record, and regain those losses. It suggests that these manuscripts provided a forum for political engagement that bypassed the printing press, making them ideal vehicles for dissenting voices. I want to offer a new definition of "loyalism" that opens a dialogue about the ways in which neutrality, disaffection, and pacifism—particularly for Quakers—were scripted as loyalism, often against the so-called loyalist's will. Women were frequently stamped as loyalists-by-association, stripped of their rights and security by property confiscation and rape, so it is important to me to study those women who wrote by their own hands their own definitions of loyalism. I am particularly interested in evaluating how manuscripts provided women a space in which they might carve out a political sense of self when other avenues were denied them.

I would not have been able to conduct this work without the help of colleagues, archivists, librarians, teachers, friends, and family. I am indebted to the Library Company of Philadelphia and the Historical Society of Pennsylvania, who made most of this research possible by awarding me a fellowship. I am also indebted to the University of Tampa for its Dana and Delo grants, which supported my scholarship as well. Many thanks to the UT librarians, especially Jeanne Vince and Marlyn Pethe, who helped me gather odd materials from far-flung places in the world. This work would not have been possible without the support of these historians/scholars/archivists/archives: Laura Keim and the Society of Colonial Dames at Stenton; Flannery Santos at the Burlington County Historical Society; Sally Van Sant Sondesky at the Bensalem Historical Society; Jim Green and Connie King at the Library Company of Philadelphia; Elaine Grublin at the Massachusetts Historical Society; and the Quaker and Special Collections at Haverford College. The idea for the book began as a seed in the American Antiquarian Society's (AAS) History of the Book Summer Seminar on Loyalty. I am in particular debt to Ed Larkin, Phil Gould, Paul Erickson, and everyone at the AAS who continued to be in touch after that formative time in my scholarship.

I will never be able to repay the Society of Early Americanists for the supportive environment they have created for young scholars, creating safe but accountable spaces at conferences that allowed me to develop my ideas. I am especially grateful for the mentorship and friendship of Laura Stevens,

Ivy Schweitzer, Sherry Harris, Lisa Logan, Sarah Schuetze, Susan Imbarrato, Karen Weyler, Mary McAleer Balkun, Theresa Strouth Gaul, Shirley Samuels, Carla Mulford, Eve Tavor Bannet, Sandra Gustafson, Chiara Cillerai, and Marion Rust. Thanks to my pen-pal and go-to sage, Chris Phillips. Thanks, Bert Emerson, my first conference friend, for helping me at the Huntington, and Jennifer Brady for saving me from loneliness in that windowless basement in Philadelphia. To Deb Holloway and Katie Foster: thanks for offering me room, board, and friendship so that I could visit all of those raccoon-haunted places in Bucks County. I was loved, supported, and held accountable by my friends, colleagues, and professors at Baylor University, the University of Mississippi, and the University of Tampa, all of whom contributed to this project. Thanks also to my professors-turned-colleagues who mentored me through the projects that would eventually become this book: Ralph Wood, Sarah Ford, Jay Watson, Karen Raber, Tom Hallock, Sheila Skemp, and Jaime Harker.

This book would not have come to fruition without my writing group to keep me accountable and offer its feedback. Thanks so much to Caroline Wigginton, Travis Foster, Abram Van Engen, Angie Calcaterra, Michele Currie Navakas, Wendy Roberts, and Greta LeFleur. You've read more of this book than anyone, and it is as much yours as mine. I also am indebted to several editors, including Joy A. J. Howard, Rachael Hoy DeShano, Margaret Hogan, and Brian Halley; thank you for helping me prepare my "rambling brat" (in print). Its blemishes amend, if so I could.

This book is dedicated to my son, Jackson, and my husband, Andrew, who gave me space, time, and love to research, think, and write. Andrew, you spent countless summers bringing Jackson to meet me at archives so that I could be with my family and continue doing what I love. You are my rock. Thanks also to Ruby Dowd, my grandmother, and Leta, Bill, and Michael Tillman, who loved me and my family through all of its trials. This book, finally, is for my mom and dad, Mary and Don Dowd. Dad, thanks for reading me those early American poems as bedtime stories. Mom, you raised me in a book-dry town and still kept me fed; thank you. You both taught me how to tell stories; I love you.

STRIPPED ﹏AND﹏ SCRIPT

INTRODUCTION

STRIPPED AND SCRIPT

I N HER REFLECTIONS on the American Revolution, the loyalist Ann
Hulton recounts how, one cold winter night, a crowd stripped Jonathan
Malcolm of his clothes, ripped his arms out of their sockets, covered him
with tar and feathers, and paraded him around town for hours. A group of
rebel soldiers in Roxbury, Massachusetts, stripped Edward Brinley's children
and wife, Sarah Tyler Brinley—then advanced in her pregnancy—and invited
other men to "see a tory woman" exposed.[1] Anna Rawle recalls how crowds
smashed her family's windows and looted their home because she refused to
celebrate the war's conclusion.[2] Elizabeth Drinker documents how the British
and Americans demanded she turn over blankets, supplies, one servant girl,
and, eventually, a room in her home—all requisitions she initially refused
but was forced to surrender.[3] Many women found themselves at risk of abuse
from all sides, regardless of their political ideology, and especially if they lived
alone. Not only were these women's bodies, friends, families, and properties
violated, but their manuscripts were as well. Women separated from their
loved ones by war extended their paper bodies across distances. These letters
bridged a gap or created an epistolary space for intimacy, despite the fact that
the revolution was a period when such intimate spaces could be violated by
interception, publication, and censorship.[4]

A common image in loyalist women's writing is stripped or violated
property, which included houses and land as well as bodies and books. This

image is key to understanding both the plight of loyalist women who stayed in America and the writing forms they used to construct their loyalties for themselves. Once stripped, these writers turned to script. By "stripped," I am suggesting that many loyalist women read and responded to the Revolutionary War through discourse that named and resisted violent abuse, oppressive political structures, and sexual assault. By "script," I do not just mean the process of writing but also the art of creating. "Scripted" is passive; "to script" is active. This term acts as both a noun and verb. It means to use manuscript writing to create a complex performance that was intended to achieve something, such as connection, evasion, protest, resistance, or allegiance. It refers to this kind of writing as performance, constructed either with careful thought and consideration or on the fly. And it also alludes to the writers' insistence on creating their own definitions of loyalty—to write into existence a space in which a person might construct themselves as a viable American citizen who is also loyal to the Crown, neutral about the war, or disaffected by all sides.

To script, for the set of writers examined here, often involves careful craftsmanship because of the possibility of discovery. Margaret Morris sent letters and diaries across enemy lines to her sister Milcah Martha (Patty) Moore; on the back of an envelope in 1781, she asks Patty to "Read This To Thyself Only."[5] She knew that her sister could not guarantee a private audience, since both Morris's and Moore's loyalties were suspect, so she scratched out names of people she did not want to implicate or offend, should the letter be read by someone other than her sister. She records and then erases. Loyalist letters plead for privacy and protection, even though no recipient could guarantee compliance with such requests. Such pleas protest losing another kind of privilege: the ability to control disseminated information and its intended recipient.

Letters that were not censored occasionally were destroyed. Rebecca Shoemaker in New York writes to her daughter Anna Rawle in Philadelphia that, though Rawle's friends had mailed letters to her, "every one that did not contain some interesting information in the Political line was destroyed."[6] After Sally Wister requests a letter of substance from her friend Deborah Norris, Norris explains that she cannot write her "sentiments freely." "Suppose some son of Adam, should unfortunately light upon it[?]" she asks. "How would his curiosity be gratified, with the perusal of such an uncommon manuscript[?]"[7] Shoemaker's, Norris's, and Wister's repeated returns to their loss of privacy challenges contemporary scholarship about loyalist rhetoric that has claimed most loyalists were concerned with the loss of "manhood."[8] Loyalist women in this archive did not emphasize the emasculation of the men in their homes but rather the penetration and violation of their own spaces, whether that space was on the printed page, in the home, or on the body.

Scholars have discussed at length the fact that rebels used the rhetoric of rape to justify war with England, but they have not discussed that loyalist women used this rhetoric to resist revolution as well. Rebels used rape metaphorically to protest legislation such as the Intolerable Acts. They told stories about violent British soldiers ravishing innocent young women to frighten Americans into joining the rebel faction once the war was underway.[9] Loyalist women likewise employed this rhetoric of rape—of the violated house and of the people in it—to frame the rebels, their supporters, and their cause as dishonorable, dangerous, and immoral. Loyalist women discursively returned time and again to the image of being stripped—of words, clothes, possessions, families, friends, land, rights, and privacy—because rebels publicly "outed" a loyalist all too often by stripping the so-called traitors naked and putting their bodies on display for the town to see.

Removing a loyalist woman's clothes served several purposes, including rape, torture, and humiliation, but stripping a woman was primarily a reminder about property. Women, children, and the clothes they wore were legal properties of the male head of household, so to strip a wife meant to strip the husband too.[10] Rebels believed that the most fitting punishment for a loyalist was to take from him all of his property so that he would be left completely impoverished and emasculated.[11] Loyalist women writers used these violent metaphors to highlight their inability to consent, neither to the people who entered their homes nor to the loyalties they or their families were assumed to hold.

My reading of loyalism as written on the body-as-property is informed by scholarship concerning the intersection of the female body and its role in national construction. Ruth H. Bloch notes that in the eighteenth century, virtue—a key characteristic of the republican citizen—implied piety, modesty, tenderness, self-discipline, sensibility, and chastity, and was inscribed on the female body. Rebels fashioned the nation as a potentially violated woman whose virtue must be protected at all costs to justify the rebellion. Katharina Erhard and Linda Frost have both noted that the nation "figured as a weak woman" whose violated body was metonymic of the vulnerable nation, "a Columbia figure over whom a whole host of potentially dangerous men attempt to gain power and control." Such a metaphor, David Waldstreicher argues, "completed the Federalist ideological alliance of the state, religion, and the nation." Michelle Navarre Cleary cites the problem with such logic, however: while the image of the nation as a female "reinforced the revolutionaries' attempt to represent a diverse people as a unified body politic," it paradoxically "placed the revolutionaries in the . . . position of using often independent female figures to depict a nation in which women remained socially, legally, and politically dependent."[12]

Loyalist families had more than just their clothes and virtue taken from them; the primary punishment for a loyalist was property confiscation and exile. Crowds, as well as Committees of Safety and Confiscation, meted out these punishments. These local committees "enforce[d] Patriot edicts" and were permitted to "ensure that dissidents were weeded out and brought to heel. Some committees acted as local governments and exercised significant power."[13] Initially, loyalist women were not at risk for loss in the same ways the men in their families were. This was particularly true when loyalist men who were exiled left behind their wives and daughters. At the war's inception, eighteenth-century British society did not view women as political creatures, since "they had no property that could be confiscated and were not expected to have political opinions."[14] Elizabeth Maddock Dillon explains that many of these assumptions stem from biological determinism:

> That is, the difference between men and women is construed as natural (rather than cultural) and as derived from physiological distinctions between male and female bodies. Women are defined as essentially (biologically, ontologically) *prepolitical* beings whose very bodies and psyches preclude them from attaining the independence necessary for entry-level competence in the liberal political arena. In the simplest of terms, for instance, women's bodies have been described as insufficiently bounded; the penetrable female body is understood to be inherently lacking in autonomy, conjoined to children and dependent upon men.[15]

Committees did not ask married women to sign loyalty oaths in the beginning of the war because men assumed that women were tied to their homes and families, making them an extension of those places and people.[16] Their legal bodies were temporarily invisible under coverture, their political identities subsumed by their husbands' identities. Effectively, women left behind had already been stripped by this law before the war began.

This invisibility enabled and disabled these women from certain political actions. "Considered weak and childlike," Judith Van Buskirk confirms, "females could go where few males dared because they were considered no threat. And since women were supposed to succor the distressed, it struck the British as natural that they should supply the unfortunates in prison with food and clothing. A man hanging around the city's prisons was usually suspect; a woman was not."[17] Some men left their wives while they fled abroad because they incorrectly assumed that state assemblies would spare their dependents. Crowds and committees quickly realized that when they tortured a woman, destroyed her property, or confiscated her house, "they were striking a blow against an absent enemy: her husband," and thus, against England itself.[18] Loyalist women left behind were political surrogates for their husband's loyalties. Women became visible just when the rebels needed to punish loyalist husbands, fathers, brothers, or sons. Once alone, without the protection of their family or their community, many of these women lost everything, including their clothes, children, husbands, houses, property, dignity, clout, faith, and their "covered" status under the law. Such is the context for most of the letters and diaries featured in this book; many of these loyalist writers put pen to paper to make sense of, cope with, or fight against these losses.

As the revolution became more heated, the definition of treason changed to be either gender-neutral or women-inclusive to suggest women could be just as politically dangerous as men, which also served to dissolve the statutes of coverture.[19] I argue throughout this book that this shift from coverture to exposure is important because, just at the time that women became politically visible, they became capable of being treated as legal citizens with their own rights. And just as they became eligible for those rights, state assemblies endeavored to deprive them for those official bodies' own gain. Epistolary/diurnal practices allowed women to script their loyalties for themselves when they were not offered the opportunity to do so in patriarchal spaces such as courtrooms, state assemblies, or Congress. These self-expressions also made women vulnerable just as they granted women agency. This book examines how women used and were used by these manuscript spaces—how they shaped and manipulated their publicity and privacy, and how they circulated the only bodies over which they possessed any semblance of control: their paper bodies.

My understanding of confiscation has benefited from several recent projects that have done recovery work of the treatment loyalists received at the hands of these committees and other rebels.[20] Maya Jasanoff's *Liberty's Exiles,* for example, notes that sixty thousand exiles—including fifteen thousand black enslaved people—escaped persecution by fleeing to Canada, England, the Bahamas, West Indies, Africa, India, and East Florida, each forming a new arm of the British Empire. Just how many people identified as loyalists is almost impossible to quantify. If exile implies political affiliation, then based on Jasanoff's numbers, at least sixty thousand people could be counted among the number of people historians might consider loyalists. (These numbers have also been challenged because they may have been based on some of the overexaggerated, myth-based nineteenth-century nationalist histories.)[21] My own problem with any numbers estimating the loyalists is that they assume a literal definition of loyalty, relying on things such as voluntary flight, forced exile, and property claims which, as readers will see throughout this book, does not capture all of the shades of loyalism. Nor does such a definition account for people such as neutralists, pacifists, and the disaffected who might have been counted among the loyalists but did not consider themselves to be of that affiliation. I would say the numbers are almost impossible to calculate, then, not only because of the unreliable statistics early historians constructed but also because scholars do not yet have an adequate means of pinpointing loyalist self-construction.

The scholars who have researched loyalist women often turn to second-hand sources to piece together their stories.[22] Janice Potter-MacKinnon's and Mary Beth Norton's invaluable research on loyalist women privileges commissioners' claims, military registers, land grants, and patriot committee minutes.[23] These sources are vital for determining sociohistorical information about where loyalists lived, why loyalists moved, and who loyalists were, but they are problematic for constructing how loyalists self-identified as such because they were not written by the loyalists. Claimants would deliver their stories to a commissioner orally (in an interview) or by writing them down (in a letter or petition), but the official claims that were filed—the claims that scholars have used to stitch together the loyalist women's perspective—were written by the commissioners, who summarized the stories they received, truncating these narratives to handle the sheer volume of material. Like Norton and MacKinnon, Linda Grant DePauw rightly notes that women "did not placidly follow the political views of their male relatives," but she does not discuss how these women chose to fashion loyalties of their own.[24] The assumption in these studies is that "rarely do the women tell their own stories in their own words."[25] In actuality, they do. I am arguing with this book that scholars have to know where to look—in loyalist letters and diaries—and how to read them when we find them.

RACE, CLASS, GENDER, AND THE DEFINITION OF LOYALISM

Most studies of loyalist history and literature begin with the question: what is a loyalist? This is a query that Philip Gould rightly names "deceptively complex."[26] How a person's loyalism was expressed, received, and regulated was influenced, in part, by their race, class, region, and gender. The letter-writers and journalists represented in this book were mostly wealthy, white women living in Philadelphia, New York, or the Delaware Valley.[27] Their privilege, connectivity to statesmen, and historical proximity to key revolutionary events means that their stories were preserved, largely because they had the resources and time to record such observations, and people deemed what they wrote worthy enough to keep.

The story of the path that black loyalists had to take to express their allegiance to the king is worthy of its own project. Take, for example, the *Book of Negroes*.[28] This fascinating manuscript, which is part ledger and part book of claims, is written by white men but records the narratives of black Americans who argued that they were loyalists so that they would receive passage out of New York City in 1783 under the British proclamations.[29] Many (though not all) were enslaved people or formerly enslaved people. Those who failed to make a convincing case were returned to the slaveholders who claimed ownership over their bodies, eradicating any title to their own political identity.

The story behind the text's creation and publication poses several problems for a project like this one, which focuses on self-authored letters and journals. The people who created the *Book of Negroes* were two groups of white men who sought to quantify black loyalists in such a way that it would further the officials' gain, rather than the loyalists' emancipation. The loyalists in the *Book of Negroes* did not write their own stories or sign their own names, but, rather, the white commissioners inscribed both if they deemed the black loyalists worthy. The book records the black loyalists' petitions and claims, but it also describes them like chattel.[30] Admittedly, the text is mediated at best, and compromised at worst. Frances Smith Foster and Barbara McCaskill suggest reading what they call "traces" of stories despite these complications; their work, along with that of Lara Langer Cohen and Jordan

Alexander Stein, has offered new ways of conceptualizing black print culture to include texts like the *Book of Negroes* in a study of American loyalism.[31] I attempted to read black women's loyalism through such traces, but this text and others are still problematic. The majority of the claimants were identified by the commissioners as male. Few of the petitions provided narratives that discussed why the claimants viewed themselves as loyalists. None of the documents in the *Book of Negroes* could be considered letters or journals. And all of the claimants were exiles, whereas I focus on the loyalist women who stayed behind. Most extant material on black loyalists concerns petitions by exiles or those enrolled in black loyalist regiments; most of the documents I found were written by black men.[32]

The petitions that black loyalists sent to Sir Guy Carleton would also be key for stitching together why black people aligned themselves with the Crown. Carleton offered freedom to anyone who would pledge their allegiance to the British government. Formerly enslaved people cited the Dunmore and Philipsburg Proclamations, which granted that asylum, to argue for their freedom and safe passage out of America and into English territory. One of the few self-authored letters by a black loyalist woman was written by Judith Jackson, a formerly enslaved person from Virginia. She wrote Carleton explaining why she believed the English should take her in:

> I came from Virginia with General Ashley When I came from there I was quite Naked. I was in Service a year and a half with Mr Savage the remaining Part I was with Lord Dunmore. Washing and ironing in his Service I came with him from Charlestown to New York and was in Service with him till he went away My Master came for me I told him I would not go with him One Mr. Yellback wanted to steal me back to Virginia and was not my Master he took all my Cloaths which his Majesty gave me, he said he would hang Major Williams for giving me a Pass he took my Money from me and stole my Child from me and Sent it [*sic*] to Virginia.[33]

How the British convinced black loyalists like Jackson to side with them so that they might be treated with basic decency is a story that scholars need to tell. Given the intricacies of the British proclamations, the reasons black loyalists enlisted and chose to flee with retreating British regiments, the format the petitions often took, the ways in which the rebels used black bodies as part of the peace treaty that ended the war, and the significance black loyalists placed on migration and exile as a political act, the subject deserves full consideration, and it would be most properly discussed in a project that did not use letters, journals, and region to limit the scope. With a broader scope or chronology, black loyalism might also be evaluated through auto-biographies such as those written by John Marrant, Boston King, John Ball, Joseph Leonard, David George, Moses Wilkinson, Cato Perkins, and Isiah Limerick.[34] For my purposes, however, none of these writers represent the loyalist woman's experience, and many of them wrote about finding meaning in religion after the revolution, rather than reflecting on what loyalist ideol-ogy meant to them during the war, which is the subject I am most interested in investigating.

Similarly, Native American loyalists are not fully represented in this project because the ways in which they had to negotiate loyalism and/or neutrality is a subject also worthy of a book-length study all its own, particularly given that Native American loyalties were negotiated by each nation, so discuss-ing Native "loyalism" would be a misnomer except in a few isolated cases.[35] And each nation often disagreed about the most prudent ways to engage or avoid engaging in the war while maintaining its own sovereignty.[36] As Lisa Brooks has noted in *The Common Pot,* Britain's Native allies were "left out of the [Treaty of Paris] entirely, and the Haudenosaunee were charged with transmitting a message to the Native nations in the Ohio Valley telling them to lay down the hatchet, without being able to offer any guarantee of their land rights."[37] Native allyship was often abused. Although rebels treated the Natives' alliance with the British as treason, as they did others who refused to support independence, few indigenous people categorized themselves as loyalists.[38]

Any study of Native women's loyalism should attend to Molly Brant, a Mohawk who convinced the Iroquois to side with the British. Brant's archive is complicated likewise in that much of what remains of her is filtered through white voices. One such letter in the Haldimand Papers in Canada is signed with the name "mari" (Mary) alongside the words "Mary Brant her mark"; both are in the handwriting of John Johnson. Two other letters in the Claus Collection also bear different handwriting, neither of which can be positively attributed to Brant.[39] Judith Gross also confirms that even the diaries and letters written by the people who worked with her as an agent are "largely speculative, occasionally bordering on prurient suggestion" regarding what she did and did not say or write.[40] Many scholars who want a sample of Molly's "voice" quote Maurice Kenny, a Mohawk, who wrote a series of poems adopting her persona in 1992.[41] But Gross rightly points out,

"The fragmentary Molly Brant who emerges from the pages of biographies of powerful males and the novels [and poems] inspired by those biographies is an enigma."[42] Although this archive is fascinating, and the ways in which Brant's voice has been filtered, sifted, and translated over time suggests the need for a discussion, that investigation falls outside of the parameters of this project.[43] Another book that does not use epistolary or journal-keeping as a limiter for evaluating loyalist women's self-expression could include other forms of print and material culture, in which case it would be possible to read additional types of public proclamations of loyalism by a more diverse group of women.

A loyalist is typically defined as "an American who favored reconciliation with Great Britain during conflicts that began with the Stamp Act and concluded with the War of 1812."[44] "Favoring reconciliation" often took place in public spaces, where the loyalist either constructed his affiliations for himself or had them constructed for him. The definition of a loyalist is problematic because it excludes anyone who lacked access to these spaces. Political alignment frequently took place via casting votes, taking oaths, writing laws, or publishing opinions—all privileges mainly granted to men. Many self-identified through the Loyalist Claims Commission, many claimants attempting to fit the definition of loyalty set out by the British government so that they might regain property or collect reparations, an economic incentive that further complicates why someone might claim to be a loyalist.[45]

Most studies of the American Revolution call rebels "patriots," which is somewhat anachronistic and problematic. The idea that patriots owed fidelity to the place in which they were born or lived currently, rather than to the country of their ancestors, developed as the war unfolded. So, while some people who favored independence may have adopted this new definition for themselves, loyalists would have defined a patriot as someone who pledged allegiance to England, not to the colonies. "Patriot" after the revolution has taken on a heroic (if not jingoistic) connotation, and it suggests that those who did not favor independence from Great Britain by definition also did not see themselves as pledging fidelity to their country, when, in actuality, they did. Loyalists saw themselves as faithful to the Crown, which was their own version of patriotism. Since the contemporary definition of patriot was still developing at this time and not used as widely as "rebel," I use the latter throughout this book when referring to those who argued for independence from England.

Gender makes the definition of loyalist and patriot even more complex and confusing to understand. Loyalist women are difficult to identify because they did not engage in public, political spheres in the same ways that patriot women did. The paradigm that notable scholars such as Jan Lewis and Linda K. Kerber have applied to female patriots of the American Revolution does not apply to loyalist women.[46] Kerber and Lewis have argued that women who served as republican mothers or wives were facilitating the nation's construction via these familial roles. Women branded as Tories, however, were uninterested in raising statesmen for the good of the nation, since they did not support the idea of nationhood in the first place. And although many loyalist wives tried to play the role Laurel Thatcher Ulrich has termed "deputy husband"—taking care of their husbands' homes, businesses, and properties while their spouses were away—local militia would not let them do so.[47] The homes these women tried to save were smashed, looted, and burned. Mobs evicted them if they tried to remain. Rebel militia confiscated the property these wives were expected to maintain. Rendered simultaneously invisible because of coverture and hyper-visible because of their family's dissent, loyalist women occupied a nearly impossible position: they could neither officially stake a claim in the revolution nor could they avoid being persecuted for their familial affiliations. Many of these women turned to letters, journals, and letter-journals—journals written as extended letters and often delivered to friends and family members—to enter conversations concerning their own political identities during the war.[48]

REVOLUTIONARY EPISTOLARITY

I am not only interested in discussing the metaphors through which loyalist women writers defined themselves; I am equally invested in examining the forms they used and adapted to disseminate their narratives. Loyalist women changed the format of letter-writing and journal-keeping to fit their purposes, and in so doing, they shaped these genres. Janet Gurkin Altman first defined epistolarity as "the use of the letter's formal properties to create meaning" and a "frame for reading letters" in novels.[49] I use the term slightly differently: to study the epistolarity of an actual (that is, not fictional) letter means to study its literary quality and form; to evaluate its language, audience, and circulation; and to identify its purpose and performance.

The form and genre with which I am most concerned is the letter-journal.

A letter-journal was a series of letters written in a journal addressed and delivered to a named recipient. This writing form might include a preface naming the audience, a salutation to the recipient that opened the book, or just an inscription that read, "Dear Husband" somewhere in the text (sometimes, naming the recipient only once and, other times, repeatedly addressing the named reader). The writer usually spoke to the reader as if he or she were present—"Oh my dear Tommy!" letter-journalist Sarah Logan Fisher writes, "how I long to see thee!"—with the letter-journal standing in the place of a face-to-face conversation.[50] I am not the first to identify or theorize letter-journals such as these. In their study of early American writing genres, Ronald J. Zboray and Mary Saracino Zboray call for more scholars to study new forms, particularly those that engage in "specific types of boundary blurring." The Zborays briefly mention "epistolary diaries" and "diary-letters," but they do not describe these genres in great detail.[51] Steven E. Kagle likewise touches on the existence of "epistolary diaries" in his larger study of Sarah Kemble Knight; he suggests that epistolary diarists were emulating epistolary novels popular in that era.[52] Helen M. Buss discusses Anna Jameson's *Winter Studies and Summer Rambles in Canada* as an "epistolary dijournal," which she defines as a genre that switches between journal, diary (two genres she reads as distinctive), and letter.[53] William Merrill Decker, likewise, has written about what he calls "epistolary diaries," which he defines as "open-ended narratives addressed to a reciprocating transoceanic readership."[54] Emily Dickinson kept "epistolary journals" as well, as Connie Ann Kirk has noted, though Dickinson's were part letter, poem, story, and diary.[55] In context, then, the loyalist writers that I discuss come from and extend a long tradition of genre-blending among writing forms, adopting and adapting their manuscripts as each situation demanded.

All of the writers in the archive I examine kept letter-journals when the war cut them off from communication with someone close to them. The space of the letter-journal allowed the writer to sustain (or maintain the illusion of sustaining) a relationship with someone that they had temporarily lost. Margaret Morris started her letter-journal for her sister Milcah Martha Moore when Moore moved away. Grace Growden Galloway began her letter-journal for her husband and daughter when they fled to London and she remained behind. Rebecca Shoemaker kept a letter-journal for her daughters when she was exiled to New York but they remained in Philadelphia. Most of these writers explained that the letter-journal was born for a very practical reason:

they were accustomed to writing or visiting their relatives, and they did not want to end communication just because letter-delivery routes were under siege. The idea behind the letter-journal was that delivering a small book one time, rather than several letters multiple times, exposed the writer to fewer opportunities for interception. Also behind the idea of the letter-journal was that writers hoped that border guards did not consider women's diaries as "epistles," so they might be less likely to search them for political information in the way letters were screened.[56]

Letter-journals, like other manuscript letters and diaries, often slip between genres for several reasons. The diaries that I studied frequently began as intimate diurnal practices, where the author addressed no one but herself, the journal, or, at best, some unnamed future reader, but then slipped into a letter to a friend when war broke out. Some of these letter-journals, such as Sarah Logan Fisher's, returned to being diaries because they were reunited with their loved ones. Some, such as Grace Growden Galloway's, never did because they never were. Helen M. Buss has suggested that people slip between journals, letters, and letter-journals because the genre combination "allows for multiple subject positions to be presented as coexisting rather than 'competing' and therefore eliminates the need for resolution into unitary selfhood that the term 'competing' implies."[57] In other words, it allows a writer to present multiple "selves" simultaneously. William Merrill Decker, on the other hand, suggests the slippage allows for one person to be in multiple places at the same time; not only are the writers updating someone across town or across the ocean, but they can address that person as if together with them while they are writing, which Decker names "virtual presence." Henry Adams does this when addressing his lover in his epistolary journal, calling his reader "her," which allowed him to play into the "trope of intimate conversation."[58] The letter-journalists that I discuss were invested in all of these endeavors: inviting intimacy across distance, calling up presence in absence, and sustaining myriad identities—social, familial, and political—for their loved ones.

The letter-journal was particularly important to loyalist women in wartime because it gave them the space to develop narrative as well as the time to decide when that narrative should be dispatched.[59] The journal's diurnal progression provided readers a gradual sense of character development that the letter did not usually afford. Safety Committeemen were often fashioned as the villains, the diarist the unwilling victim. The journal's linear narrative also allowed a coherent train of thought; unimpeded by the traditional letter's time lapse, the journalist was able to include minutiae and story development. The interesting details of war, such as descriptions of soldiers boarding in the city, cannons firing in the distance, or rations dwindling at an alarming rate, were often teased out. Not pressed for time by the servant standing in the doorway or the boat leaving the harbor, the writers had time to engage in a "moral vocabulary of warfare," which Jill Lepore explains in *The Name of War* as being "the language by which combatants justify their own actions while vilifying their opponents."[60] Letter-journals, if they were not burned or lost, allowed the writer to have the last say, existing beyond the death of the journalist. Loyalist women used this medium not only to recount their oppression but also to thank or praise charitable people who aided them, or to blame or chastise husbands who abandoned them. These journals permitted the writer to engage in the contest of interpretation—the war of words—via this writing form.

For the reasons listed above, I engage in some discursive slippage between letter, journal, and letter-journal in this book, though I attempt to be clear when a writer began moving among genres. My slippage exists because the distinctions that modern-day audiences make between autobiographical genres did not exist in eighteenth-century America. Ronald and Mary Saracino Zboray's research on early American manuscripts confirms that life-writing genres tended to shift and mix over time: "While the folks who created these literary items recognized each one's distinct form and purpose (the diary to record daily events, the commonplace book to transcribe extracts from printed matter, the household account book to track expenses, and the scrapbook to house clippings), in practice they often merged formats, so that a diary, for example, could easily morph into a scrapbook or a scrapbook into a commonplace book."[61] Letters that began as short entries meant only for the writer changed into long, sometimes footnoted essays that were occasionally published later in the writer's career.[62] Both Mercy Otis Warren and Judith Sargent Murray kept copybooks of letters they later incorporated into published essays or history textbooks. Sarah Logan Fisher began a so-called private journal at the war's beginning that she later mailed to her husband and his friends in prison. Deborah Norris Logan kept a journal that she excerpted in a published biography of her husband, George. These blended genres allowed the writer to adapt her purposes as she saw fit, using the most appropriate writing form for the subject and occasion.

For the writers I consider, the rich critical history of letters-as-performance is not only useful but the foundation on which my own interpretation rests.

Scholarship about epistolary art in England, France, Italy, and Turkey has proven that seventeenth- and eighteenth-century writers saw letters as paradoxical: they were both performative and genuine. Scores of letter-writing manuals, for example, claim to teach writers to affect a letter that reads as if it has been written spontaneously and straight from the heart, when, in actuality, every word and intonation has been carefully weighed.[63] Most scholars agree that letter-writers carefully constructed their epistles, whether those writers were enacting this performance by manipulating the letter's form or through speech acts.[64] Anyone who has studied letters has also recognized that letters were neither wholly public nor wholly private, existing in private-turned-public spaces where manuscripts circulated and were often made public by their readers, leading to a vast transnational and transatlantic eighteenth-century epistolary tradition.[65]

Inherent in most studies of epistolarity is the implication that letter-writers were geographically mobile, an assumption that I suggest does and does not apply to the loyalist women in this book. Loyalist women used letters to metaphorically cross political dividing lines, reaching out to friends and family members in other regions or an ocean away to maintain connections with them. The result in many cases, however, was not connectivity but further isolation, a confirmation of a growing suspicion that the loyalist left behind just might die alone, an exile in her own house, targeted by mobs and hostile soldiers from both sides of the war. Local militiamen policed loyalist letters after learning that women were smuggling intelligence in their correspondence. This surveillance inspired the writers to embrace paranoia, coded dialogue, and resentment borne from alienation, not the confidence, transparency, and greater intimacy across distances many epistolary scholars have claimed. The results were conflicted; some relationships adapted and thrived, while others withered and died. Anna Rawle maintained a close correspondence with her exiled mother, Rebecca Shoemaker, and their relationship resumed following the war's conclusion. Grace Growden Galloway, however, resented her husband Joseph's abandonment to such a degree that she stopped writing to him altogether, opting mid-letter-journal to begin addressing her daughter instead. Galloway never saw her family again. While some loyalists—particularly men—were able to flee their homes, many women stayed behind to guard the family property. Most scholarship about letter-writing is about the men who possessed the opportunity, money, and freedom to travel. This project is about the loyalist women who possessed none of these advantages.

PUBLICITY, PRIVACY, AND THE POST

In the chapters that follow, I return often to the concept of "audience" for letters and journals during this tumultuous time, whether or not these writers knew or hoped anyone would read their work. If manuscripts are vehicles for political engagement and permit women a space for self-fashioning, it seems important that someone would be on the receiving end of those entries. But just how public were these epistles? Part of the challenge in recognizing the significance of eighteenth-century epistolarity lies in defining the terms "public" and "private." As early American scholars already know—or at least suspect—letters and journals were rarely private in the sense that only the author or only the named recipient would read them. While the details within them may have been intimate, and although the writer may not have wanted others to read their content, these manuscripts were intercepted, edited, published with and without permission, read aloud, used in court, quoted, circulated, paraphrased, and discussed. Every writer who picked up a pen knew these conditions to be true. Keeping letters private was futile, even in the best of circumstances, but writing them was still completely necessary.

Letters composed in early America were public, in part, because no reliable form of letter-delivery existed. The British government established the first post office in North America in Massachusetts Bay in 1639, but this system allowed people to communicate with England, not other American colonies.[66] The Penny Post, which decreed that people could receive letters for a penny a piece, changed this situation. In 1685, King William III appointed the colonies' first postmaster in the hopes that such a position might unite Maryland, Virginia, New York, Delaware, New England, East and West Jersey, and Pennsylvania.[67] Post roads, which were former trade routes established by Native Americans, were put into use for mail delivery. Colonists did not trust the post office, however, because they thought the government would read their mail. They were right. "Throughout the long eighteenth century," Eve Tavor Bannet explains, "successive governments routinely treated the post office as a convenient depot of intelligence, by detaining, opening, copying and when necessary deciphering 'private letters' in transit to find out what was going on in the nation, in the empire and in the world."[68] Many people, as a result, elected to send letters by hiring private deliverymen or by relying on the generosity of travelers going in the same direction as the missive.

The Continental Congress established its own post office in 1775 and named Benjamin Franklin as the postmaster general.[69] Once the war was underway, writing letters was even more futile in terms of reliable delivery but, again, still completely necessary.

The revolution made the Franklin-era post office just as unreliable as its British-run counterpart. Both the British and American governments still read the private letters of people they suspected of treason. Ships carrying correspondence from abroad were attacked. Even if the enemy did not seize the mailbags sloops often carried, crews dumped letters into the ocean to protect the writers when they saw approaching hostile ships. If letters did make it to shore, they were still not guaranteed to reach their intended recipients. Deliverymen hung mailbags on the walls of coffeehouses so that people could grab letters—their own or someone else's—as they pleased.[70] War made many private letters public, as soldiers searched postbags for intelligence or evidence of treason. People delivering missives on horseback were ambushed for war intelligence. This intelligence was then circulated among congressmen, printed in meeting minutes, and occasionally published in newspapers (see chapter 5). When Benjamin Franklin acquired Governor Thomas Hutchinson's letters to Thomas Whatley, printers Benjamin Edes and John Gill published them as a *Copy of Letters Sent to Great-Britain, by His Excellency Thomas Hutchinson* (1773), permanently damaging Hutchinson's political career, since his correspondence suggested he meant to betray Massachusetts to England.[71]

Hutchinson's case was not isolated. When writing her husband John, Abigail Adams recognized that their letters discussing contested issues surrounding the new republic's formation might be intercepted and made public, which she feared would damage John's career and her own reputation. The Adamses' fears came true when in 1775, the British published in a loyalist newspaper John's letter describing his fellow statesmen as vain, capricious "fidgets."[72] Adams's derogatory opinions about his colleagues and the overwhelming nature of his assignment to organize a vast nation suddenly entered the public domain. A so-called private letter could become public overnight, without the writer's permission or intention. Letters that did arrive to their intended readers often did so weeks after the writers sent them, making the contents within them unreliable.[73] The anxiety that the news within the letter was outdated or that the letter itself could be seized and exposed, coupled with the writer's insistence on capturing the present moment, makes the letter a curious artifact. While few people trusted letter-writing, letters provided the only means of communication and, therefore, acted as one of the most important lifelines to friends and family who lived elsewhere.

Not all letters and journals were publicized without the author's say; many shared their work through letter- and journal-reading. When Margaret Morris asked her sister to "read this to thyself only," she was likely asking for "privacy," a concept Patricia A. M. Spacks distinguishes from things that are "public" and "private." "Privacy," she explains, "always implies at least temporary separation from the social body. . . . A man might feel the need to seek privacy in a public setting; a woman might find the private realm quite devoid of privacy."[74] Public and private need not be distinct when considering a letter or journal's privacy.

Acts of privacy or intimacy often still contained elements of rhetorical performance. What modern audiences might see as randomly capitalized words could point to the common rhetorical practice of reading letters aloud to a larger audience. Capitalization of the first letters of words served the letter's reader as a "guide to pronunciation or reading aloud," like "notes in music" or stage directions; capitalization taught readers which words to emphasize, much the same as underlining or italicizing today. (Spelling and capitalization had yet to be fully regularized in the late eighteenth century, and this also accounts for some of these textual inconsistencies.)[75]

Punctuation served a similar purpose, showing the reader where to pause or breathe when reciting a letter. Sarah Logan Fisher, for example, used punctuation and capitalization to underscore her distress when her infant son Billy was dying. She writes to God, crying, "Oh wretched Parent; how can I come at Resignation, as I ought, Oh my Baby, my dearest Baby, will thee leave me, what shall I do." The words she emphasizes here are "Parent" (which is what she calls God), "Baby," and "Resignation," as she struggles to accept that God would take her son away. This journal entry is riddled with commas, despite the fact that the rest of the journal is punctuated in a way that would be fairly standard today. The rhetorical effect is that one thought rushes into the next without a stopping point. The comma symbolizes her breath, and Rawle is struggling to catch hers. Her punctuation and capitalization change when Billy passes away. Her grief renders her speechless. Her punctuation speaks for her instead. She draws thick black lines in place of words, marking the passage of days with meaningful silence (fig. 1). Thus, these elements of expression and performance—the capitalization, dashes, commas, and other rhetorical devices—combine to express a sense of self that is anything but transparent. "These documents do not function as open windows on the soul," as Spacks has observed. "On the contrary, the windows all have, at the very least, Venetian blinds."[76]

Women's journals, like women's letters, also moved in and out of various realms of privacy and intimacy and could occupy all of these spaces and purposes simultaneously. Rebecca Steinitz rightly notes that a text could be for the diarist only, for an unnamed reader, for a friend, or for a selected group, all at the same time. The key to navigating these audiences was "containment." "The manuscript diary was not something to be randomly or broadly exposed," Steinitz explains; "rather, diarists took rhetorical and material steps to control and limit their audiences, even as they accepted and often embraced them." Such precautions allowed them to "police the bounds of intimacy" to the best of their abilities.[77] This slippage between audience types

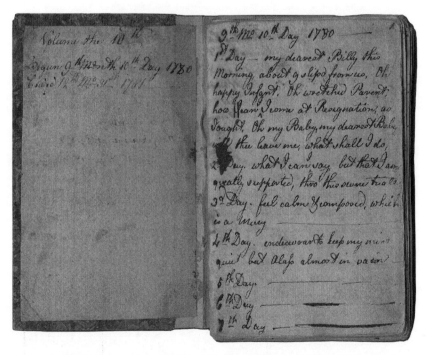

FIGURE 1. Grief lines in the journal of Sarah Logan Fisher. Sarah Logan Fisher Diaries, Historical Society of Pennsylvania.

is so readily observable to those of us who study early American manuscripts that one scholar even developed a sliding privacy scale, as follows:

1/ Diaries written solely for the diarist

2/ Diaries directly addressed to the diarist, or addressed to an external addressee who will never read the diary

3/ Diaries addressed to an external addressee who might read the diary

4/ Diaries which the diarist allows to be read by an intimate acquaintance

5/ Joint diaries

6/ Diaries addressed and presented to a group of friends

7/ Diaries which the diarist allows to be published, either posthumously or while living.[78]

The texts I have studied often begin at one level and end at another, occupying any number of levels in between before their conclusion, thus illustrating the ways in which the letter and journal participated in the literary, political, and printed public spheres while masquerading as private or intimate documents transmitted from one home to another.

Modern audiences should interpret a so-called private epistle or journal in the eighteenth century as intended for a select, rather than a singular, reading audience. The public sphere as Jürgen Habermas and Michael Warner defined it was not a viable outlet for loyalist women's self-expression because women discussing politics in coffeehouses and newspapers would have been taboo but also because these spaces were public, and loyalists were unwelcomed dissenters.[79] Engaging with the public sphere can be advantageous for those who desire change and seek a forum to demand it, but the public sphere causes complications for people who want to maintain the status quo. Any engagement with the public sphere after the treason laws were rewritten to punish dissenters painted a target on the loyalists' backs, drawing what some might have thought to be unwelcome attention. Such attention would have been particularly loathsome to loyalist women, who possessed not one but two reasons for sidestepping the public sphere. Not only were they risking their femininity, but they were also announcing to their communities that, if they were given the opportunity to pledge allegiance for themselves, they would voluntarily categorize themselves as traitors to the colonies. Public sphere theory paints these spaces between the family and the state as democratic safe havens; this theory claims that these were the places that gave birth to what would eventually be the new republic. But public sphere theory fails to account for the people who never wanted a democracy in the first place.

Paci⁵sm, Disaffection, and Loyalism's Sliding Scale

This book proves how and why loyalist women used letters and letter-journals as a vehicle for political engagement. It offers a departure from typical studies of the American Revolution in general, and of loyalism specifically, since most scholarship on war writing and rhetoric focuses on essays, pamphlets, and broadsides traditionally published by men. *Stripped and Script* notes that women used public, if not published, letters and journals to protest property confiscation, spy on rebel soldiers, deliver intelligence to the English, and free imprisoned pacifists, all while redefining notions of loyalty for themselves and others. My book uses a literary analysis of extensive archival correspondence by statesmen's wives, Quakers, merchants, and spies—particularly Grace Growden Galloway, Elizabeth Drinker, Margaret Hill Morris, Anna Rawle, Sarah Logan Fisher, Elizabeth Graeme Fergusson, and Deborah Norris Logan—to dismiss the privacy prejudice that has, for decades, excluded women from discussions about the war. It also offers a new definition of "loyalism" that goes beyond the white, male property owners who were privileged to possess the ability to vote, fight, or legislate.

The chapters in this book are divided by the different shades of loyalism as they existed in the manuscripts that I study. Some writers self-identified with the Crown. Some were treated as loyalists because they were married to male loyalists. Some were disaffected or neutralists but were treated as loyalists because they would not join a side. Chapter 1, "Scripting Disaffection," argues that most women were categorized as loyalists by blood or marriage and suggests that women who sought to distinguish their loyalties from their families used manuscript writing to do so. This chapter examines that argument through the journal of Grace Growden Galloway, a writer who used letters and a journal addressed to her daughter and husband to craft a disaffected identity that she hoped would save her social standing and considerable property in Philadelphia.

Chapter 2, "Scripting Pacifism," suggests that women's loyalties were also determined not only by their familial relationships but also by their religious affiliations. This chapter highlights the ways in which Quakers, specifically Sarah Logan Fisher and Elizabeth Drinker, reconstructed their political identities from traitors to pacifists in order to save themselves from prison and exile, convincing state assemblies that they were not loyal to England but to God.

Chapter 3, "Scripting Neutrality," explores the predicament of neutralists in the Delaware Valley. It illustrates how Margaret Hill Morris sought neutral ground in Burlington, New Jersey, but when she was denied the privilege of remaining uninvolved in the revolution, she used her letter-journal to script neutrality as she defined it.

"Scripting Loyalism," chapter 4, explains how some women used letters and diaries to become "active loyalists," or loyalists who sought allegiance to the Crown through an action they voluntarily undertook. In this chapter, that "action" involves delivery of intelligence between Anna Rawle, in rebel-occupied Philadelphia, and her mother, Rebecca Shoemaker, in loyalist-occupied New York. It also focuses on the ways in which loyalist women coded rape and sexual assault as political acts by which they might cast aspersions on the rebels' cause.

The penultimate chapter of my book features a loyalist woman who used her manuscript to convince the public and state assemblies that she was a patriot. "Scripting Patriotism" concerns Elizabeth Graeme Fergusson, a writer who delivered intelligence for the British but was so successful in her reinvention as a patriot that scholars today still classify her as one.

Stripped and Script concludes by tracing, not the evolution of the loyalist women's narratives but the disappearance of them. "Scripting Ellipses" examines the disappearance of the loyalist narrative through the writings of Deborah Norris Logan, who kept correspondence during the revolution and a journal after it. Logan's postwar journal—which served as a rough draft for two other history books and one biography—erases the loyalties with which she would have been affiliated during the war. The conclusion explains Logan's revisionist history of the American Revolution and suggests that loyalists may have been complicit in their own erasure from the nation's origin stories.

The majority of the women in this study were Quakers. Quaker loyalists are somewhat different from other loyalists because many initially wanted to stay out of the war altogether, citing pacifism, but the rebels forced their participation or punished them for their refusal, branding them as traitors. Local militiamen "requisitioned property, required military service or payment of a substitute, imposed loyalty oaths, and issued paper currency" that financed the war, and they refused to make exceptions for religious people. As Quaker historian Sydney V. James explains, "Passive noncompliance looked like covert disaffection to Revolutionary patriots."[80] Many Quakers were loyalists by default, at least at first. Some Quakers eventually embraced loyalism for themselves as the revolution progressed.[81] Because these loyalties were both actively assumed and passively embraced, Quakers throughout the colonies were rounded up, refused trial, jailed, and exiled. The letter-writers and journal-keepers who documented this treatment reflect a wide spectrum of reactions, ranging from disbelief and hopefulness to indignation, anger, and despair. Quakerism writ large during the American Revolution is not the primary preoccupation of my study, but the Society of Friends' commitment to pacifism informed the ways in which Quakers politically framed themselves and were framed by the founders, so the theories about the ways in which their religion informed their citizenship do play an integral role in this book.

Despite the fact that some of the Quakers in this project would not have self-identified as loyalists, they are nevertheless important for understanding the gradients of loyalties during the war. Some people assumed the loyalist label while some had it affixed to them without their permission or intent. Political identity was not always voluntary. History has focused largely on active loyalists, or loyalists who took some kind of action to align themselves with the British. Philadelphia assemblyman Joseph Galloway cast votes and wrote proposals to construct an American version of Parliament. James Rivington ran an eighteenth-century newspaper distributing loyalist propaganda. Some loyalists, on the other hand, were what I term "passive loyalists."[82] The line demarcating an active loyalist from a passive one was often crossed and blurred. The blanket term "loyalist" does not recognize the ways in which external bodies, such as lawmakers, confiscation committees, crowds, and townspeople, forced their will on people. There were loyalists-by-association, convicted by their connections to relatives (such as husbands or fathers) or to associations (such as the Society of Friends) who had been branded loyalists. Loyalists-by-association were identified in a number of ways, but these were the most prominent: nonimportation agreements, abjuration oaths, and kinship. Several loyalist women did self-identify with the British—acting as spies, merchants, and, in rare cases, soldiers—but many also had that label forced on them, at least at the beginning of the war. A woman branded a loyalist by someone else might later take up the label and adopt it for herself, or she might reject the label altogether and exchange it for another of her own fashioning. Many women convicted of loyalism thought of themselves as neutral. The distinction between loyalism actively or passively assumed became a gray area when the loyalist crossed from one category into the other or rejected them all, for any number of reasons. Much of this self-fashioning was constructed, for loyalist women, via writing. And much of this writing was circulated in manuscript form, which was then occasionally publicized, read aloud to an audience, revised and submitted to a press, or copied in books and submitted to friends or relatives.

I am not concerned only with recovery, although recovery is important if scholars are to comprehend the narrative of the nation's inception outside the scope of the perspective of white, propertied men. I read manuscript culture anew, creating a theoretical shift in the way people understand the medium of intimate political writing conducted in domestic spaces. This book insists that letters and journals were not only historical artifacts; they were also literary texts that writers used to construct the war's narrative. Envisioning these texts this way involves revisiting the construction and reception of this kind of eighteenth-century manuscript culture—how letters and diaries were drafted, edited, footnoted, circulated, read aloud, bound, and occasionally printed. Such a study revises what constitutes literary culture during the American Revolution by suggesting that unpublished, privately circulated manuscripts were political tools that were as vital as the books and pamphlets that have been credited with the formation of America's national narrative.

CHAPTER ONE

SCRIPTING DISAFFECTION

Grace Growden Galloway

I travel over 1,000 miles to reach the mansion of loyalist Grace Growden Gallo-way in Bensalem Township, Pennsylvania. One research grant, two car rides, one airplane, one train, and multiple sleepless nights later, I stand at the front door of the Growden Mansion with my tour guide, Sally, a volunteer for the Bensalem Historical Society. There's only one problem: the tenant who lives in the mansion will not let us in. She has, in fact, already slammed the door in our faces, reluctantly inching it back open only when Sally reminds her that allowing guests inside is part of her lease agreement. "Go away!" the occupant shouts. "This house is full of dead raccoons and it reeks. My husband is naked and refuses to put on pants. You can't come in." I begin to speak, but the tenant ignores me. She focuses on my guide, pointing a finger in her face. "The last time you were here, you brought those paranormal investigators. We can't have that. They stir up ghosts!" She punctuates this last accusation by slamming the door a second time. I turn to Sally for an explanation, but she refuses to meet my eyes. "I may have evicted her last night," she mumbles by way of explanation, which explains both the U-Haul and the tenant's terrible mood. "Great timing," I think, and I put both palms to the door. I lose any shred of dignity I may have once had and begin pleading for the woman to let me in. "Do you know about Grace Growden Galloway?" I shout through the wood. "She's fascinating, and I have to tell her story." Nothing happens for several beats. I turn to leave, but I pause when the door hinge creaks. The tenant stands there smiling, and this time she is looking at me. She crosses her arms, leans on the doorframe, and sizes me up. I surreptitiously wedge my foot between the door and the frame, aware that this might be the last opportunity I have to convince her to let me see the place where Galloway wrote her letters and journals. I can barely make out the hallway—which is long, dark, and raccoon-free. "Oh yeah, I know her," the tenant says, putting her shoulders back to stand up taller. "I was Galloway in our school play." And with that, she kicks my foot away and slams her door shut one final time. She does not open it again. I never get inside.

I TELL YOU THIS story not only because it is bizarre (and it is bizarre) but
also because this tenant acted almost exactly as Grace Growden Galloway
acted when the confiscation committee came to evict her over two hundred
years ago.[1] It is as if the house itself creates inexorable people. This tenant
embodied Galloway's resolve when asked to leave a place she believed to be
rightfully hers. She exemplified her entitlement, her defiance of the state, and
her resentment that anyone would breach her private space.

Galloway owned Trevose because it was gifted to her by her father, Lawrence
Growden (fig. 2). Growden ran the Durham iron furnaces, owned ten thousand
acres, and held a prominent position on the Pennsylvania Assembly. When
Grace married Joseph Galloway, who was also a Pennsylvania assemblyman,
Joseph inherited Grace's share of the property, which her father bequeathed to
his daughter following his death in 1770.[2] The trouble for the Galloways began
after Joseph argued that a centralized government, chosen from titled aristoc-
racy, would prevent the colonies from fomenting rebellion born from con-
tention.[3] The vote narrowly missed passing, but Joseph Galloway still became
the face of treachery, his vision of the colonies as an extension of the British
political system providing a useful foil for his opponents.[4] The Pennsylvania
Assembly viewed him as an unwelcome dissenter, and in 1774, it removed him
as speaker, replacing him with John Dickinson. The Galloways became the face
of treason. Crowds descended on Trevose but could not find the occupants,
who had fled ahead of the mob. Furious, they fired on the home, and the bullet
holes remain to this day. Joseph joined Sir William Howe's army in 1777 as an
intelligence official. He fled with Howe to England, his daughter Betsy in tow,
after he evacuated with the British troops. The Pennsylvania Assembly thereafter listed treasonous citizens whose property the state would seize if they failed
to pledge allegiance to the rebels before April 20, 1778, including that of the
Galloways. Grace was left in Bensalem Township to guard the family's estate.[5]
She refused to flee with her family because she assumed if she lived in the house
the commissioners wanted, the men would pity her as an abandoned wife and
leave her alone. She was wrong. She barricaded herself inside her home when
the men came to evict her and stood in the dark as they beat on her doors.
She would not be moved. It was this image of Galloway standing stock-still,
furious, immovable, that flashed before me when the tenant slammed the door
in my face. I had to smile. Galloway would be proud, I thought, that this tenant
would not go quietly from her house.

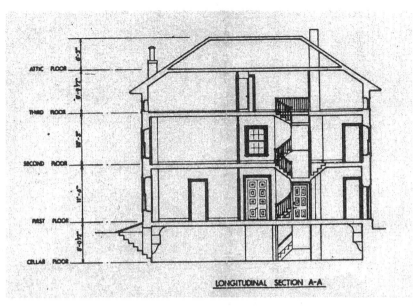

FIGURE 2. Trevose layout. Courtesy of Historical Society of Bensalem Township.

I read Grace Growden Galloway's journal as an alternative political space where Galloway could script her loyalties for herself. Her journal could easily be interpreted as simply the story of a miserable, abandoned wife, but when read this way, we miss her ingenuity as she attempted to manipulate the legal system, and we run the risk of overlooking her adept writing ability. The space she created was disaffected. That is, she used the space in her journal to cut ties with both the British Empire and the Americans opting, in the end, to abandon her families' loyalties. I also explore how a *feme covert*'s political, and sometimes literal, body became uncovered during the American Revolution. And, finally, I explore the metaphor that runs throughout loyalist letters and diaries from this period: the metaphor of forced entry of the home, body, and even the journal itself.

Studying the disaffected perspective during the American Revolution unlocks a series of rhetorical complexities about the way people saw themselves during the war. If pacifists eschewed war on moral grounds, and if neutralists wanted to opt out of making a decision altogether, the disaffected vehemently resented being placed in any political position in the first place. As a result, writing by the disaffected is often characterized by anger, hostility, and active rejection of both the loyalists and the rebels. Neutralists were unwittingly caught in the middle of a warzone, whereas the disaffected spoke out against both sides to decry the entire operation altogether. The former is passive; the latter is active.

The story of any war is often about the winners, occasionally about the losers, but rarely about those people in between. By saying this, I mean to emphasize an important fact: when we study the rhetoric of the disaffected—and Galloway's letters and journal is an example of this kind of rhetoric—we are able to glimpse a much more nuanced vision of the gradients of loyalty that existed in the moment between the Boston Tea Party and the dawn of the early national period. I want to further emphasize that to study this group of people means to study how Americans came to think of themselves as citizens of a nation, rather than emblems of an empire. This is the story of the space Grace Growden Galloway created to script her disaffection. This is also the story of that moment of hesitation that all citizens had—or still have—whether fleeting or permanent, as they reflected on what it meant to be asked to pledge allegiance to a country born out of violence, chaos, and betrayal.

STRIPPED PROPERTIES IN GALLOWAY'S JOURNAL

The fear and resentment that transformed Grace Growden Galloway's life between 1777 and 1779 dominates her journal, which documents the confiscation of Galloway's properties—her land and her body—and the evolution of Galloway's own loyalties. Galloway eventually explored her political quandaries, but the journal seems to have begun as a daily account of her ordeal during this troubling period, kept for her own information and well-being. In these passages, she rarely addressed a reader beyond the journal or herself, and she did not gloss or contextualize any of the people or events that she recorded. Galloway shifted to address Betsy, her daughter, as a named reader, at which point she began to explain her legal situation in detail. And, finally, Betsy received the journal after Galloway died, which further complicates the ways in which we might categorize this text's genre.[6] Much of the latter part of the journal documents Galloway's attempt to regain her daughter's inheritance, so it seems safe to assume that the journal that records these efforts was shipped to Betsy at her mother's request. We might then read this text as a posthumous letter-journal since it includes a salutation to Betsy, a valediction, and a series of messages in between that Galloway wanted dispatched to an intended recipient. We might just as easily, however, read it as a "contained" journal, as discussed in the introduction, insomuch as it was meant for a narrow/named reader, falling along the sliding scale of privacy and publicity somewhere beyond "for-the-author's-eyes-only" but before "published at her directive for a broad readership's amusement." At times, the journal moves between all of these categories, sliding between genres as Galloway negotiated various subject positions. I suggest that recognizing the ways in which Galloway manipulated and defied these generic conventions is more important than stamping her text as one thing or another. It is also important to note that she engaged in such slippage while trying to make sense of the impossible legal situation of the "covered" wife of an exile as well as distancing herself both from the Americans who stripped her of all she cared about and from the Crown who abandoned her.

Given that Galloway was suffering for her husband's loyalties, it is perhaps unsurprising that the majority of the journal is a discursive exercise attempting to achieve both ideological and literal separation from her husband. She strips herself of any ties to the man who caused her to suffer. She achieves this by remaining what I would describe as politically "still." She stays where she is, in Trevose, and remains steadfast in her refusal to swear allegiance to either side. In her version of what happens after the rebel men come to inventory the estate, Galloway emphasizes that she resisted all efforts to be moved. Galloway's journal opens by focusing on her treatment by the commissioners of forfeited estates—Robert Smith, Charles Willson Peale, William Will, Samuel Massey, and Jacob Schreiner—whom the Pennsylvania Assembly charged with arresting traitors and confiscating loyalist lands.[7] Pennsylvania chief justice Thomas McKean ordered these men to confiscate all of the property that Galloway inherited from her father: Trevose (400 acres), Belmont (550 acres), Richlieu (439 acres), and King's Place (312 acres).[8] The considerable amount of property involved in this confiscation would help finance the war and would send a strong message to people in the nearby area that no loyalist, no matter how wealthy, would be spared repercussions. On July 21, 1778, Grace Growden Galloway writes that McKean sent the commissioners, who "took an inventory of everything, even to broken china and empty bottles," because "they must advertise the house" as they intended to sell it. She writes that the committee would have to take her "by the force of a Bayonet" if they wanted her to leave.[9] Galloway rhetorically distances herself from any blame for this confiscation; she reminds Joseph that he is the cause of her suffering. His politics, not hers, have stripped her of her home, companions, and social standing. "I expect every hour to be turn'd out of doors, and where to go I know not," she writes. "No one will take me in, and all the men keep from me. . . . I am fled from as a pestilence," she laments, adding, "I have No friends."[10] Many of the women in my archive talk about loyalism and patriotism as a disease, and Galloway is no exception.

The infection, as characterized by these disaffected women writers, begins in a man's body—typically the body of an exiled or imprisoned husband, soldier, looter, or rioter—and spreads to the women and children who suffer by proxy. The writers framed their experiences in such a way that women's bodies became metonymic for their relatives' loyalties: they were exposed, violated, and humiliated so that the absent husbands were vicariously punished. These loyalties infected Galloway, eroding not only her body, which became sick with stress, but also her social standing. She was unaccustomed to asking for help, particularly since she was one of the wealthiest people in that region, so when she approached a "Mrs. [Polly] Wharton" to ask for transportation and boarding, she felt deeply ashamed. Her humiliation magnified when Wharton refused her request. Galloway reflects on the depth of her fall by saying, "My heart was ready to burst at the mean figure I must cut in begging to go to another persons house & be told I cou'd Not. . . . I was so Mortified & Troubled that I cou'd not sleep all Night about it."[11] Her greatest fears came true on August 3, 1778, when she received a letter from George Bryan, president of the Commonwealth of Pennsylvania, informing her that the state had officially confiscated her property, despite her husband not living there any longer and despite the only person occupying the home being supposedly apolitical as far as the law was concerned. The insomnia that Galloway mentions in relation to her endangered property is also present in the letters and diaries featured in the other chapters, particularly in those manuscripts written by passive loyalists. I return to this restlessness in chapter 2, when Sarah Logan Fisher connects her spiritual disquiet with the attacks on her home, and in chapter 4, when Anna Rawle refused to sleep until her house was safely secured, fearing the crowd outside would harm her family. As Galloway frames her legal battle for her family's estate, Joseph's loyalties spread to contaminate all aspects of her life, infecting her ability to rest, heal, and shed worry.

Perhaps unsurprisingly, 1778 also marked Galloway's entry into a lengthy discussion about the construction of the eighteenth-century political female, most notably in the absence of a still-living husband. She writes that she asked George Bryan why she was being punished for Joseph's vote. She then studied his reply to try to make sense of her situation, but, unfortunately, Bryan was just as confounded as she was. He writes,

> When a lady marries, (unless by a special reserve of her lands in the hands of Trustees, made before the contract,) the use and profits of the real estate belonging to her rests in her husband for and during their joint lives, and if children be born then for his life. This estate, so acquired by wedlock, the gentleman can sell. It may be seized by creditors and applied to their relief; And it may be lost by attaint, and then it devolves to the publick as a forfeiture. But the moment the husband dies it returns to the widow, or if she be deceased to her children or other heirs. . . . In every case of attaint for treason, support for the wife and children shall be awarded by the Judges of the Supreme Court, out of the estate of the husband. What may be thought proper in your case I profess myself very ignorant, yet it is probable it will be most convenient for you and the publick too, that such allowance be made out of the paternal estate, lost by you, for the uncertain term of Mr. Galloways natural life.[12]

Bryan's letter explains what Galloway already knew. The commissioners removed Grace Growden Galloway from her house because the name on the deed was Joseph's. Since he had committed a crime against Pennsylvania, the courts could—and did—decide to take what was his. Trevose would belong to Grace if Joseph were dead, but while he lived, the assembly felt justified in taking it from him. While Bryan could explain the court's logic, he admitted that her situation seemed odd. Joseph lived but was absent as an exile. Grace remained but was theoretically covered by a man who was not there to protect her. She would have to appeal for mercy as a wife with little authority of her own, emphasizing her status as a *feme covert,* casting herself as an unfortunate bystander in war.

Galloway did not take Bryan's advice. This moment is crucial because if students of loyalist women writers are going to understand how women achieved agency by using their pens, they need to make note of how those women navigated the men who attempted to control their limited options. Galloway framed herself as both helpless and willful, unmoved and defeated, all of which aptly describes the female loyalist's predicament. The commissioners' forced entry was a physical violation; Galloway described it as she would her own rape. The violation of her home was a violation of her body. When Charles Peale and his men arrived to evict her, Galloway writes that they "try'd every door but coud get none open," so "they went to the Kitchen door & with a scrubbing brush which they broke to peices they forced that open." They met with "the Women"—Galloway and her servants—"standing in the Entry in the Dark." These women were not running or hiding; rather, they had stayed to make their stand. While the committeemen were breaking down the door, Galloway went through the house and opened all of the windows she had previously barred, so when they finally entered the kitchen after much exertion, they saw that their first attempted point of entry was now completely unblocked. Galloway writes that this made them "very mad."[13]

Galloway failed to successfully bar the door, so she implemented a legal argument, likely the one written by George Bryan, to get them to leave. That did not work either. "I spoke first," she says, reminding her audience that she was doing all she could to control this situation, "& told them I was . . . ill." (She does not say what has made her ill, but she implies she is trying to appeal to their empathy. She hopes that they will not evict a sick woman.) Galloway "show'd them the opinion of the Lawyers. Peel [Peale] read it but they all dispised it & just said he had studied the Law & knew they did right." All of the legal opinions in the world could not save her. The men were not interested in her treatise on coverture and property ownership; they were there to throw her out and make a point to the community around her that no one was immune to these new laws. Again, Galloway stands her ground: "I told them Nothing but force shou'd get me out of My house. Smith said they knew how to Manage that & that they wou'd throw my cloaths in the street." Robert Smith in Galloway's recounting does not say if he means to strip Galloway of the clothes she is wearing, or if he means to take all that she owns and put it in the street, but since other loyalists had been punished both ways, Galloway likely understood the threat's full implications. Smith tells her that Grace had this humiliation coming to her not because of anything she had done but because Smith sought to be as cruel to her as Joseph was to others. Galloway writes that Smith "hinted that Mr G had treated people Cruely," which was why he was evicting her as publicly as possible. Galloway does not respond to these accusations; instead, she reiterates that Trevose is hers to own and sell. "I was at home & in my own House," she told Smith again, "& Nothing but force shou'd Drive me out of it." The committeemen see her threat as empty and mock her for it. Smith replies that she would not be the first woman he had forced to do something she did not want—another thinly veiled rape threat that Galloway fully understands. Specifically, "he said it was not the first time he had taken a Lady by the Hand an insolent wretch." Peale then called her chariot and asked her to get in it so that the driver could take her away. "Indeed I will not," she says, "nor will I go out of my house but by force." So, Peale then forced her to move. She writes that "he then took hold of my arm & I rose & he took me to the door." Galloway clung to the sides of the doorway and writes that she "said pray take Notice. I do not leave My house of My own according or by my own inclination but by forse & nothing but forse shou'd have made me give up possession."[14] I highlight the way that Galloway tells this story in her journal because it is metonymic of the ways in which she rewrote her own narrative to make herself the victor, rather than the evicted. It is important to compare how these writers scripted what happened alongside the alternative narratives—the white, male narratives that claim to tell the full story—if we want to understand how women attempted to construct their loyalties themselves.

Galloway framed this battle of wills as an issue of forced entry; she asserted that the issue was a metaphorical and literal violation of the home and the family inside. Men came into the parlor and kitchen, pushed their way into domestic spaces uninvited, and made threats of rape and confiscation that seemed to blend together. This was an intimate intrusion of her private space and of her family's legacy. By threatening to take both her mansion and her clothes (either what she was wearing, what she owned, or both), they stripped her of outward markers of wealth. But property loss cut deeply in many different ways. They were confiscating Betsy's inheritance, Grace's safe space, and at least one source of the Galloways' revenue (an apple orchard).[15] Galloway returned to her resistance in the journal, and this repetition suggests this part of her narrative is just as important as her removal. She told her audience— Joseph and Betsy, and anyone reading the work after them—three times that she refused to go quietly. When she interrupts her story to say, "Pray take notice," the implied second-person subject is twofold. She is talking to Peale and his committee, but she is also talking to her readers. "Remember," she is telling her readers, she did not give consent. No one asked her for her consent, but she did not voluntarily yield at any point. Her story suggests that, even though loyalist women refused or tried to refuse to grant access to the spaces and political ideologies they sought to control, external groups—such as legislators, confiscation committees, and crowds—ultimately regulated the loyalties that determined who possessed the right to entry.

FEMALE LOYALISM AND COVERTURE LAWS

Galloway's letter-journal reads like a legal treatise that challenges the eighteenth-century concept of coverture. The journal provided the space for her voice to be heard when other venues, such as courtrooms, were closed to her. William Blackstone's definition of coverture claimed that once married, "the husband and wife are one person in law: that is, the very being or legal existence of the woman is suspended during the marriage." The wife then lived under the husband's "wing, protection, and *cover*"; he is "her *baron, or lord*." On paper at least, a *feme covert* could not own property, make contracts, sue, or be sued. According to British law, wives, like children, were "dependents." A woman's political identity was suspended after marriage, but it was not erased. "When the cover is gone," after the wife's husband died, "she [could] pop back into view."[16] The political identity of the female loyalist's husband—his affinity for or loyalty to the English Crown—subsumed her own because of the law of coverture. Such a distinction mattered because what the British called "loyalty," the patriots called "treason," which was punishable by law. Historian G. S. Rowe confirms that as covered women, wives' "marital status and the nature of their criminal associations, in theory at least, cast their legal liability onto the shoulders of their husbands." Under English law, men went to court and prison on their wives' behalf. Coverture also implied that since women were incapable of taking political action independently or apart from their husbands, they should not have been able to suffer for their husbands' transgressions, which explains why many husbands left their wives at home in America to maintain the family property. Legal custom, however, did not always mirror legal theory. In theory, coverture stated that husband and wife were one person; in practice, they were occasionally accused or tried separately. Blackstone dubbed women "civilly dead," but before the nineteenth century, Pennsylvania tried 3,700 women in court. In some cases, courts treated women as people with a legal and political will of their own: "In 276 charges between 1750 and 1800 wives were prosecuted with husbands; in 266 prosecutions wives were alleged to have committed the same offense as their spouses."[17]

The Revolutionary War introduced new situations in which rebel-run legislatures deemed women capable of acting as legal entities independent of their husbands. The first situation concerned treason, and the second property confiscation. Susanna Adams of Philadelphia, Susannah Longacre of Coventry Township, and Rachel Hamer of Providence Township were convicted of treason separately from their husbands, but in other cases, only the husband was charged.[18] While the law occasionally punished the husband for his wife's crimes, it rarely condemned the wife for the husband's. To justify the latter, the courts would have had to recognize women as political figures in their own right so that the wives could suffer alongside their spouses. The courts tried women separately from men for treason so that, in Pennsylvania at least, the assemblymen could hold them liable. This decision meant that women's legal bodies became politically visible just when it became necessary for men to exploit them. Such an act threatened to strip those same women of any rank, wealth, property, or agency they might have gained via such a decision.

The second complex legal situation that proved difficult for rebel lawmakers and local committees concerned property confiscation. The colonial governments sought power through estate seizure, thereby proclaiming themselves to be legitimate authorities to the American people. Following the Intolerable Acts, provisional governments sought to bolster their economic infrastructure through seizure and sale of loyalist properties, which were often quite large. By November 1777, the Continental Congress was recommending confiscation to all the colonies. By April 30, 1779, two confiscation bills made these suggestions official acts: "An Act to Confiscate the Estates of Certain Notorious Conspirators" and "An Act for Confiscating the Estates of Certain Persons Commonly Called Absentees." The first sanctioned property seizure for twenty-nine officials; the second cast a much wider net, resulting in losses for thousands.[19]

The rebels did not initially deem women capable of independent political thought, so they did not require them to sign the association that declared loyalty to the colonies. But this presented a tricky question: how would the committee members know a female loyalist if they saw one? The Americans addressed this conundrum by expanding the "test laws," or loyalty oaths, to women throughout the colonies—specifically in New Hampshire, Massachusetts, New York, and South Carolina.[20] But once the rebel committeemen enacted their authority to both define other people's loyalties for them and punish them accordingly via exile or property confiscation, they did not know what to do with the exiles' wives, who often stayed behind to guard the family property. Some vigilantes and state committees alike treated women as if they had made a "choice of allegiance," a decision that had broad ramifications.

Ruling that wives were independent political beings capable of independent political actions would usher in questions about other legal rights, such as suffrage. Ruling that they were dependents and within their rights to keep their homes and property meant, essentially, returning the house and property to the loyalist husband.[21] Some colonial governments decided to address these questions by allowing loyalist wives to purchase their own family's property back from the rebels, requiring them to declare loyalty to America in order to take advantage of the offer. This solution caused more problems than it attempted to solve since many women's political identities were yoked with their families' identities. As soon as they pledged allegiance to the colonies, their property could be stripped a second time, and the women who purchased the property could be tried for treason in their own right. Such was the predicament of Grace Growden Galloway when she began her journal. If Galloway's journal provided her a space where she could script her loyalties—or her lack of them—for herself, to whom was this performance directed? Who did she hope would receive this legal treatise?

Most loyalist letter-journals possessed at least three audiences, and this stands true for Galloway. The first was the self. The second was the named audience, usually a relative. The third, however, was what I call the "unnamed reader," a term that could refer to a variety of people. Unnamed reader could be descendants who might inherit the journal, the social circle affiliated with the named audience, or more generic future readers: scholars, students, or historians. This journal's primary audience was Grace herself, the secondary audience was Joseph and Betsy, and the tertiary audience was Betsy's friends, Grace's descendants, and anyone else who might care to read her story. If we read her journal with these audiences in mind, we see that her legal proclamation of neutrality and independence would have been public. It would not have been public via a traditionally published venue through a printing press; rather, the journal was public in that it gave her access to the court of public opinion through which she sought the trial she was denied through coverture. This use of her journal was comparable to the ways in which other loyalist women used their letters and journals. Sarah Logan Fisher, featured in the next chapter, writes to herself, her husband, and her husband's friends, all at the same time. Margaret Morris, about whom I write in chapter 3, speaks to her sister, her sister's friends, and to posterity. Elizabeth Drinker wrote for herself and to the broader Philadelphia Quaker community, whom she knew published and circulated the journals of prominent people after they died. The journal's form offered the female loyalist the ability to address all of these audiences simultaneously. The hybridity of Galloway's chosen genre permits personalization and narrative unity while also allowing her narrative generic and political fluidity; that is, the journal's form allowed her text to take the form she needed it to take (journal, letter, legal treatise, open protest), address the people she needed to reach (self, relative, posterity), and assume the identity that was most advantageous or desirable at the time (mother, *feme covert*, disaffected, aristocrat).

Following her eviction, Galloway used her journal to form an argument that she made to the council: that she should not have been removed from Trevose for Joseph's treason. Galloway was (mostly) correct from a legal perspective. Trevose was hers, not Joseph's. Her father willed the house she lived in and the Durham lands to her when he died. When she married Joseph, she instructed her husband to keep her name on the property. Joseph, however, did not honor this request. Upon Grace's eviction and Durham's confiscation, Grace learned that her husband had signed the deed but left Grace off of it. "Had ye Deed for ye 24th share of Durham & find it made in J G's Name only," she writes Betsy when she discovers his betrayal. "Oh how has the Unhappy man injured me & my child[,] for this deed Cuts of[f] all ye water from me estate yet he was so base as to take it out of My family."[22] Still, she moved forward with her petition to the Supreme Executive Council in August 1779. She argued that Pennsylvania could not take away property she inherited from her father because, under coverture, the councilmen were only supposed to punish the person who could be considered capable of possessing a political identity in the first place. She wonders if she could purchase it back from the Supreme Executive Council so that her daughter might have some form of inheritance, writing, "it seems these people have not yet advertised it but if they do we Must buy it: the Unfair conduct of this man has quite . . . ruin'd me & as I cannot tell ye world I abuse the English Army for their base & treacherous conduct."[23]

Galloway was attempting to achieve several things simultaneously in these entries. In some ways, she was trying to separate her loyalties from Joseph's so that she could regain the property she believed to be rightfully hers. In other ways, she was further yoking her legal body to his, claiming that as Joseph's dependent, she should not have had to suffer for his political beliefs. Finally, she turned on the English (not the American) army for her treatment, suggesting that she and other loyalist wives were being unjustly punished—a lament she sent her daughter because she "cannot tell the world." Galloway's journal entry, which indicts both the British and the rebels, marks the beginning of an ideological shift that she did not complete until the end of her life, a move to an alternative space that aligned neither with the British Empire nor with America, but rather apart from them both; Galloway resented that both seemed complicit in her erasure.

As Galloway's subject position began to shift, so too did the genre she used to explore it. She stopped addressing the journal to herself as the book's reader and began writing journal entries as letters to her daughter, Betsy, on November 23, 1778. She also rhetorically divorced her husband in these passages. She admits that she is "happy not to be with him. . . . I want not to be kept so like a slave as he will always . . . prevent every wish of my heart."[24] She aligns wifehood with slavery, and this move points to her problematic subject position. Both enslaved people and wives were considered property during the war, and confiscation committees initially tallied them as such. During this period of upheaval, however, it became profitable to treat enslaved people and women as capable of independent political thought.[25] Later, Galloway writes,

> My ever Dearest Child what can I do for thee as to J G tho I have some affection for him yet I dispise & abhor his vanity & baseness & am Now truly set against him yet I do not tell anyone this makes it worse to bear but all his Unkindness is in my mind & all within Distress and Confusion; I seems quite an Out Cast of Mankind & my soul struck with a Thousand Daggers to find how this man has imposed Upon me as well as treated Me Unkindly. . . . I will never live with him more.[26]

Galloway's text at this point begins to move quickly between the privacy scale I discussed in the introduction; she is keeping score for herself, an external addressee, and an intimate acquaintance. Her writing appears to be occupying various realms of privacy and intimacy simultaneously. She is ashamed of her husband's betrayal while also outraged, loathe to have people mock her fall but compelled to share her agony with her daughter. Thus, she shares the journal but contains the audience. The generic shift reflects an internal rift while also opening up the level of degree of privacy for this text. From this point on, she rarely mentions Joseph again, choosing instead to speak only to Betsy in her entries. Galloway replaces her legal ties—to her husband and to England—with a blood bond—to her daughter. She furthermore creates a sovereign self that does not answer to Joseph or to the statesmen that seek to punish him (and her). The journal hereafter documents Galloway's efforts to regain Betsy's inheritance. Galloway marks for posterity her refusal to be legally erased by Joseph's treachery and by the Pennsylvania Assembly's arbitrary application of the law by writing about the Supreme Executive Council's wrongdoings and her efforts to regain her property. These passages echo the one that opens the journal, where she demands that her audience "Pray take notice"—nothing but force should convince her to abandon her case. In so doing, she reshapes the definition of coverture during wartime, suggesting that women should be treated as legal entities in their own right so that they might retain their own property and avoid being convicted for their husbands' crimes. She also collects evidence in case the assembly revisits her petition to regain her property. The journal allows her to explore her predicament, to communicate with a daughter far away from home, to gather evidence that might be useful in the future, and to record for posterity her position about her legal status as an almost-but-not-quite covered woman.

The Exile-at-Home

Grace Growden Galloway's journal presents a bifurcated narrative, divided between before and after the eviction. Before her eviction, Galloway scripts herself as disaffected to avoid losing her home. After losing it, she fashions herself as an "exile-at-home" to regain it. Abandoned by her family, shunned by her friends, targeted by the rebels, Galloway becomes a stranger in a once familiar land, and her letter-journal's narrative reflects her alienation as it focuses on the physical and emotional aftereffects of trauma and grief: sickness, depression, anger, and withdrawal. This latter reaction, particularly, would have been key to the recovery of Galloway's properties, since the believability of her suffering and alienation after Joseph abandoned her would have been reliant on a successful symbolic divorce from one of the most vocal loyalists in Pennsylvania. The latter part of Galloway's journal borrows from sentimental tropes that were popular in novels of her era. The end of her story reads like *Clarissa* or *Pamela,* once Galloway's transformation as an exile-at-home is complete. That is, once she is alienated from her familial and social circle, she becomes ill and weak from an unnamed sickness although her symptoms are reminiscent of what we could label grief or depression today.[27] Her infirmities would have helped successfully plead her case that she should be granted an exception and restored to her home since her current situation was killing her. (Such a strategy was not unusual and was successful on a few occasions, which I discuss in greater detail in the next chapter.) On January 1, 1779, adopting a new voice in a new year, she recounts that she has narrowly survived a grave illness, "with vomiting and coughing and fever." This illness marks the onset of multiple illnesses that cause her to fear for her life. "Oh My dear Child," she exclaims, "how did I then think of you," presumably because she worried she would never see Betsy again.[28] Her brush with death makes her realize that she may die before securing the Galloway properties, and she begins to use her journal to document her efforts to argue publicly for her property rights and to regain her lost land.

Once she described how the rebels' treatment weakened her, she separates herself from their target, Joseph. He continued to spend money he did not possess while living in London, placing the family in debt, a fact that Grace discovered after she learned she would lose her home. "He conceals all he can from me," she tells Betsy. "Was it Not for My child I wou'd Never care anything about him for his base conduct to Me . . . & his takeing no care of me in his absence has quite Made Me indiferant to him."[29] He has left her weak and sick, with no contact with her immediate family, no control over her property, and little income.[30] These problems were exacerbated when the Supreme Executive Council denied her petition, and she officially lost her house. She became a refugee, moving from house to house until finally settling with Deborah Morris, a Quaker who took her in. Galloway's passages about the lasting implications of the confiscation of her home underscore the physical toll Joseph's loyalties took on her. She reminds her reading audience again that she is a victim, not a perpetrator, when she emphasizes her vulnerability. She does not say if she presented her physical deterioration as part of the case she made to the council, but it seems likely, since she writes that she enumerated the other ramifications in her petition. Galloway has transferred the abuses done to her physical and personal space into her journal, inscribing them onto her paper body to retain them as proof of permanent injury. She then presents those marks—the arguments she makes in the pages of her book—to her family and the state assembly as evidence. The ink stains remain longer on the page than bruises and diseases endure, so these words serve as permanent evidence that the assembly was guilty of violence against a woman who denied all ties to the man it sought to injure.

Galloway's journal emphasizes not only her physical deterioration but also her mental diminishment as well. She is plagued by nightmares, the majority of which concern being stripped of all she holds dear. Shortly after moving in with Morris, she dreams that her husband's and daughter's ship crossing the Atlantic to London had sunk "and that they were all lost." "I then thought the News True," she writes, "& awoke in a fright." Despite her best efforts to shake the dream, she could not lose the image of death by water. Upon returning to sleep, she recalls, "I . . . dream'd my dear child was going home with Me to Trevose & that it rain'd & she was but poorly." In her dream, Betsy has caught the disease from which Grace suffers, and both of them are ill because of Joseph. Echoing the moment where she was taken away from Trevose in her own carriage, Galloway says that in this nightmare, she and her daughter "were obliged to walk" but the "roads was full of water & she got wet in her feet & I was greatly destress'd." The carriage then arrives at a "Narrow place" in the road and is in danger of being swallowed up by the surging waters. Just before she and her daughter drown in the deluge, Galloway says that she "awoke in great horror."[31]

That Galloway recorded her nightmare in her journal would not have been unusual; dreams during this period acted as tools thought to predict outcomes, practice agency, and brainstorm dilemmas. Mechal Sobel in *Teach Me Dreams* notes that diarists between 1740 and 1840 frequently recorded their dreams because this was the period in which "many people in America first came to accept that they had an inner self that controlled their emotions and actions." These dreams, or more precisely, writing about these dreams, acted as a Foucauldian "technology of self" that served as a "catalyst for change." People often recorded acting on what they dreamed or waiting for visions they received while sleeping to inspire them to take action. Sobel notes that the rebels supporting the American Revolution often recorded liberty as a dream they had before they decided to fight for it; the language in these entries often makes the revolution seem preordained.[32] I am suggesting here that if the revolution could be dreamed, then its resistance could be also. Nightfall brought for patriots images of rebellion, victory, and freedom, but for Galloway, sleep brought visions of chaos, separation, and loss. Rather than being a "catalyst for change," her dreams predicted the death of her family as they attempted to cross the ocean and were swallowed up by the waves of war. Her dreams were not windows into possible action that she might take. Instead, she believed they warned her of a dark fate.

Galloway's emphasis on her terror and restlessness suggest that her suffering invaded the interiority of her mind—there is no moment in her day or night when Joseph's treachery and her separation from Betsy did not plague her. These are the emotional aftereffects of trauma that proved her victimization to anyone who might be looking for verification of her allegiances. Her torment suggests that they most certainly were not with her estranged husband, a strategy that I analyze in chapter 5, when Elizabeth Graeme Fergusson takes similar measures (but with a different outcome). Galloway's losses underscore her role as a victim, rather than as a perpetrator. She interprets the dream to be about the anguish of being forced to leave home and about the dangers of writing letters. In the journal entry to her daughter recounting this nightmare, she explains that the day after her dream, she discovered that Joseph Galloway's letter to his sister had been intercepted and printed in the local newspaper. While it did him "no dishonor," its interception—a violation of her intimate communication with her family by people who claimed to be fellow countrymen—further underscored both her family's and her nation's division. "What pain I feel," Grace writes, "to think my dearest child Must be drove from her Native Country & all she has taken from her & Incapable of doing anything for her[.] No one can imagine but those who have had the like Tryal: God grant them a speedy & a prosperous Voyage."[33] The Galloways *were* drowning, particularly socially and economically. Their former prestige was dwindling, Joseph's status as a powerful politician had faltered, their home was lost, and their finances were in jeopardy. By describing her family in this way, Galloway was fashioning the loyalists and their families as victims, rather than as traitors. Galloway refused to view her family's losses as Abigail Adams viewed hers; this loss was not a sacrifice made for the good of the nation. Her family's symbolic death was unwarranted. As she saw it, they did nothing to deserve their fate. Rather than adopting the labels that the executive council wanted to foist on the Galloways, namely loyalist, traitor, and defector, Grace refashioned her family as hapless victims of an overwhelming tragedy.

Galloway's image of the drowning family returned in the journal less than one month later, on November 12, 1778, when she has what she believes to be a premonitory dream. "It rain'd very hard," she writes, and "I was so wet in my feet & pettycoats as if I had been dipp'd in water." She makes it clear that she sees this deluge as an omen that her prior dream has come true, which is what Carl Jung would later name "synchronistic phenomena," when someone dreams something happens before it does.[34] She writes that she believes her husband and daughter are now dead, having drowned or been captured and killed on the voyage overseas. Early Americans tended to be symbolic in their dissection of dreams: "dry land . . . often represents the terra firma of ordinary ego-consciousness," suggesting all is well, whereas storms, thunder, and lightning were thought to signify disruption, death, and/or grief; dreaming of lightning was often interpreted as an omen of God's wrath.[35] Galloway's passive construction—Betsy "has been drove" from her native home—displaces the actor behind her misery, though Galloway certainly intimates the fault lies with men rather than gods. When she describes her family's descent into unknown depths, she may have been drawing from a universal and historically reoccurring image that Jung called "the *nekyia*, or night-sea journey," which involves being swallowed, either by darkness, a creature, or other unknown depths. It repeats itself in the myth of Osiris, in the biblical story of Jonah, and, for Galloway, in the vision of her husband and daughter sinking to the bottom of the Atlantic. These visions could symbolize Galloway's desire to heal from grief or trauma, particularly since this dream occurs when two people who are linked by a strong bond are separated, as was the case of Galloway and Betsy.

Galloway was so shaken by this vision that she had to confirm it was not a premonition come true. She immediately "went into Owen Jones's & they told me to be easey for Mr G was Not taken"; he and Betsy remained safe. Galloway's rhetoric here has shifted. Betsy is no longer "you," as she had been before, nor is Joseph. Her daughter is "she," and her husband "Mr G." Galloway does not seem to know to whom she is speaking any longer. The journal has lost its named audience—Betsy, she fears, may have drowned—and yet she keeps writing, to herself and to the unnamed reader she hopes will hear her story. Her next entry sheds light on the cause for this discursive alienation. "As I was walking in the rain My own Chariot Drove by," she writes. It was the same chariot in which she was taken away from Trevose, only someone else was driving it. Being passed by this symbol of her once-great wealth underscores the depths of her descent. "My dear child came into my mind," she reflects, "& what she wou'd say to see her Mamma walking 5 squares in the Rain at Night like a common Woman & go to rooms in an Alley for her home[.] I dare not think."[36] She flashes back to her nightmare where Betsy drowned in a rainstorm just shy of the protection of the chariot and believes what she feared has come to fruition. The chariot—in this case, a symbol of the Galloways' affluence and mobility, as well as a persistent reminder of her eviction—is just out of the women's reach and leaves Galloway literally and figuratively standing still. Both Betsy and Galloway have "died" with the financial and social shelter the chariot promises just out of arm's reach. Joseph is nowhere to be found (in the dream or in real life), either to be held accountable, make amends, or rescue them, which suggests again that Galloway was fashioning herself as the protagonist of a sentimental novel. Scenes like this one divert the reader's attention away from Joseph's loyalties and place them instead onto Grace's and Betsy's losses. The larger implication of this literary moment is that, as a female loyalist, Galloway is politically and economically unable to move forward, to regain her property, wealth, or status. She is also unable and unwilling to flee to London. She wants to remain near Bensalem Township and Philadelphia to preserve what is left of her father's estate so that her daughter might have something to inherit when the war concludes. She casts herself as metaphorically caught in the war's downpour, stuck at a standstill as her life rolls past.

Toward the end of her life, Galloway became convinced that people— even other loyalists—relished her social descent, evincing a paranoia that would eventually cause her to live as a shut-in. The most notable incident preserved in her journal occurred at a social gathering at her friend Billy Turner's house, where she seized the opportunity to return to the metaphor of the nation as a drowning family. When in public, she inverted the image. She discursively reconstructs it in the journal, however, so that her enemies drown while she looks on. "I ... got My spirits at command & Laughted at the whole [W]ig party," she writes, and "I told them I was the happiest woman in twown [town] for I had been *strip[p]ed* & Turn'd out of Doors Yet I was still the same." This part of her speech gives way to memorable braggadocio. She proceeds, "[I am] Joseph Galloways Wife & Lawrence Growden's daughter & ... it [is] not in their power to humble Me for I shou'd be Grace Growden Galloway to the last." She then points at the partygoers and tells them that she has suffered all that they can heap on her, and now she has decided to "act as on a rock to look on the wrack of others & see them tost by the Tempestuous billows while I was safe ashore." Galloway rhetorically elevates her body so that she can look down on everyone else. She watches others sink instead of drowning herself. She judges, rather than being judged. She is empowered, instead of being stripped. In this moment, she also allies herself with the paternal heads-of-household in her life—her father, Lawrence, and her husband, Joseph—and simultaneously distances herself from them, concluding the entry by inscribing her own name. That she writes such a contradictory statement makes sense in light of the loyalist wife's legal limbo. She was, in fact, a dependent of her father and then, once married, a dependent of her husband, although the war uncovered her legal body so that it too could be stripped. She concludes this entry: "Defye the Villans," distancing herself from everyone who looked on.[37] Her misanthropy allows her to shun all possible political affiliations and replace them with her own construction, which permits her to build an identity that does not rely on charity, loyalty, property, or marriage for self-worth.

THE RECLAMATION OF TREVOSE

Galloway's self-construction as a victimized woman who suffered the ills of a man who abandoned her—starring in her own prequel to *Charlotte Temple*—worked. The Supreme Executive Council invited Galloway to buy back her own property and put it in her name on January 30, 1779. The opportunity she had been waiting for had arrived, but she could not take it. Galloway explains that buying any of these properties would legally and politically "uncover" her, which would then make it possible for the assembly to charge her with treason: "First shou'd I Claim & they Grant me the whole I then made Myself a subject to the state & owning their Authority subject Myself to All the Penalties of their Laws & there by banish myself from my husband & Child or render Myself liable to an Attainder." By this, Galloway means that if she officially becomes the proprietor, she has essentially sided with the rebels who now own the property. She must recast her loyalties if she is to reclaim her house. She also means that she must pay taxes to the Americans, an act that violates multiple convictions she possesses since such money would fund a military she does not support. Second, she writes, if the property were in her name, she could be "Try'd for . . . life [or have her] whole Estate Confiscated" if she openly sided with the British after reclaiming her estate.[38] Owning property would make her legally visible. The irony, of course, is that Galloway's family loyalties had already made her legally visible. She lost her furniture, house, and land because of Joseph's political leanings. At the time she wrote this entry, she possessed almost nothing she could call her own. She may have possessed the possibility of regaining what was once hers, but purchasing her estate would put her in debt. This solution was untenable because once she put the property in her own name, her loyalties—not

Joseph's—became the conditions under which she kept her home. Ultimately, she refused to side with anyone in the war.

Galloway decides to resolve this dilemma by claiming an alternative space in her journal that is neither loyalist nor rebel. "[I] am determin'd to sit still," she writes; "[I am] quite Vext with the english, but I hat[e] the others," meaning the Americans. Angry because of the rebels' persecution and frustrated with England's refusal to support its loyal subjects, she denies them both. "I would turn Rebel rather than hold such a Wretch to be My King," she explains to Betsy. "There was No Justice in the English more than the Americans. . . . I hate the King & all his Court, . . . & I Renounce the Nation." She tells Betsy that she has decided to belong to no one for the rest of her life, writing, "oh My Child had I my fortune again I wou'd Defye them all," a pledge she admits rings hollow without her considerable fortune behind it.[39]

These sentiments reflect the general opinion held by loyalists—particularly by exiles—about the British Empire following the war's conclusion. The Crown had promised those who stayed in America or who fled to the Bahamas, Sierra Leone, Nova Scotia, London, and St. Augustine compensation for remaining faithful to the king, but it did not always follow through. England promised black loyalists freedom and then helped white loyalists export their slaves in bondage. It swore to Native American allies that it would grant them land in exchange for their fealty, but it largely abandoned those Natives after 1783. It pledged to compensate people like the Galloways for confiscated property but did not always do so. Parliament "tightened the reigns of administration" throughout the world, believing that part of what caused the rebellion in the thirteen colonies was "too much liberty, not too little," which embittered many British subjects of the diaspora toward their home country.[40] Galloway's renunciation of America and of England is part of this larger protest spreading throughout the Atlantic world. She appears to have been separating herself from any greater political agenda England or America possessed by divorcing herself from both. This act was one of her last ones, a final assertion of self as her life drew to a close. Her property sold in 1781, and Grace never fully regained it in her lifetime.[41]

One of Galloway's other final acts, becoming a recluse, might, at first, seem like the most apolitical decision she could make, but her inaction *was* action. Once again, she was deciding to sit still. She told her daughter in 1782, the year she died, that she rarely left her house and was "as ignorant of all the grand bustle of life as any recluse or pious person in this or former ages. . . . I care little for the world."[42] She ignored Joseph's invitation that she join him in London, preferring instead to remain where she was—in America, but not part of it.[43] She seems to have preferred her own sovereignty, constructing a political identity that shunned the labels "loyalist," "wife," and "property" that men had created on her behalf. The only thing that sustained her was the possibility that she might be able to save Betsy's inheritance: "If by it I save my child[,] all will be right." Her final act in 1782 was to will her confiscated estate to Betsy, despite the fact that legally she could not do so. She used her pen to restore to her daughter what had been stripped from them both, a final, symbolic act of her defiance. Following the Treaty of Paris in 1783, Belmont, Richlieu, and King's Place reverted back to Grace's heirs. And the Pennsylvania Council granted Betsy the opportunity to buy what remaining property she desired. By 1787, Betsy owned all of the family's property except Durham and Trevose. After the death of Joseph Galloway, the Pennsylvania Supreme Court decided that Grace should not have suffered for Joseph's treason and posthumously awarded the original Growden real estate—including Trevose—back to Grace and her heirs.[44] Grace Growden Galloway finally had returned that which was taken from her, but the decision came twenty-six years too late.

Galloway's journal is not merely the product of an insightful critic living through difficult circumstances; it is representative of many other women left behind. As we see in the chapters that follow, loyalist wives and daughters used manuscript writing to construct their own political personae, though not all used them to carve out a neutral or disaffected space. Philadelphia Quakers Elizabeth Drinker and Sarah Logan Fisher used their diaries to carve out a space for pacifism, a position that confiscation committees deemed traitorous because Quakers refused to pick a side. All of these women found themselves exposed because of war. Their legal bodies, and sometimes their physical bodies, were uncovered and put on display so that others could exploit them. And all turned to writing to script a new self. These women wrote daughters, generals, and assemblymen so that they might declare their personal loyalties (and sometimes their lack of them) and regain what metaphorical or literal property they deemed to be their own.

CHAPTER TWO

SCRIPTING PACIFISM

Sarah Logan Fisher and Elizabeth Drinker

Wakefield, the home of Sarah Logan Fisher, is supposed to be located squarely in the middle of a park just north of Philadelphia. Or it's on the corner of a lot across the street. Or it's somewhere inside the border of La Salle University. Fisher was a Quaker in the third trimester of a pregnancy when the rebels came to arrest and imprison her husband for refusing to take the loyalty oath to the colonies. She was raided time and again by rebel soldiers while he was away, but she refused to give them what they wanted. Additionally, all the while he was imprisoned, she wrote letters and signed petitions protesting his unlawful detainment. The only document I can find about the location where her standoff took place comes from a permit for her home's historic preservation. It offers few details and multiple addresses for Wakefield. I'm here to try all possibilities. My first stop is Wakefield Park, which stretches out for blocks, a wide expanse of discarded Styrofoam cups and weeds as tall as an SUV. It's flanked by buckled concrete sidewalks long in disrepair. I see no house. I cross Fisher Avenue, walk down Ogontz to Lindley, and peruse the row houses. The streets I walk are breadcrumbs on a trail. Fisher, Olney, Wister, Logan are all named for the people I'm trying to find. My last option is La Salle University, which purchased the Fisher property. La Salle is guarded at each entrance. I meet a security officer and tell him I'm looking for a historic house, Wakefield. He leans out of his security booth to study me. "Who?" he asks. "It's a house. The Fisher house. The Fisher of Fisher Avenue right over there," I say, pointing to the sign in the distance. He shakes his head. "Never heard of them, but you're welcome to come in," he says. I realize I've been holding my breath when he opens the gate. I'd expected another Trevose—steps from my goal but denied a way in.

I drive to a rise in the hill where the historic permit suggested Wakefield may have once stood. It is 96 degrees in July in the city, and the heat ripples off of the sidewalk in waves. I'm looking down at my map, my blistered feet, and my notes dotted with drops of sweat, so I don't see the building until I almost run into it. It's a cheerful, two-story white house with green shutters—an unmistakable image I've seen a dozen times before. I wonder if the heat has affected my head. This is not Wakefield; it's Belfield: the Charles Willson Peale House. The same Peale that took away the Galloway house. One of the commissioners of confiscated estates. The loyalist's house is gone. The rebel's house remains. I take out my phone while I rest on a blistering stone bench to search for explanations: Belfield, Wakefield, Fisher, Peale. The answer makes me laugh. Although Wakefield burned in 1985, the Fisher family purchased Peale's house in 1826 and folded it into their estate, along with twelve acres. The prisoner's family members bought the jailor's property and made it their own.

M Y SEARCH FOR Wakefield is not unlike my search for information about the Fisher and Drinker families, who were caught up in the Spanktown controversy of 1777. Their story is full of selective silence, their journals at times gaping, open, weed-filled lots without markers about what happened there. The Spanktown story in particular is full of false starts where the facts about the truth behind the matter became falsified and twisted, the people caught up in it shuffled from street to street, and then city to city, until, eventually, they sat in exile.

Congress published a spy letter in 1777 written by Quakers from the Spanktown Yearly Meeting and used it as an excuse to round up thirty people and interrogate them, citing them as a security threat. The Spanktown Yearly Meeting, however, did not exist.[1] Congress fabricated the hoax to justify arresting some of the most powerful men from some of the most prominent Quaker families in the Philadelphia area, in part because they refused to accept Continental currency and also because they were "notoriously disaffected."[2] This missive allegedly broached intelligence about George Washington's army and suggested that the Quakers, who claimed neutrality in the name of pacifism, were actually latent loyalists. Until that year, the Quakers' refusal to support the revolution because of their pledge to pacifism was begrudgingly tolerated. The Spanktown letter changed everything. After seeing it, General John Sullivan issued a statement saying that Quakers were inclined "to communicate Intelligence to the Enemy."[3] He labeled the Society of Friends "the most Dangerous Enemies America knows" hiding behind "that Hypocritical Cloak of Religion."[4] Sullivan's reaction was published in papers throughout the colonies, and word spread like wildfire that the Quakers sought to sabotage the rebels. Never mind that no one could verify the intelligence. The Friends, already suspect, became a target. The Pennsylvania Committee of Safety then searched the houses of suspected spies, and between September 1–4, 1777, exiled twenty-two people to Winchester, Virginia, without trial.[5] The damage was already done by the time the fabrication of the letter became public knowledge. The accused Quakers sat sick in prison, the colonists questioned their loyalties, and only an aggressive public relations campaign saved those men and the people they represented.

Whoever wrote the Spanktown letter did not account for the Quaker wives. While waiting on their families to return, these women suffered physically and spiritually as proxies for their imprisoned spouses and fellow Quakers. They refused to suffer silently, however. Historical accounts of the American Revolution have thoroughly documented the Virginia Exile Crisis, but much of the emphasis has been on the prisoners, rather than on their families.[6] This chapter explains how exiles' wives used the crisis as a touchstone for exploring and proclaiming their loyalties in light of these arrests. They wrote letters, journals, and letter-journals in response to the Spanktown missive to launch an epistolary campaign of their own. These texts challenged the viability of a fledging American government and demanded the right to religious pacifism. The collective letter that may have grown out of these texts perhaps even influenced George Washington to free the exiles. I trace how Quaker women such as Elizabeth Drinker and Sarah Logan Fisher used letters and journals to map their fluctuating loyalties to the British monarchy, the Society of Friends, and the new nation, and I track how they created a localized identity that refused allegiance to anyone outside of their faith. And, finally, I explain how these women used journals and correspondence to create a counter-rhetoric defying Congress's insistence that Friends should be categorized as traitors and spies.

The Virginia Exiles' letters, like the journal of Grace Growden Galloway, underscore the point that revolutionary-era loyalty (broadly speaking) and loyalism (specifically) should be studied as a spectrum rather than a fixed point, despite what the Continental Congress attempted to codify through treason laws, exile, and confiscation. If the disaffected violently opposed the idea that they must fall somewhere on that spectrum—in fact, rejected the notion of the existence of a spectrum at all—then pacifists questioned the morality of the people who created this conundrum in the first place. Like the disaffected,

Quaker pacifists defined themselves by stating what they opposed, but they differed from other kinds of loyalists in that their opposition tied them to a powerful and recognizable collective: the Society of Friends.

How Quakers Became Loyalists

Before considering how Quaker women writers defined "loyalty" and used their letters and letter-journals to disseminate that definition, I must first explain how the Society of Friends became the "most dangerous enemy America knows." This moment is crucial for understanding how Quakers went from being begrudgingly tolerated as pacifists to actively hunted as traitors. The Pennsylvania Assembly demanded that everyone take a loyalty oath, or "Test," to the new ruling body on June 18, 1776. The Quakers opposed the action that the new Congress took in the early summer of 1777, requesting all men above the age of eighteen pledge the following:

> I, A.B., do swear (or affirm) that I renounce and refuse all allegiance to George the Third, King of Great Britain, his heirs and successors, and that I will be faithful and bear true allegiance to the commonwealth of Pennsylvania as a free and independent state, and that I will not at any time do or cause to be done any matter or thing that will be prejudicial or injurious to the freedom and independence thereof, as declared by Congress; and also that I will discover and make known to some one justice of the peace of the said state all treasons or traitorous conspiracies which I now know or hereafter shall know to be formed against this or any of the United States of America.[7]

Quakers refused to swear this oath because they believed it would signify their support of the revolution, and the war violated the principle of the Inner Light. This religious tenet argued that if all people contained the light of God, then both lying and killing contaminated that light (which was the basis of their belief in pacifism as well).[8] Quakers also resented being asked to swear allegiance to the colonies because the Sermon on the Mount instructed believers to "Swear not at all."[9] Friends believed that all words, not just oaths, should be an "expression of Truth."[10]

Colonial governments, for the most part, respected (though consistently tested) what the Quakers called their Peace Testimony in the years before the revolution, but after the Spanktown letter, Congress disregarded all informal agreements to leave the Quakers to worship as they wished. Congress even began targeting Quakers, much as they did with known loyalists. The

Continental Congress passed a resolution on March 12, 1776, requesting that states "donate" supplies to the colonial troops. Quakers believed that granting requisitions meant choosing a side in the war, so they refused in the name of pacifism. The commissary of the Continental Army responded to this refusal by demanding that the Pennsylvania Board of War supply blankets, and on May 2, the Supreme Executive Council authorized the requisition of 4,000 blankets from the state, 667 of them to come from Philadelphia. Quakers were singled out for this requisition, in part because they refused to support the war in other ways.[11] A war against these peaceable people had begun.

THE DIARY OF SARAH LOGAN FISHER

Sarah Logan Fisher considered herself a pacifist but was treated as a loyalist during the American Revolution. The *Pennsylvania Magazine of History and Biography* sixty years ago claimed that Logan's name is "overshadowed only by those of William Penn and Benjamin Franklin," and the Fisher family was "one of the community's outstanding families before the outbreak of the Revolution."[12] As the granddaughter of James Logan, William Penn's secretary, Sarah Logan became even more well-connected when she married Tommy Fisher, a successful merchant, in 1772. Tommy Fisher's arrest, like Grace Growden and Joseph Galloway's property confiscation, broadcast a message to the community: everyone, regardless of social status before the war began, must pledge fidelity to the colonies or suffer the consequences. After Tommy was arrested, his wife penned her journal—which she titled "A Diary of Trifling Occurrences"—to him, which he received while in exile and shared with the other prisoners by reading it aloud.[13]

Fisher's diary, as she called it, resembles Grace Growden Galloway's both in the way that it developed and in that it moved between sliding scales of privacy and publicity over the course of its history. She began the journal in October 1776, about one year before Tommy's arrest, and she continued writing until her death in 1795. She had filled twenty-five volumes by then.[14] She wrote to herself and God in the diary primarily, though she also addressed her relatives in the text. She addressed Tommy as a reader during the Exile Crisis, but later she included salutations to her children. For example, in 1786, she writes,

> Dear objects of my most affectionate wishes & care,
>   May you be preserved in innocent simplicity & kept free from the pollutions of the World, but how hard it is to stem the torrent in a great City, where

there is so many temptations, so many avenues to vice, by a constant Watch I belive we may set a good example to our Children & insensibly conquer our own defects, by carefully gaurding against doing anything improper least our example should be influencing to our Children.[15]

It is as if she hopes that the children reading her journal will use it to live according to the principles their mother hoped to instill, which would have been a common Quaker practice. Quakers often published posthumous journals so that others could emulate the good they did while living. The back of the last volume of her diary has the name "Hannah"—a daughter born in November 1777 during her family's trials—centered perfectly on the page in Fisher's handwriting; this appears to be a book dedication.[16]

Fisher's diaries were willed to Esther Fisher Wistar, Sarah Logan Fisher's granddaughter (likely via Hannah), who passed them to Mary Helen Cadwalader, her cousin, who gave them to her sister Sophia Cadwalader, who gave them to Benjamin R. Cadwalader, who passed them to the historian Nicholas Wainwright and asked him to publish them.[17] The manuscript and published volumes, then, moved between several different states and audiences. As discussed in the introduction, the writings express an intimate grief over the loss of her child Billy, in an exchange between herself and God (whom she calls the Parent). She uses the diary as a letter-journal for a time to Tommy, when she both addresses him and sends him the book. After the Exile Crisis resolved, she reverts to writing to herself while simultaneously overtly talking to her children, naming them either specifically as she did with Hannah or collectively. The diary is, at times, an autobiographical diary dictating an historical event, occasionally an epistolary journal, and sometimes a conduct book that was public but not widely circulated outside of the family, at least until its publication many generations later.

While Galloway constructed her political identity by opposing her husband's, Sarah Fisher scripted her loyalties by writing about her resistance to any rebels' demands for food and supplies during her husband's absence. And as with Galloway's journal, Fisher's journal also focuses on forced entry. Fisher, more than any writer featured in this book, spends most of her letter-journal challenging the legitimacy of the rebel cause and the paper on which that cause was printed. The revolution was a fabrication from Fisher's perspective because the rebels invented much of the material on which they based the Virginia Exiles' arrests.

Fisher's status as a woman prevented her from writing a publicly acknowledged proclamation or declaration, loyalty oath, or arrest warrant, but her
diary offered her a space in which she could confirm her loyalties to the
Quakers, rather than to the Americans. One passage in which she does this
occurred in 1777, just after Pennsylvania began demanding that everyone
take the abjuration oaths. She reflects on this mandate by writing,

> This Evening a Paper came out from the Committee of Safety unlike anything I
> ever before heard of, except the Spanish Inquisition, declaring that every person
> who refused the Continental Money, should be liable for the first offence to forfeit
> the Goods & a Sum of equal value, for the second offence to forfeit the same, &
> to be banishd what they are pleased to call this State, to what place, & in what
> manner, they shall judge most proper, that all those who have been imprisoned,
> & whose Stores have been shut up by them, on the account of their refusing it
> formerly are to be opened, & they are to be subject to this new Law, after having
> experienced all the vigours of the old one—a most extraordinary instance of
> arbitrary power, & of the Liberty we shall enjoy should their Government ever be
> established, a tyranical Government it will prove from weak & wicked Men[.][18]

The Committees of Safety to which she refers assembled after the Second
Continental Congress convened in May 1775. These groups formed the ad
hoc governing bodies that Congress appointed to administer the first colony-
wide loyalty oaths of 1776, which Fisher here references as the "old law." The
Pennsylvania Assembly constructed the "new law" she protests, asking each
county to swear to be "true and faithful to the commonwealth of Pennsylvania."[19] The old law was national; the new was regional. Fisher sees through the
rhetoric that the Safety Committees were using to justify search and seizure
of loyalist and Quaker properties. The Test Laws (like our own Patriot Act
in the twenty-first century) were enacted in the name of greater liberty. That
is, their creation was based on the idea that Americans must sacrifice their
privacy to achieve the improved standard of living that the rebels promised
would come at the war's conclusion.

Fisher's letter rejects this justification. She did not see her country as a
budding republic; rather, she claimed that the colonies had traded one greedy
tyrant for many. Fisher compares the revolution to the Spanish Inquisition
to suggest that the rebels were concerned more with orthodoxy than with
freedom, more concerned with obedience than with liberty. As with the
inquisition, committee members were going door to door to impose arbitrary definitions of faith. A self-appointed governing body had decided what

constituted faithfulness—or loyalty—and, if the accused were found wanting, they could be punished. She had been stripped of liberty in the name of liberty. The parallels disturbed Fisher.

Fisher did not open her home, Wakefield, and her cupboards willingly when faced with the demand that she fall in line with the government's mandates. Instead, she responded to this forced entry by analyzing the arrest warrant for the Virginia Exiles, a document that symbolized for her the legality of the revolution itself. Fisher writes on the day that the Safety Committee arrested the Philadelphia Quakers, "An affecting trying scene presented itself this Day, for our further refinement, as we are told it is thro suffering we are to be made perfect.—About 11 oClock our new made council sent some of the deputies to many of the inhabitants who they suspected of Toryism & *without any regular warrant or any written paper* mentioning their crime, or telling them of it in any way, committed them to the confinement." The Fishers demanded again to see the warrant for themselves, so the rebels "read over a Paper *which they called one* which was an order from the congress, recommending to the executive Council, to fall upon some measure, to take up all such persons, who had by their conduct or otherwise shewn themselves enemys to the united states, & the Council gave orders for the taking such persons, as they thought proper."[20] Fisher here underscores the rebels' inability to produce a document (or figurehead) that legitimized their authority; therefore, the rebellion they constructed also lacked viability.

It is important to understand what Fisher's examination of the charges in this document meant in order for us to understand the ways in which female loyalists used letters to subvert a nationalist narrative that threatened to consume them. The Exile Crisis tested the legitimacy of Congress's new authority and exposed the tension between local and national governing bodies. In other words, by questioning the Exile Crisis, Fisher questioned the provisional government itself. No one could decide what to do with the Quakers once the Philadelphia Assembly contained the so-called threat. The Supreme Executive Council refused to grant the prisoners a trial, arguing that the present crisis required that it skip such formalities. Congress likewise denied the Quakers a hearing on the grounds that the Pennsylvania legislature should try them, both because Pennsylvania initiated the arrests and because the Quakers were "inhabitants of Pennsylvania." Each governing body pointed fingers away from itself, refusing to accept blame or responsibility.

This stalemate stemmed, at least partially, from the fact that no one could

produce a legitimate reason to arrest these men in the first place. Offering
a trial ex post facto would only underscore the rebellion's lack of structure.
Trying the Quakers would have highlighted the cracks in Congress's plan to
build a new republic: what were the laws? who was in charge? what did it
mean to be loyal or treasonous, and to whom? Instead of addressing these
questions, George Bryan, president of the Pennsylvania Supreme Executive
Council (and the man who advised Grace Growden Galloway), sent the prisoners three hundred miles away to Virginia, putting them out of sight and
mind. This move caused an uproar throughout the colonies about Congress's
and the state assemblies' authority during the war.[21] Accordingly, when
Fisher commented on the Quakers' exile, she was also questioning the colonies' legal limitations.

THE QUAKERS' LETTER WAR

After the Friends were rounded up and imprisoned, Congress published a
series of resolves to justify the arrests and name the guilty parties in the newspapers. The Quakers in these articles found themselves on trial in the court of
public opinion despite being denied a formal hearing (and, of course, despite
the fact that Congress had fabricated the letter in the first place). American
general John Sullivan wrote that the nation was on the eve of a "single battle"
because the "war is at an end" (it was not), but the nation had to be vigilant
against those who wished it to fail. "Now is the time for our strenuous exer-
tions," he wrote, for "one bold stroke will free the land from rapine, devastation
and burnings, and female innocence from brutal lust and violence."[22]

Congress followed that declaration with eleven papers which "proved"
their accusations to be true, the most damning of which was the falsified
Spanktown missive. This publication concluded with the list of the prisoners'
names: "Joshua Fisher, Abel James, James Pemberton, Henry Drinker, Israel
Pemberton, John Pemberton, John James, Samuel Pleasants, Thomas Wharton, Sen. Thomas Fisher, son of Joshua, and Samuel Fisher son of Joshua."[23]
These letters and their context are essential to understanding the archive
of loyalist women authors I examine because the publication of this list of
names and its accompanying resolves forced the Quakers to publish their
own counter-explanation of what happened. Elizabeth Drinker and Sarah
Logan Fisher seem to be in conversation both with Sullivan's accusations and

with the Quaker's official rebuttal of them, which Israel Pemberton published in response on behalf of all Friends.

Pemberton's "The Remonstrance of the Subscribers, Citizens of Philadelphia," written by Pemberton and several other Friends, offers this refutation: "Most of you are not personally known to us, nor are we to you," but the "liberty, property, and character, of every Freeman in America, is, or may be endangered." The plight of the Quakers represented the plight of all Americans. Everyone, they write, would have to "appear before the Tribunal of Divine Justice"—God. They had been charged to "live peaceably with all men," so they should not engage in war. "Many of our houses have been stripped of the leaden weights used for the hanging of windows," another letter laments, and the "houses of several Friends have been wantonly abused, and their windows broke and destroyed by a rude rabble, *for not joining with the present rulers in their pretended acts of devotion.*" "Some of our members," the pamphlet authors continue, "have also had soldiers forced into their houses and kept there for some time, . . . Our peaceable testimony disregarded by the authors of this imposition." The rebuttal is signed, "Your *real* Friends," "Israel Pemberton, James Pemberton, John Pemberton, Thomas Wharton, Henry Drinker [Elizabeth's husband], Thomas Fisher [Sarah's husband], Samuel Pleasants, Samuel R. Fisher."[24] Congress's list of names targeted the entire Quaker community. The Quakers' list of names absolved the Friends of these accusations.

In this chapter, I read Sarah Logan Fisher's journal as part of the Friends' communal rebuttal of Sullivan's accusations against them. Rather than reading her journal as derivative or merely an echo of Pemberton's public note, I interpret it as a bullhorn for the Quaker's collective message. Her journal joins the Quakers' outcry against Congress's unjust treatment of them and seeks to redeem their good name. When the exiles were removed to Virginia, she too enumerated the people who were taken, naming them "the most respectable inhabitants" in Pennsylvania, particularly "Viz. Edward Pennington, Joseph Fox, Parson Coombe, Thomas Affleck, Thomas Gilpin, Myers Fisher, Phineas Bond, Thomas Pike[,] Elijah Brown, William Smith, William Drewet Smith, Thomas Wharton, John Pemberton, Henry Drinker, Owen Jones Junr, Charles Jervis[,] Charles Eddy, Isarel [Israel] Pemberton, John Hunt, Samuel Pleasants."[25] Fisher's list, unlike the Friends' or Congress's meeting minutes, did not go to the newspapers. She sent it to her husband who read it to the other exiles, yet I assert that her inscription achieved a similar purpose as that of the other publications.

I mean to emphasize a few points about female epistolarity and journal-keeping during the war by reading her journal in this way. The journal engages with traditionally published, public dialogues, even though it may not have circulated through the printing press as these other publications did. It is also a source for female political engagement that exists outside of Michael Warner's and Jürgen Habermas's definition of the public sphere. And, furthermore, it underscores my assertion that writing was a legitimate outlet for discursive resistance in that, once stripped, women turned to script. Fisher's journal both protests a great betrayal (as Congress's list of names served to do) and renames the exiles as "respectable inhabitants," rather than traitors. She may have used her journal and its list of grievances as a lifeline because it went to Tommy. While the diary acts as a letter-journal, it reestablishes the relationship that her friends and loved ones' removal threatened to erase and countered Congress's imperative that they be excluded and forgotten. The letter-journal closes the loop between those forcibly sent away from the community and those who remained behind. Its entry into the public sphere mirrors the newspaper articles that publicized the feud between Congress and the Quakers, and it represents Fisher's public-but-not-published entrance into that debate. Fisher manipulated her semi-private journal into the public sphere as a letter-journal just as the Quakers circulated meeting minutes from the semi-private meetinghouse into the papers.

Fisher's list of names serves as a visual representation of her discursive resistance. The question of who possesses the authority to label people as subversives, terrorists, rebels, or traitors has long involved a broader struggle for the right to name, categorize, and control those people. In a feminist treatise on naming, Dale Spender explains that "groups that have a marginal status are denied the vocabulary to define (and express) their own experiences. . . . By assigning names we impose a pattern . . . which allows us to manipulate the world."[26] Those in power often seek total domination through labeling or naming, which they look to control, as any student of postcolonial theory knows. Congress achieved domination over the Quakers by rewriting both the connotation and denotation of pacifism. These labels, once printed, can be "infectious," "created to spread quickly, . . . proving hard to shake off and determining the boundaries and key reference points of future debates and

discussions." Just as the loyalists often described the revolution as a conta-
gion, so the rebels described any resistance to the revolution as a virus. The
purpose of such propaganda was to create a discourse that created an "us"
versus "them" dichotomy "to justify action through labelling."[27] Labeling the
Quakers "dissenters" allowed Congress to exile the Quakers to Virginia, but
labeling them as respectful members of society allowed Fisher to resist that
sign and its signifier.

Fisher did more than just list the exiles' names, of course; she also insisted
on the falsehood of the charges lodged against the Society of Friends. She
writes, "Nothing more than divers[e] testimonies . . . have been wrote at different times, for this two Years past." She expresses outrage at what she calls
"paper number 11, it being a Paper signed Spank Town Yearly Meeting when
no Yearly Meeting ever existed." She adds, "Any impartial person must see
how great a falsehood it is."[28] The Spanktown letter, like the warrant that Congress sent to justify the arrest of Fisher's husband, was yet another counterfeit
document that the rebels used to justify violence against the Quakers. The
protest that Fisher lodged here formed just one thread in a large web of epistolary communications, all versions of which were vying for legitimacy, just
like the groups that penned them. Congress reified the falsified Spanktown
letter when it discussed it, reprinted it in its minutes, and distributed the
minutes, papers, and ensuing resolves. The Society of Friends then engaged
in counter-rhetoric by fighting letters with letters when they signed the collective epistle that the exiles issued. The Quakers entered that collective in
the public sphere the newspapers provided, as Congress had done, and the
papers redistributed their protest so that the same readers who condemned
them might form an alternative perspective on the matter. When Fisher then
copied and supported the primary arguments articulated in the Friends'
open letter and sent her letter-journal to her husband and fellow inmates,
who read them aloud to others, she transcended the boundaries between
intimate, private writing and public, political work. Her letter-journal
allowed her to move between intimate and public, religious and secular,
printed and manuscript, domestic and political spaces as she borrowed from,
copied, responded to, and challenged the missives that moved rapidly among
minutes, missives, blacklists, resolves, and responses.

QUAKERS IN ZION

Fisher frames the exile and the rebels' repeated demands for access to her home as part of God's efforts to test her faith. She was in the last stages of her pregnancy with Hannah when Tommy was taken away, which exacerbated these trials. She believed that if she were able to keep the soldiers out of her house until her husband returned home safely from prison, she would pass God's test. She writes, "But Oh thou Almighty Being who sometimes for a season permits wicked men to bear sway, perhaps . . . we may see, how much their ruling ends in confusion, when thy Law does not rule in their Hearts."[29] Quakers did not want to be part of the new nation. They believed they could make their own "holy nation" located in the colonies but not part of the colonies.[30] In this regard, they saw themselves as—and often deployed metaphors relating to—Zion.

As the Israelites were chosen, persecuted, and exiled, so too were the Quakers in this metaphor. And as the Israelites wandered in search of a space in which they could abide by their own laws and customs, the Quakers did likewise. Quakers saw themselves reflected in Leviticus, which says God's chosen people would be "scatter[ed] . . . among all the nations, from one end of the earth to the other," with "no resting place for the sole[s] of [their feet]."[31] The Friends' exile in 1777 seemed biblical, the completion of a prophecy they had been waiting out. Fisher's journal allowed her to interpret her family's trials as part of a divine plan from God. The chosen had to suffer to expose the rebels' wickedness; she believed the Friends' persecution would both remind Quakers to guard against intruders in the holy nation and expose the wicked will of the pretenders. "Home" possessed as many layered meanings for Sarah Logan Fisher as it did for Grace Growden Galloway; it signified not only Fisher's literal house but also her spiritual one.

Fisher frames her ability to resist the soldiers' requests (both material and sexual) as evidence of God's providence, much in the way that she contextualizes her husband's exile as proof that God is testing her faith. When a group of men came to her door, demanding blankets from her home, she temporarily blocked their entry by emphasizing her status as a *feme covert*. She told the men that they "had robd me of what was far dearer than any property I had in the World, . . . my Husband, & that I could by no means encourage War of any kind." The soldiers pushed past her anyway and made two demands: first, that she grant them access to the rooms upstairs, and next, that she give them "some person" to take with them to search those rooms. Fisher interpreted the latter request to mean that she was either being asked to sacrifice herself or one of her female servants. She refused to do either. These men then surprised her by deciding to neither harm nor rob her. When faced with her resolve, they turned around and left the family unmolested. "Tho there was a Carpet on every floor," Fisher writes, "& a Blanket on every Bed, they came down & in a complisant manner told me they had had the pleasure of viewing my Rooms, but saw nothing that suited them. This I looked upon as a singular favor & an encouragement to trust still further to that Hand that hitherto mercifully supported me."[32]

Fisher's narrative at times is as remarkable as it is implausible. Two soldiers barged into her home, demanded to search her rooms with the company of one chosen person, and then, when faced with Fisher's staunch denial, chose to leave the house empty-handed. Rebel soldiers were known for abusing women who refused to cooperate, with punishments ranging from beatings and torture to rape, robbery, or property confiscation.[33] Fisher's story at least initially mirrors that of Sarah Tyler Brinley, whom we heard about in the introduction, but it quickly departs. Brinley, her husband away from the house, was stripped by the rebels even though she was "then advanced in her pregnancy" and pushed out into the snow.[34] Could Fisher's encounter have happened as she said it did? Such a question is less productive than examining how Fisher framed the encounter. To say she refused the soldiers' entry sent a message to her readers, both the prisoners and the descendants who would eventually inherit the journal: the rebels might strip her of her husband, her peace, and her safety, but they would not take her home or her faith. Or, put another way, though the rebels might gain access to her physical space, they could not penetrate her body or will. Her message signaled to her readers that she was willing to risk violence, abuse, and loss to stay true to the tenets of her Quaker faith and to her husband and Friends exiled three hundred miles away. The men left her unmolested because God favored her, according to her interpretation, which suggested that her pledge of faith— and the broader commitment the Quakers made to adhere to the Peace Testimony—had not gone unnoticed by a power with more authority than a rebel militia.

Fisher's journal draws from and challenges familiar Christian metaphors that pitted one's earthly "house"—the body and/or its material entrapments— against the heavenly one a Christian would enjoy in the afterlife. Both bodies and houses symbolized life's impermanence; believers were supposed to spend less time worrying about material goods and more time enriching their souls. This idea was represented in biblical passages that suggested the body was a "tabernacle" easily "dissolved" but quickly replaced by a "building of God, an house not made with hands, eternal in the heavens."[35] Because bodies are the "temples of the Holy Spirit," Christians were taught to internalize the idea that "you are not your own."[36] Christ told his disciples before his crucifixion, "In my Father's house are many mansions. . . . I go to prepare a place for you."[37] Quakers turned to passages such as this one to make sense of and cope with their own tribulations during the Revolutionary War as their bodies and houses were ransacked. The nature of their attacks, like Galloway's dreams of her drowning daughter, seemed prophetic. The Bible taught them that if material possessions were fleeting, then the supplies the soldiers sought should have been of small consequence. But the Bible paradoxically also suggested that the houses these women were guarding symbolized a more sacred temple. That is, if their houses were metaphors for their souls, then they should guard these spaces against the soldiers.

Fisher's barred door thus becomes a spiritual conflict. Clinging to her material possessions indicates her weakness. Giving over her home or the goods inside violates her faith. Such a conundrum becomes particularly difficult when we consider that some soldiers wanted the women inside of these houses; their bodies were the possessions in need of protection. Rape, in the context of these biblical imperatives, poses an unspeakable problem. Because most people in the eighteenth century assumed that women could not be raped because sex did not require their consent, a woman writing about rape implies that she was guilty of secretly wanting it to happen. (I discuss this in detail in chapter 4.) Fisher may have addressed this problem by carefully scripting her encounter with the rebel soldiers who ransacked her home and wanted to take her upstairs to her bedroom alone. She writes herself as victorious when she recalls the events for her husband in her letter-journal. The soldiers leave empty-handed and unsatisfied, a version that would have been quite powerful to any women who possessed limited legal control over their lives or homes.

THE DIARY OF ELIZABETH DRINKER

The events that Sarah Logan Fisher documents in her diary/letter-journal were also covered by the diarist Elizabeth Sandwith Drinker, who, like Fisher and Galloway, focuses on the metaphor of forced entry. But unlike Fisher and Galloway, Drinker constructs her loyalties in opposition to forced quartering and requisitions. She uses her opposition to these practices to script her dedication to the Society of Friends and to counter the rhetoric that attempted to label her and her husband as treasonous loyalists. It is important to see the way in which Drinker writes her resistance into her diary because it suggests that pacifism possessed striations during the American Revolution and was just as fluid a concept as loyalism. Also, her refusal to grant lodging or supplies—and the fact that she writes about this refusal in her journal— highlights yet another subtle way that women created spaces in which they could act as political agents with wills of their own. The diary provided a natural outlet for her worry and grief over this ordeal, since she had begun keeping it in 1758, when she was twenty-four, and it had become part of her daily ritual of spiritual accountability. She was a dedicated chronicler. Her diaries amount to thirty-three manuscript volumes, the equivalent of two thousand typescript pages, by the time she died at age seventy-two in 1807.[38] Her diary's audience and its privacy is different from Fisher's in that she did not send it to her husband, Henry, while he was in prison. She was a forty-two-year-old mother caring for five children when the Committee of Safety came for Henry (whom she called HD).[39] She does not address him by name in her journal, nor does she address anyone else.

The only way in which her journal engages with publicity practices is that it acts as what Richard T. Vann calls a "spiritual account book in which [Quakers] could record their spiritual credits and—more often—debits."[40] These account books were supposed to be kept in Quaker plainstyle, the prose as unadorned as their dress or homes, in part to avoid the sin of pride.[41] Journals provided a way of reflecting on divine revelations and decentering the self, a spiritual goal that could be attained if the writer recognized God's will and became aligned with it. Diaries of this sort were read aloud, passed along, and returned to the owner, like a letter that comes full-circle, but we have no proof that this happened to Drinker's in her lifetime.[42] She may have suspected it could circulate posthumously because she read the diaries of other Friends. The Society would often publish these journals after the writers had died, their work a testimony to a life well-lived. Quaker journals were therefore semi-private manuscripts that allowed for passage into the public sphere.[43] Drinker's journal offered her a space to reflect on the choices she made, but it also stood as her testimony to her faith, which other Quakers might read after she was gone. The thirty-three volumes she left would have been an impressive legacy for anyone who might care to read them.[44]

Many of Drinker's entries are brief chronicles of daily activities. Events that would later go on to make history sometimes receive only one line. Her entry on the Boston Tea Party reads, "an account from Boston, of 342 Chests of Tea, being thrown into the Sea." Others are quite detailed, however. After her husband Henry was arrested in 1777, for example, she writes,

> Wm. Bradford; one [Bluser] and Ervin, enterd, offering a Parole for [HD] to sign—which was refus'd. they then seiz'd on the Book and took several papers out of the Desk and carried them off; intimating their design of calling the next morning at 9 o'clock. . . . [The committee took Henry to Mason's Lodge] in an illegal, unpredesented [unprecedented] manner—where are several, other Friends with some of other proswasions, made prisoners;—Isreal Pemberton, John Hunt, James Pemberton, John Pemberton, Henry Drinker, Saml. Pleasants, Thos. Fisher, Saml. Fisher, Thos. Gillpin, Edward Penington; Thos. Wharton, Charles Jervis, Ellijah Brown, Thos. Afflick, Phineas Bond, Wm. Pike, Mires Fisher, Charles Eddy, Wm. Smith, Broker—Wm. D Smith, Thos. Comb, &c I went this evening to see my HD. where I mett with the Wives & Children of our dear Friends and other visitors in great numbers—upwards of 20 of our Friends call'd to see us this day.[45]

This list of names, and her opinion about the legality of the arrests, echoes Sarah Logan Fisher's, Congress's, and the Society of Friends'.

This entry sheds light on the many ways the Committee of Observation and Inspection could have impoverished her. First, it tried to take Henry's loyalties. The "parole" he was asked to sign was likely an oath, which he refused. Then, it took Henry's personal belongings—his book and papers—to see if it could find proof of treason. And, finally, it took Henry himself, along with a group of other Friends. Drinker's emphasis on the illegality of the committee's actions underscores that the Friends had all been stripped of their basic rights as citizens. Neither the Continental Congress nor the Supreme Executive Council possessed the proper authority or probable cause to detain the men, and neither wanted to properly prosecute the prisoners, which led to a stalemate. Both governing bodies literally distanced themselves by moving the prisoners to Virginia. Drinker, like Fisher, counters the attempts at erasure when she lists each prisoner's name in her diary, solidifying their treatment by inscribing it on paper for everyone to see.

Much of Drinker's diary, like much of Fisher's journal, documents how she denied the rebels access to her home, which signified her chasteness in body and spirit. She writes, "an Officer call'd this Afternoon to ask if we could take in a Sick or Wounded Captain; I put him off by saying that as my Husband was from me, I should be pleas'd if he could provide some other convenient place, he hop'd no offence, and departed." She describes a few days later how another officer "call'd . . . to know if Genl. Grant could have quarters with us; I told him my Husband was from me, and a Number of Young Children round me, I should be glad to be excus'd—he reply'd, as I desir'd it, it should be so."[46] Drinker argues that the army should leave her home unspoiled because its commanders had already taken what mattered most to her: Henry. This strategy worked, for a time. She eluded being forced to house soldiers or grant requisitions by reminding the officers that they had already arrested the man responsible for "covering" and protecting her and her children, an argument that echoes Grace Growden Galloway in her struggle for Trevose. Also, like Galloway, Drinker had to render herself metaphorically, legally invisible in order to accomplish this feat, a task made more difficult by the fact that her husband had been arrested for treason.

Each time that Drinker turned a soldier away from her home empty-handed, she also turned away the imperative that she support the revolution. Each time that she wrote of this denial, she reaffirmed her loyalty to the Society of Friends despite being tempted (or threatened) to abandon her principles. One particular incident was explicitly sexual and emphasized the threat to three sacred spaces: body, family, and home. Drinker writes that one man came on November 5, 1777, "to *demand* Blankets," which she says she "did not in any wise agree to," but this time, she is unable to stave off entry. "Notwithstanding my refusial," she recounts, "he went up stairs and took one, and with seeming good Nature beg'd I would excuse his borrowing it, as it was G. Howes orders." She then came upon a British officer—Captain John Tape—attempting to seduce her servant Ann. She ordered him to leave, and he became belligerent. Tape "shook his Sword, which he held in his Hand and seem'd to threaten." Her neighbor, Chalkley James, twisted the weapon from Tape's hand and collared him with it, which forced the officer to stumble away. He soon returned "with the Sword in his hand." The women had locked themselves into the parlor during his brief absence, but he beat on the door, "desiring entrance." When Drinker (like Galloway) would not admit entry, the "enrag'd, drunken Man" stomped "swareing about the House." She reminds her reader a third time that he moved about "with a Sword in his hand." Tape left the house with Ann, whom he "stole . . . over the fence." The intrusion left Drinker shaken for weeks; one month later, she writes, "I often feel afraid to go to bed."[47] These passages are undeniably phallic. Tape's sword symbolizes the many threats he brought with him into Drinker's home, including murder, rape, and robbery. The entry concludes with a scene that amalgamates all three when the soldier abducts Ann and, Drinker implies, violates her.

Ann still had not returned three months later, but Drinker saw Captain Tape in the streets and explained to him that he owed her a debt. Drinker asked him if he possessed "no sense of Religion or Virtue." "I should think," she adds in her account, "that what your Soldiers call Honor would have dictated to thee what was thy duty after thy behavior some time ago in this House." The soldier feigned innocence until Drinker pressed him, when he confessed, "I han't got your Servant." "I don't care who has her," Drinker says. "It was thee that stole her." "Well," he replies, "if you'll come up to my quarters up Town," but Drinker interrupts him. She demands not Ann but remuneration. Drinker then threatens Tape. If he fails to pay for the servant he took, she claims she will knock on every house in town that is also quartering officers and "tell all I meet with" what he has done. "I told him if he did not bring the Mony or send it soon he should hear further from me." "He stutter'd," aghast, and could only respond, "Well well well." Then "away he went seemingly confus'd."[48] Drinker has rewritten Tape's violation of her home by categorizing Ann as an economic loss, turning Tape's intrusion into a business transaction gone awry. He controlled her space and all of the people and things in it when he was in her home. Drinker remakes Tape into her debtor when she sees him a second time. The diary provided her a space to mark how she held him accountable, writing down how she confronted, controlled, and baffled the man who had dominated her home and traumatized her family three months prior.

Captain Tape, for Elizabeth Drinker, was metonymic of the revolution itself. The war asked her to align either with God or country when she desired to be a member of a separate but amicable "holy nation." The men carrying out the war asked her to donate to its cause when she desired to be left in peace. The war violated her belief system, and it physically and spiritually imperiled her. Such a depiction of the revolution foiled the rebel rhetoric that justified separation with England, which rebels often couched in terms of rape as well. Revolutionary narratives suggested that the king was a rapist—a man with a mighty sword with power gone awry—and the colonies his victim. America in art and literature was often depicted as "a Columbia figure over whom a whole host of potentially dangerous men attempt to gain power and control."[49] This rhetoric suggests that the nation's "assailed virtue should elicit the colonials' outrage and stir them into taking action against the British villain."[50] Drinker changes the story. In her version, the colonies are the rapists—violent men waving about their swords—and the dissenters are the victims. She discursively revises the war's justification to make herself—and, by extension, the Quakers—righteous. The Friends did not act as covert loyalist spies secretly carrying out meetings in Spanktown; they were faithful but hapless casualties of war.

Drinker's consistent refusal to house soldiers of any stripe stands out in stark relief to the moment when she ultimately decided to quarter a British soldier in her home. She labors in these passages to prove that this decision did not imply consent. Before Tape's drunken sword-waving and servant-stealing, British major John Crammond had approached Drinker about moving in to her home. She had denied him, as she had all of the others. One too many encounters with violent soldiers and too many bouts of insomnia later, however, Drinker wondered if she had made the right decision. Crammond approached her again on December 19, 1777, and again Drinker hesitated. "I expect'd that we who were at present 'lone women, would be excus'd," Drinker protested. "He said he fear'd not, for tho I might put him of[f] . . . yet as a great number of the Forign Troops were to be quarterd in this Neighborhood, he believ'd they might be troublesome." Crammond meant that he and his men were safe while the rebels, the colonists he labels as "foreign troops," were potential rapists. The rebels, he told her, would not ask to billet there; they would simply occupy. Drinker wrote that this logic made her pause. Captain Tape was a British officer, so she knew that Crammond's men were just as dangerous as the rebels. She also knew that billeting so-called trustworthy people did not always result in protection. Her friend Owen Jones and his family had "been very ill used indeed, by an Officer who want[ed] to quarter himself," she recalls. Jones's officer, like Captain Tape, "drew his Sword, us'd very abusive language, and had the Front Door split in pieces."[51] When Crammond returned to repeat his proposition that Drinker should quarter him in the name of "safety"—that is, to protect the women of her household from compulsory entry "rather than wait until a soldier was *forced* on her"—she acquiesced.[52] This gray area of consent was not consent at all. While it is true that Crammond did not brandish his weapon and break down her door, Drinker also did not want him in her home. It seems important to Drinker that she let her potential readers know—and perhaps that she note for herself—that she made this decision only after she weighed it carefully. Henry still lived in exile, so she had to act as the deputy husband, protector to her children and servants, but because she was a woman, she lacked the (phallic) power of Tape's "sword," so her agency could also be conscripted.

Drinker began using her diary after Henry was sent to Virginia to focus primarily on two subjects: the crowds that stripped her and her neighbors of their peace and property, and her attempts to regain what she had lost. The looting in Drinker's neighborhood began on September 16, 1777, when Washington evacuated Philadelphia and the British occupied it. Thieves stole flour from the Drinkers' stable, and Elizabeth and her neighbors feared for their safety. Crowds also attacked Drinker's husband and the other exiles in protest of the prisoners' arrival in Reading, Pennsylvania. Drinker immediately began appealing to Congress and the Pennsylvania Executive Council to issue writs of habeas corpus, a procedure Congress (conveniently) suspended shortly after the Virginia Exiles' families began requesting them.[53]

THE EXILES' RELEASE

The fight for the right to entry went both ways. As the soldiers wanted access to Fisher's and Drinker's homes, so Fisher and Drinker wanted access to the Quaker exiles, which was particularly difficult to obtain once the men were moved so far away to Winchester, Virginia. The rhetoric that the Quaker women used to pen their collective letter to demand the exiles' release shares similarities with the rhetoric these same writers used in their own private diaries and letter-journals. This suggests that the private or intimate diurnal practices these loyalist women cultivated at home may have inspired or found an outlet in public protestations and loyalty proclamations in the political sphere.

Elizabeth Drinker learned that Thomas Gilpin had died on March 27, 1778, and on April 3, she heard that John Hunt had too. Henry Drinker was also gravely ill.[54] The publication of the prisoners' conditions renewed public interest in the exiles' case, and Quaker women decided to act. Elizabeth Drinker and three other Quaker women gathered information about the exiles' poor health and used it to pen a collective letter (which Sarah Logan Fisher also signed) making a case for the men's release. These four Friends then marched to Valley Forge to deliver the appeal to George Washington, who had named these women as traitors.[55]

The letter that the women presented to Washington echoes the anxiety in the Quakers' diaries, but the tone is more supplicating. The women did not initially ask for the prisoners' release; instead, they requested access to them so that they could provide them with medical care. This collective missive uses the rhetoric of sympathy and argues that exile was killing the prisoners, dooming the wives to become widows. "What adds to our distress in this sorrowful circumstance is the account we have lately received of the removal of one of them by death," they write, "and that divers of them are much indisposed; and as we find they are in want of necessaries proper for sick people, we desire the favour of General Washington to grant a protection for one or more wagons, and for the persons we may employ to go with them, in order that they may be accommodated with what is suitable." The arguments so prevalent throughout the diaries and letter-journals are missing from this petition. The writers do not focus on whether or not the Friends were loyalists, pacifists, or traitors. They do not attack the justification of the warrants or the loyalty oaths. They completely omit any discussion of Congress's right to exile these men, a point to which they often return in their journals. Their sentimental appeal emphasizes a woman's dependence and innocence in matters of war. On one hand, the epistle signified a protest against what they had been told to accept: their husbands' imprisonment and their lack of legal recourse to do anything about it. On the other hand, the women seemed to realize that Washington held the ability to grant them a pass to cross enemy lines. Their request played on his pity. Furthermore, the writers signed the letter "on behalf of the whole." The group insisted that they spoke for the entire Quaker community, which served them in two ways: it demoted them to mere representatives, since it reminded Washington that they sought not personal favors but rather justice for the larger group, and it called up the formidable power of the Society of Friends. These strategies worked. Washington considered their pleas, then wrote ex-Quaker Thomas Wharton, Jr., president of the Supreme Executive Council, to request that the prisoners be allowed to cross enemy lines, citing the women's petition for his decision. "They seem much distressed," Washington wrote by way of justification; "humanity pleads strongly in their behalf."[56] Washington was convinced and let the women pass.

Once the Quaker women succeeded at Valley Forge, they presented a second missive to Congress in Lancaster, which served as the Pennsylvania capital and headquarters for the Continental Congress, Supreme Executive Council of Pennsylvania, and Pennsylvania Assembly.[57] The wives' appeal suggested that the council extend "Christian charity and compassion" to a group of people who have a "strong attachment to their native country" and to "mankind in general." Like the first collective missive, this epistle also employs sympathetic rhetoric. It argues that the wives were too emotionally frail to handle the stress of losing a spouse in wartime. "No doubt many of you have wives and tender children," the women told the council, "and must know that, in time of trial and distress, none are so proper to alleviate and bear a part of the burden, as their affectionate husbands." This letter to Congress, like the letter to Washington, bears few traces of the journal entries that depicted women as square-shouldered defenders of their homesteads, pushing away inebriated, armed, cantankerous soldiers. They are described, instead, as weak, sorrowful, and unable to shoulder the burden of their husbands' exile, fearful the ordeal would kill them as well as their husbands. This final letter to Congress closes by arguing for religious liberty. If the council failed to muster enough sympathy for the prisoners or their wives, at least it could admit that the exiles were only guilty of holding fast to religious beliefs, "a steady and firm adherence to their inoffensive and peaceable principles," which was hardly a punishable offense. The women conclude by insisting that they wrote the letter without their husbands' approval, and then they signed it:

> Hannah Pemberton
> Isabella Affleck
> Rebecca Jervis
> Phebe Pemberton
> Sarah R. Fisher
> Mary Eddy
> Sarah Pennington
> Rachel Wharton
> Esther Fisher
> Mary Pemberton
> Eliza Drinker
> Sarah Fisher
> Susanna Jones
> Mary Pleasants
> Mary Brown
> Elizabeth Smith
> Eliza Jervis
> Rachel Hunt

This list mirrors that of the male exiles' names printed in the Fisher and Drinker diaries and in Quaker meeting minutes.[58]

The similarity is not coincidental. Printing their names for the council meant that they, like their exiled husbands, refused to be invisible, either politically, as loyalists and Quakers, or legally, as *femes covert*. They used the arguments they developed in their letter-journals and diaries, and aggregated those signatures to demand a presence before the statesmen who could free the prisoners. This letter to Congress, like the one written to Washington, worked; what had been stripped was returned to them. Timothy Matlack delivered the news on April 10, 1778, that the Executive Council had approved the prisoners' release.[59] It is possible to argue that the women made it easier for Congress and the Pennsylvania Assembly to extricate themselves from a public-relations nightmare, but such a suggestion underestimates the Quaker writers' prowess. I instead am suggesting that sympathy prevailed where logic had failed.

The effectiveness of the Quakers' rhetorical strategy is obvious and confounding. Rebels used sentiment and sympathy—which Andrew Burstein has called "the most distinctive emotional force[s]" of the eighteenth century—to launch the war. Americans could not be united through a monarch, so they would be joined by affection, an imperative that "required heart, affection, unselfish feeling."[60] Sympathy connected nerves, heart, and mind and was integral to the well-being of both physical and political bodies.[61] The prevalence of sympathy in rebel rhetoric justifying the rebellion might explain the Quakers' use of sympathy as a rhetoric in their own appeals to free the Virginia Exiles, except that rebels did not think the loyalists were capable of such heartfelt emotions. Rebels often oversimplified the revolution as a war between two groups of people: those who could feel and those who could not. Those who were able to feel were good and just, and those who could not were tyrannical and corrupt. Americans were able to feel. The English—and anyone who sympathized with the English—were not.[62]

This dichotomy placed the Quakers in a difficult position. The rebels counted the Quakers as loyalists and assumed all loyalists were unable to feel, so the rebels would therefore have assumed that the Quakers were incapable of fully comprehending sympathy and sentiment. This assumption would have excluded them from full consideration by the nascent American government. Ultimately, this logic meant that the Friends possessed an impossible, circular position to defend, but the Quaker women defended it well. They appealed to George Washington's sympathies by reminding him that if their husbands died while the men were imprisoned without trial, they would become widows. The women's argument used the rebels' rhetoric against them. Although Matlack, Washington, and the Philadelphia Assembly might have changed their minds about the Virginia Exiles for any number of reasons, it is important not to discount the Quaker women's ingenious strategy to call the statesmen on their commitment to create a republic of sympathetic people united by their affections for one another.

LIFE, LETTERS, AND JOURNALS AFTER EXILE

The Friends' journals and letters went silent for a time after they completed the task of returning their loved ones to their homes. Sarah Logan Fisher did not record her husband's homecoming until May 29, 1778, one month after the Friends reached Philadelphia. She explains that "a fit of illness & many engagements has prevented me continuing my Journal to this time."[63] Elizabeth Drinker also wrote very little about the reunion; instead, she returned to chronicling and notes only that Henry looked "much hartier than expected . . . fat and well."[64] As it were, their woes were just beginning. The British evacuated the city on June 9, 1778, and the Americans arrived on June 18.[65] Under rebel occupation, both Drinker and Fisher continued to suffer hardships, including heavy taxation, property loss, mobs, and hostility. The same month the exiles were released, the Pennsylvania legislature created a law requiring all men over eighteen to swear allegiance to the state before June 1, which must have caused the former Quaker prisoners a dreadful feeling of déjà-vu. Many refused and lost their properties and/or the rights to sue in court, make a will, or act as executor of any estate, but in the few days that followed the exiles' release, these writers did not discuss these events.[66]

Sarah Logan Fisher's and Elizabeth Drinker's manuscripts both clarify and complicate our understanding of how Quakers constructed loyalty during the American Revolution. Drinker wrote about all soldiers as robbers and rapists. Fisher saw them as illegitimate madmen drunk with power. These letter-diaries suggest that these gray-area loyalists would identify primarily as pacifists if given the opportunity, but they sometimes shifted their loyalties to fit their situations when under duress. Many of these writers were treated as if they possessed affiliations all their own, even before it was clear to the writer herself whether or not she did. These journals, letter-journals, and collective missives also affirm and enrich what early American scholars have suspected was true of these kinds of texts: they were neither wholly public nor wholly private. Although the audience for these letters and journals was limited, the texts were shared with other people, making them a quasi-public proclamation of political identity. Fisher performed her loyalties for her husband and the other exiles, and Drinker for herself and any other Quakers who might read her story. Furthermore, these letters and journals shifted genres. They sometimes acted as an intimate space through which the writers might communicate with close family and friends. But occasionally they were written for public consumption in the papers, or delivered to Congress and debated in a public forum. Sometimes the sentiments, arguments, and ideas in them were later reflected in published, collective petitions, such as the letters to Washington and the Pennsylvania Assembly, signed "on behalf of the whole." The generic categories of letter, diary, petition, newspaper article, autobiography, and spiritual account resist classifications that seek to bind and hold them, much like the women who wrote them.

These writers teach us that finding a safe space to voice dissent has, since the nation's inception, been both an imperative and a fragile undertaking. Their work explores the hegemony that a label—whether rebel or loyalist, thug or terrorist—can place on marginalized people who must bear its burden. These women's stories suggest that external groups with the privilege of surveillance—legislators, confiscation committees, and crowds—ultimately regulated the loyalties that would determine who possessed the right to entry, but the writings also prove that our earliest medium for hyperlinked communication provided those marginalized people with an outlet for resistance that could achieve tangible results.

CHAPTER THREE

SCRIPTING NEUTRALITY

Margaret Hill Morris

I would like to tell you that I traveled thousands of miles to Margaret Hill Morris's home in Burlington, New Jersey, to learn more about war in the Delaware Valley, but, really, I am here to learn about a secret attic in her house. I'd been studying Morris's diary for years, and one part dogged me. Morris, a Quaker, broke her vow to adhere to pacifism by hiding a loyalist spy in the attic. Technically, it was William Franklin's attic. He'd built the Green Bank house overlooking the Delaware River several years before the American Revolution, and Franklin's blueprints apparently included the construction of a mysterious hiding place, accessible only by prying off the back of a trick bookshelf. The room boasted a large sandbox—which, for some reason, was the detail that always disturbed me the most—and some kind of alarm. A person standing at the door downstairs triggered the bell with a secret switch to let the occupant in the "auger hole" know to hide. I have many questions. Why did Franklin build a secret room? Where was the room now? And why did a pacifist decide to hide a loyalist inside of it?

What I find when I arrive in Burlington leaves me with more questions than answers. Green Bank has been replaced with a one-story brick building that now serves as a meeting-place for the Veterans of Foreign Wars. A large American flag whips in the breeze coming off of the Delaware. A stone marker outside the house commemorates the founding of Burlington in 1677. An eagle statue as tall as a horse perches on the other side of the road. Its head is swiveled toward the place where Morris's house once stood. Despite rebels and loyalists alike docking their boats just a few feet away, despite Morris's journal giving her readers a front-row seat of the war, despite Morris being a prominent healer/doctor, there is no sign that Margaret Morris ever lived here. It is simultaneously fitting and insulting that a VFW has replaced her memory. She, too, survived a war. She, too, served her country—mending soldiers, tending armies, healing sickness. She, like the veterans who gather here, lived with trauma. Morris would neither recognize this flag nor like it. If she were alive today, she would be a twenty-first-century Rip Van Winkle who had awakened to find all the signs in town swapped from pro-Crown to pro-colonies. The VFW Hall is locked as tightly as Grace Growden Galloway's house and twice as dark. I was lucky at La Salle, but not here. As I was at Trevose, I am, once again, denied entry.

THE QUAKER MARGARET Hill Morris, at first glance, seems like a failed pacifist. She used both a hidden room and an alarm system to help a man she was hiding escape a group of "Tory Hunters." Each time that British, Hessian, or rebel soldiers besieged Burlington, New Jersey, they asked her to declare what side she supported so that she could be categorized and, if necessary, searched. Each time, Morris resisted such categorization. She instead proposed an alternative: neutrality. There is "a great deal of talk in the neighborhood about a neutral island," she writes in her letter-journal, and "I wish with great earnestness it may be allowed."[1]

When Morris's sister Milcah Martha (Patty) Moore moved away from Burlington during the war, Morris began writing her a letter-journal so that they could stay in touch. It names Patty as the reader in its salutation and commences diurnally with dated entries. The letters are bound together with thin metal rods and twine, forming a booklet. The booklet contains a preface, which states that Margaret does not intend her journal "for mixed companies or general communication" but that she has "no objection to them reading it out to our own family, provided you turn the critic out of doors, and let only the partial friends hear the thoughts of my heart at the time I wrote them." "Part of it was written in a serious, others in a waggish mood," she explains, "and most of it after the family were abed, and I sat up to keep guard over my fences, &c., while the soldiers were next door, for fear they should pull them down to burn."[2] Her "paper island," then, was intended as an echo-chamber meant for people who, if not in the same situation, could sympathize with her conundrum. She sought in these letter-journal pages a space for neutrality when she was denied it elsewhere. Her thoughts came to fruition while Morris was waiting and watching—waiting to see if soldiers would pull her home apart, watching to see if men would scale her walls. Her diary acted as a sentry, keeping watch and allowing others to keep watch alongside her.

Morris's readers included the members of Patty Moore's salon, fellow Quakers, relatives, friends, and authors, some of whom presided over or participated in salons of their own.[3] The salon's members included Hannah Griffitts, Susanna Wright, and Elizabeth Graeme Fergusson (the subject of chapter 5), who exchanged information with another salon in New Jersey, each group forming concentric circles that made the network of possible readers astoundingly large. The journal's readers might also have included Moore's, Griffitts's, Wright's, and Fergusson's friends and relatives, all of whom were connected by "birth, education, religious, socioeconomic status and affinity."[4] Moore wrote a commonplace book that featured several of these writers, including large excerpts from Elizabeth Fergusson's journal, but she did not include Morris's letter-journal in this book.[5] Morris's writings to her sister should be seen as being in dialogue with Moore's broader system of exchange, albeit through reading aloud to the group (and possibly through epistolary excerpts that no longer exist) rather than transcription into her own text.[6] Morris's acquiescence in her sister's sharing the journal with sympathetic friends suggests she considered herself in conversation with Moore's correspondents, which means that Morris's unnamed audience included a vast, well-connected group of women of great intellectual acumen and social status.

Her readers, as historian Karin Wulf puts it, were "by no means a politically homogeneous group."[7] Moore's circle represented an array of loyalties. She promoted pacifism, and Griffitts encouraged moderation. Fergusson may have served as a loyalist informant, but she revised her position later to align with the patriots to regain confiscated property. Morris gives no indication that the neutrality in her letter-journal was performed for their benefit, either; rather, it appears that she considered herself on a sliding political scale, and that she found solidarity and empathy among these writers, many of whom also longed for a neutral island where they could live out their days in peace.

NEUTRALITY IN MORRIS'S LETTER-JOURNAL

Political neutralists often claim neutrality for epistemological, moral, or pragmatic reasons. Margaret Morris argues for all three in her letter-journal. Epistemological neutralists say that they should be exempted from participating in war to "defend an 'epistemic abstinence,' according to which it is better not to justify policy decisions on perfectionist grounds, given our degree of uncertainty about what kinds of life are best." An epistemological neutralist would suggest that non-neutrality violates the citizen's attempt to live a good life according to his or her own personal definition of that term. Moral neutralists, however, argue that a "plurality of values" exists in all societies—that not everyone can or should agree on what is morally right—and so the state should take a position of neutrality in times of war to avoid violating "individual autonomy," which includes people's religious or spiritual principles. Pragmatic neutralists promote neutrality because war would "pose unacceptable risks of oppression, instability and error."[8] Such logic suggests that, because fallible human beings might inflict unnecessary suffering on innocent civilians while waging war, their decisions could easily plunge that society into chaos by toppling its infrastructure and turning people against each other. Continuing from that logic, neutrality is preferable to war. Morris uses her journal to implement all three reasons—epistemological, moral, and pragmatic—for promoting neutrality, building a case that she and her fellow residents should be permitted to form that "neutral island" they so ardently desired.

Morris's political body, and the letter-journal she used to define it, held contending loyalties, mirroring the geopolitical space in which Morris resided: the Delaware Valley. This area encompassed 130 miles along the Delaware River and included Burlington, New Jersey.[9] Discussions about loyalism often focus on how it played out in Philadelphia, Boston, New York, or Charleston, the strategic cities the rebels and loyalists sought to control for economic and political advantages. The Delaware Valley, unlike other contended revolutionary spaces, served as a kind of weigh station as people from both sides paused to gather strength or wait out the winter before advancing to Trenton or Philadelphia. As such, this area and many in it fluctuated politically.

Morris's own diary, like the backdrop against which it was set, struggled—or refused—to delineate the line between loyalists and rebels. The resulting text forces the reader to struggle—or refuse—to determine the political affiliation of the key players in the narrative. People like Morris who lived in cities like Burlington often resisted making political allegiances. Her writings offer people a perspective that differs from Galloway's, Drinker's, and Fisher's because she lived in this space. Galloway was disaffected, completely disillusioned with both the rebels and the loyalists, and Drinker and Fisher were pacifists, opposed to the war's violence for religious reasons. Morris, on the other hand, identified as a neutralist. Renunciation distinguishes the former categories from the latter. The pacifists in this book actively rejected war, and the disaffected adamantly shunned all sides; this neutralist, however, occupied a tenuous middle ground. Although a neutralist is typically someone who remains impartial, Morris used that terminology to mean someone who constantly adapts. She picked *all* sides rather than picking *one*, a discursive strategy that saved her family's lives and allowed her to maintain a modicum of control among chaos in one of the most contested areas of the country during the Revolutionary War.

Morris's letter-journal theoretically broadens the concept of "neutral ground" from place to page. The most commonly studied neutral ground is Westchester County, New York, and its periphery, situated just north of Manhattan Island and east of the Hudson River. Other neutral areas included the shores of Long Island Sound, the region surrounding Philadelphia (from 1777 to 1778), and parts of the South after 1779. Neutrality did not mean impartiality in these areas, just as it did not mean impartiality in Morris's journal; rather, neutrality meant that residents' allegiances fluctuated as rebels and loyalists gained and lost traction in these spaces. And as violence and property destruction became commonplace, residents' allegiances often soured into disaffection. George Washington argued that he who could control these neutral grounds could make significant strides toward winning the war.[10] The same could be said about whoever controlled letters in this area. Stemming the flow of intelligence across borders was paramount for winning the war, which explains why the first treason laws drafted during the revolution included the charge of correspondence with the enemy, weighing it equally alongside fighting for the British (a point that becomes more germane in chapter 4). Letters were as contested as the spaces in which they were written. Tensions among the letter-writer, courier, soldiers, and recipients mounted as the war escalated. As these tensions increased, so did the imperative to create spaces for political self-definition. Margaret Morris responded to these mounting pressures to pick a side by constructing for Patty and any other unnamed readers her own paper "neutral island" that was otherwise denied her.

BLESS ME, ARE YOU HESSIANS?

When Margaret Morris saw a fleet of ships approaching her house on December 6, 1776, she picked up her pen and began writing to Patty, who had fled the war and settled in Montgomery Township, roughly thirty miles away.[11] Washington's troops were marching to Pennsylvania, and the British were retreating to New York. Hessians remained behind to preserve the loyalists' interests in the region. Burlington, New Jersey, was caught in the crossfire (fig. 3). The Hessians swept through the town on December 11 in search of any "persons . . . in arms [or] any Arms, Ammunition, or other effects, belonging to Persons that were in Arms against the King."[12] The continentals ordered a similar sweep two days later, though this time for Tories—an order that brought a group of rebels to Morris's front door. She writes that her sons John (who was seventeen) and Richard (who was fourteen) wanted a better view of the soldiers conducting the raid as they went house to house, so John "caught up the spy-glass, and was running toward the mill to look at them." He then brought the glass to Richard so that his brother also could see, but then "both . . . were observed by the people on board, who suspected it was an enemy that was watching their motions." As Richard and John were watching, so too were they being watched. The soldiers they were observing quickly dispatched a small group of men to discern the threat at the Morris house. The soldiers demanded that Margaret Morris deliver the "D—d tory . . . spy," meaning one of her sons.[13]

What happened during this raid—and the way in which Morris recorded the Tory hunters' invasion—provides a useful introduction to how Morris constructed her own political identity in the Delaware Valley as she sought to navigate among pacifism, loyalism, and neutrality. Neither John nor Richard were

FIGURE 3. *Scene of Incidents Described in Revolutionary Journal of Margaret Morris. The View from Green Bank in Burlington, New Jersey.* From the collection of the Burlington County Historical Society.

spies, but their mother was hiding one—a poet and Anglican minister named Jonathan Odell. After Odell wrote a series of letters criticizing the "Whig Congress," Congress had placed him on parole in Burlington. He had violated that punishment by interpreting for the Hessians and publishing a series of poems calling for an end to the rebellion. His overt public dissent, which he refused to temper even after being captured, made the Tory hunters target him, which explains why he had taken shelter in Morris's home.[14] Morris tells Moore that when the rebel soldiers approached her house to search for Odell, "the Name of a Tory so near my *own door* seriously alarmd me, for a poor *refugee*, dignifyed by that Name, had claimd the shelter of my Roof & was at that very time conceald, like a thief in an Auger hole" in the secret chamber of Green Bank, her home. Morris says that she "kept locking and unlocking [the door]" so she might have time to get her "ruffled face, a little composed" and think of a plan. She then "[rang] the bell violently, the Signal agreed on, if they came to Search," and bought time by stalling with her inquisitors. Opening the door, she put on a "very simple look" and "cryd out, 'Bless me, I hope you are not Hessians—say, good Men, are you the Hessians?'" The men replied, "Do we look like Hessians?" to which Morris replied, "Indeed I don't know . . . but they are Men & you are Men."[15] She redirected the soldiers to her neighbor's house, but they could not find Odell there. "Strange where could he be[?]," Morris jokes to her sister. After the rebels left empty-handed, she transferred Odell to another home, from which he escaped to New York, eventually resettling safely in New Brunswick, Canada.[16]

Morris capitalizes on her political fluidity in this passage, which has multiple, layered meanings. She cleverly plays on the performative nature of political identity by insisting that she cannot distinguish rebels from loyalists because "they are Men & you are Men." Such a moment provides a prime example of epistolarity. She wants the soldiers to leave, so she answers their questions with a question: are you Hessians? The troops' smart retort—do we look like Hessians?—suggests their frustration with Morris for being unable to recognize them as patriots. She refuses to identify their political affiliation, just as they fail to identify theirs. When she says that Hessians are "men," as the soldiers are "men," Morris reverses what the soldiers have done to her (and all women in the war): she identifies them by their sex, rather than by their loyalties. Although she may have used this maneuver to buy Odell time to better secure his position, it also allows Morris a chance to fashion her own definition of loyalty (while simultaneously questioning the soldiers').

One can assume that she possessed even more time to fashion this interaction in her diary, as she sat down to her desk later that night to write her story the way that she wanted it to be remembered.

Knowing a bit about the Hessians adds to the many layers of Morris's question to the rebel soldiers. The British hired the Hessians—men from Hessen-Kassel in Germany—as auxiliary troops to aid them in the war.[17] They possessed a reputation for being violent, cruel warmongers and villainous, licentious plunderers. They also were undiscerning; they violated, robbed, and injured allies and enemies alike. When Charles Cornwallis ushered a group of British and Hessian soldiers into Hackensack, New Jersey, for example, the loyalists there "welcomed them as liberators" until the Hessians began ransacking the loyalists' homes. The locals expressed dismay to find that these men "could not"—or perhaps *would* not—"distinguish a Tory from a Whig." Hessians often ignored other loyalists' protection papers and robbed their own allies, choosing profit over patriotism.[18] Morris's question, "Bless me, are you Hessians?" purposefully holds up a mirror to the rebels and informs them in no uncertain terms that they resemble the enemies they seek.

The other semantic wordplay happening in this entry occurs when Morris recategorizes Odell as a "refugee," rather than a "damned Tory spy." On one level, Morris subtly corrects the soldiers' terminology because their label—Tory—would have been a pejorative. But on another, Morris is redefining Odell in a way that would have justified her decision to help him, despite the Peace Testimony that demanded she remain uninvolved. Quakers historically have always quibbled over what constitutes political engagement.[19] They believe that fighting or killing someone in battle clearly violates their principles of pacifism, but they have quarreled over whether helping someone in distress or curing an ailing soldier would. The Quakers decided during King Philip's War that Friends, in good faith, could offer sanctuary to anyone—civilians or soldiers—whom they categorized as "refugees and casualties of the war." "To offer sanctuary," they decided, represented a "purely benevolent service, expressing sacrificial love, and so appears an appropriate replacement for military participation."[20] Morris likely was correcting the soldiers' categorization of Odell, then, because doing so not only defended him but protected her.

Morris's wordplay in her letter-journal highlights the way assumptions about women's apolitical status could work in their favor. Readers could read her letter as a straightforward account of a woman who feared armed men would find a known loyalist hiding in her house, a discovery that would endanger both Odell and her family. Her fear would certainly explain why she assumed a "simple look." I suggest, however, that her letter should be read as experimenting with the soldiers' labels. If read this way, the subtle means in which women engaged in political discourse and in which they turned that discourse into active resistance becomes apparent. Odell, to Morris, was a refugee, a word that highlighted his victimization as a byproduct of war; to the local Safety and Confiscation Committees, he was a traitor. According to new laws, Morris betrayed the colonies too. Her willingness to hide Odell would have made her a loyalist in the rebels' estimation, regardless of how she classified herself. The men asked if she was concealing a Tory, and the answer stood before them, but they could not see it because Morris was female. They sought the man under her roof, but they were looking for the woman in the doorway. Morris's transparency also harmed her. Her neutrality endangered her because rebels treated Friends as subversive loyalists. She could easily lose this war of words. As I discussed in chapter 2, Quakers constructed, distributed, and read aloud letters at various regional meetings urging Friends to avoid fighting or lending aid. Congress already suspected Quakers because they refused to take oaths, so Friends were not afforded the luxury of being neutral. Their neutrality acted like a blank page onto which rebels could inscribe the loyalties they assumed Quakers held. External forces may have wanted people such as Margaret Morris to publicly proclaim their allegiances via oaths, but many were uninterested in making such proclamations.[21]

LOYALTY LOST IN TRANSLATION

Morris, a pragmatic neutralist, often used her diary to record the ways in which misinformation and translation complications plagued soldiers on both sides, leading to instability and mistakes. By highlighting these communicative failures, Morris's diary calls into question the impetus for the war. She writes in the winter of 1776 that Washington's aide-de-camp John Laurens rode out to meet a group of gondola men, or rebel auxiliaries, who would soon overtake the town. Laurens told these men to hold their fire when they reached Burlington and then returned to await their arrival. Imagine his surprise when these same auxiliaries—his own allies—crossed into the city a few hours later and greeted Laurens by shooting at him. "Not believing it possible this could be designedly done, [Laurens and his fellow officers] stood still," Morris writes, and were fired on again. The new arrivals began attacking Burlington residents, aiming cannons at their houses and setting fire to their properties. The auxiliaries later explained that they "believe[d] that the houses were full of Hessians."[22] Morris underscores the futility of this revolution by suggesting that the auxiliaries were firing randomly at any house that seemed to be occupied—rather than targeting specific locations that might help advance their cause. Why is anyone fighting at all, she asks, if no one can accurately identify the enemy?

Her observations also suggest that she believes the revolution to be disorganized and misguided, a common critique among loyalists. Morris makes this belief clear by highlighting the proliferation of misinformation during the war. This second interpretation is important because, without it, the diary can be read as merely a chronicle of life interrupted, rather than a text engaging in coded discourse that, in Morris's day, would have signaled a particular stance on the war. She may have hoped for a neutral island, but her diary leans heavily on standard loyalist rhetoric. Her passages suggest that, rather than being the "commonsense" movement of valiant men seeking liberty for all Americans, this war was led by bumbling fools who preferred violence and chaos to peace and order. Morris's diary sounds like Samuel Seabury's "Free Thoughts on the Proceedings of the Continental Congress."[23] As with Seabury, Morris argues that confusion is contagious in that it ripples out into the community and causes good citizens to fear for their lives. Citizens struggle to discern between rebels and loyalists. Morris tries to get news about troop movements to see if she could safely resume her daily routine, but living in the eye of the skirmish meant that the delivery of information had been frozen; nothing went out and nothing passed through. Friends and neighbors cautiously crept out of their houses after each attack on their neighborhood. As soon as the residents emerged, the rebels returned to extrapolate hidden spies. "The suspicions of the gondola men still continued," Morris recalls, "and search was made in and about the town for men distinguished by the name of Tories."[24] The result appears to be a pointless cat-and-mouse game. Soldiers fired aimlessly at houses occupied by innocent civilians. The civilians fled. The other houses were also randomly searched, and their occupants fled as well. The result as Morris imagines it was a desolate town emptied of good people who only wanted, all along, to be left alone.

The language barrier between the residents and the soldiers—namely the

Hessians—only exacerbated the tensions in the Delaware Valley. Morris tells her sister that she taught her children to say *"vegates . . . like a Dutchman"* so that they might escape the Hessians' ire.[25] This pleasantry—*"How* are you?"—suited her purposes better than interrogation—*"Who* are you?"—perhaps because the latter question was more difficult to answer than the former. She searched the town for someone who could speak the soldiers' mother tongue so that she and her family might learn more than pleasantries that would help her navigate this situation. She discovered that her neighbor's maid spoke Dutch and declared, "We resolve . . . that she shall be the interpreter of [Green Bank]." The cultural divide among the Hessians, British, and rebels ultimately proved too great to overcome. Some people procured papers that confirmed their loyalties to the Crown and assumed these documents would allow them to move freely. These documents often proved worthless if they were written in English, however, because many Hessians spoke only German. An anxious Hessian without a translator would likely bypass the form if he could not read it and would either harm the possessor or plunder his or her house anyway. Such difficulties were complicated by the fact that the citizens who lived in neutral areas would occasionally sign these British loyalty oaths out of convenience, rather than ideology. Hessian captain Friedrich von Münchhausen attested to "having written out thousands of protection papers in German, so that the auxiliary troops should not molest the loyal," but "many of these papers were subsequently found on the bodies of American soldiers slain in battle or captured." The captain assumed these soldiers procured the papers themselves (rather than stealing them from other loyalists) so that they could move easily between opposing geopolitical locations. "Not speaking the language, [the Hessians] could not distinguish between friend and foe and plundered indiscriminately."[26] Hampered by language barriers and what appeared to be a dizzying fluctuation of political identities, the Hessians defaulted to that which would best serve themselves. Morris belabors this point to bring to light the war's futility in her region. With loyalists robbing loyalists in a babel of corrupt, confused, scared soldiers, Morris suggests that leaving the rebels alone provided the most sensible solution to the conundrum. She focuses on the ideological confusion between the warring parties and the citizens they were attacking in order to support her claim that the rebels and loyalists should leave her, and anyone else who agreed with her, in peace.

This journal also makes the point that the chaos the soldiers created in the

Delaware Valley sowed seeds of misinformation, which rendered making an informed decision about the revolution nearly impossible. She writes, "The *lie* of the day runs thus; that the New Englandmen have taken Long Island, are in possession of King's Bridge, that Hen[ry] Lee is retaken by his own men, the regulars in a desperate condition intrenching at Brunswick, and quite hopeless of gaining any advantage over the Americans in this campaign."[27] Just as Grace Growden Galloway in chapter 1 argues that she should be simultaneously considered a free agent and a *feme covert,* and as Anna Rawle in chapter 5 labels political women "unsexed" while acting as a loyalist informant, so Morris contains contradictions. She resents the lack of reliable information, yet she spreads rumors. She resents the chaos that misinformation spread, yet she contributes to it. Her thirst for intelligence of any kind—even gossip—compels her to pass along these snippets of stories as she receives them. The war siloed people in such a way that they were only exposed to limited information as it was passed to them through biased sources (such as other soldiers, supporters, or detractors). Morris writes that such restrictions frustrate her: "Wonder the men in town don't think it worth while to step down here and tell us what they are after—get quite in the fidgets for news." She sent her son Richard to see if he could gather intelligence, but "he return[ed] quite newsless." Upon meeting him empty-handed, she has a "good mind to send him back again."[28]

The volume of misinformation was further aggravated by the fact that much of the news during the war was delivered by word of mouth, which resulted in exaggerations and dramatizations as the information traveled away from its source. Morris recalls hearing about a refugee woman who hired a servant to retrieve some of her belongings in Burlington and bring them to her in the nearby town to which she had fled. A group of soldiers attacked her hired man, robbed him, and released his horse. The story became a tall tale by the time it reached the refugee and her family. Morris says that the small group of soldiers swelled to include "10,000 wagons, ... Gen. Washington, Lee, Howe, and all the Americans," and, instead of one robbed servant, the narrative changed to involve "Washington ... mortally wounded, ... the streets ... full of dead bodies, and ... the groans of the dying" echoing throughout New Jersey. The entire family felt certain that all of their loved ones were dead, their homes razed to the ground, all possessions lost forever. They tore open their letters "in fearful haste" but "found nothing relative to what the [news had] told them."[29] Morris's description of a town whose communication has been replaced with gossip and rumor adds another layer to her depiction of the problems that continued to plague the Delaware Valley. Not only were the soldiers attacking and robbing each other, unable to recognize or speak to one another in the street, but also the citizens and newspapers were incapable of sorting out the confusion. Bypassing the fourth estate through letter-writing was difficult as well, since the refugee family's letters had been held behind enemy lines until their hired hand could deliver them. The revolution disintegrated the fundamental communication between the state and its citizens. The only viable "estate" left was the epistolary one, where Morris was able to underscore these absurdities for her sister and friends.

A Holy Nation on a Neutral Island

Morris's letter-journal not only makes a convincing case for a neutral island but also explains how her definition of neutrality aligned with the Peace Testimony of the Society of Friends. The Quakers labeled their most trying moments as the "times of stripping." When a Friend was stripped, they experienced an annihilation of the self, an "inward crucifixion," when all of the believer's earthly attachments fall away to reveal God's purpose for their lives.[30] Stripping was essential to the Christian's growth. Morris returned frequently to the notion that her trials had baptized her, much in the way that Sarah Logan Fisher did, removing her of all of her worldly attachments so that she could grow from these persecutions. This echoed Quaker rhetoric that suggested the best alternative to supporting nationalism would be forming a New Zion—an ideological space that allowed Quakers to reside in America but pledge allegiance to the Friends. Morris's letter-journal provided her with the space to develop this New Zion. In her writings she documents her tribulations, rectifies them with her faith, and uses her trials to align herself with the Quakers' faith-based alternative to the notion of nation.

Quakers framed themselves as citizens united by faith because they could be neither with the nation nor against it without violating their principles. They launched a mission to establish a "church militant upon earth" as an alternative to becoming the "citizen-soldiers" that nationalists demanded. Their goal was to be in the nation but not of it. The concept of Zion appealed to the Quakers because they, like the Israelites, were forced to endure exile and oppression. And they, like the Israelites, took solace in spiritual unity with fellow believers in the face of a diaspora. The "Zion tradition was predicated on a future in which nations and empires would fall away and their violence and corruption of worldly government would be replaced with the peace and purity of divine rule. . . . As citizens of Zion, it mattered not where one lived, but what one believed."[31] At the point in the journal when Morris begins calling for a "neutral island," she also begins emphasizing how her faith informs her political decisions, moreso than any other identifier. Such language signals an allegiance with and acceptance of the Friends' call to establish that church militant, a neutral space aligned with God, rather than with soldiers, and one that championed peace rather than revolution.

Her allegiance to the New Zion is most clearly reflected in the passages where she eschews political markers in the stories she tells her sister about the soldiers who occupy Burlington. The diary's discourse refuses to delineate between loyalists and rebels. Such a decision at least partly signals her desire for neutrality in the traditional sense of the word, while it also aligns with the Quaker imperative to see all people as equals. The reader must struggle to determine the affiliation of the key players in Morris's narrative. She identifies them solely as "soldiers," "men with guns," or "gondola men," the latter a phrase she fabricates to suit her purposes, a corruption of men who sailed in gundalow boats.[32] She fashions these men as a blur of boats and gunpowder, the language representing and resisting the contending forces where she lived. She writes in January 1777 about a group of soldiers whose political affiliation she does not identify, staying in a nearby house:

> I went into the . . . house to see if the fires were safe and my heart was melted to see such a number of my fellow-creatures, lying like swine on the floor, fast asleep, and many of them without even a blanket to cover them. It seems very strange to me, that such a number should be allowed to come from the camp at the very time of the engagements, and I shrewdly suspect they have run away— for they can give no account of why they came, nor where they are to march next.[33]

The key phrase in this passage is "fellow-creatures." Morris emphasizes their suffering—their humanity—rather than their uniforms. She renders them (and her own diary) neutral by rendering them helpless. Both she and the people she pities are linked by their vulnerabilities.

Morris does not tell her readers that these boys served George Washington. A cold front on January 2, 1776, swept across the Delaware Valley, and temperatures dropped rapidly. No one could see well on that starless night. The soldiers became confused, then panicked in the predawn hours.

Someone cried out that the army was surrounded by unseen Hessians, which spooked the soldiers in the rear, who broke rank and fled toward one of the nearest towns, which happened to be Burlington. They arrived frozen, confused, hungry, tired, and afraid. Morris writes that they seemed like they had defected because they had. She lingers neither on this fact nor on their affiliated politics; rather, she focuses on their cold and suffering. This sympathetic rhetoric closes the gap between the writer and her subject, eradicating the difference between citizens and soldiers and bridging the divide that would have isolated them from one another. Her discourse thus mirrors the rhetoric that Elizabeth Drinker and Sarah Logan Fisher, who were also Quakers, deployed to convince George Washington to free their husbands. As Morris's diary demonstrates, claiming a political identity was a challenge in these tumultuous spaces, particularly if someone found or intercepted her journal. She could be tried for treason if she claimed the Crown while hiding Odell. She could be robbed if she claimed the colonies while helping the Hessians. She could be disowned by the Society of Friends if she claimed a side at all.[34] Focusing on the soldiers as people, rather than as tools of the state, she avoids all of those pitfalls. The letter-diary served as a space where she could map the fluid identities she assumed and discarded, rarely willing or able to adopt just one perspective on the war.

Morris strips the soldiers of their political markers when she describes the deserters as nothing more sinister than cold, hungry, lost boys. She reveals, beneath the uniforms, the common desire for people's most basic needs: food, shelter, and warmth. She uses the language of illness to achieve a similar result elsewhere in her letter-journal. The same soldiers that threatened to kill her children for wielding the spy-glass early in 1777 later that same year approached her home a second time. An illness had spread quickly among the men, infecting them and their wives, so the rebels asked Morris to heal them because she was known in town for her medical expertise. She expresses bafflement at such boldness, considering that the rebels' "late attempt to shoot [her] poor boy" made her an unlikely caregiver. She was wary. "At first," she writes, "I thought they might have a design to put a trick on me, and get me aboard of their gondolas and then pillage my house, as they had done some others." She realizes that desperation, not artifice, drove the rebels to seek out a woman they considered to be a loyalist for aid after she saw the extent of the fever. She observes how dysentery, smallpox, typhus, and many other deadly diseases ravaged their ranks.[35] She remarks that she "treated them according to art, and they all got well." One of the sick men promised to repay Morris by seeking out Patty Moore—to whom the letter-journal was addressed—to relay communication from behind enemy lines, but Morris assumes he made fevered promises that he would forget. The man surprised her by arriving unannounced at her home in the middle of the night bearing "a letter, a bushel of salt, a jug of molasses, a bag of rice, some tea, coffee, sugar, and some cloth for a coat for my poor boys—all sent by my kind sisters."[36] She gave him molasses, salt, tea, sugar, and coffee to send back to Moore. Both Morris and the soldier kept their word.

Morris's exchange with these rebel soldiers put her in a compromising position with the Society of Friends, who, like the rebels and loyalists, also pressured her to adopt their concept of loyalty. Could pacifists (or neutralists allied with pacifists) serve sick soldiers while remaining true to their principles? Quakers struggled to address such moral quandaries, according to the minutes for the Philadelphia Yearly Meeting's Meeting for Sufferings.[37] On one hand, mending a soldier meant repairing a weapon, an agent of the destruction of another person's Inner Light, but on the other hand, an ailing soldier was a brother in need, regardless of the color of his uniform. Some meetings supported serving the "less fortunate," suggesting all Quakers should be "ready to distribute, & communicate toward the Relief of their suffering Brethren, not only of our own, but of every other Society, & Denomination," while others argued about who were the "less fortunate." Should they aid only innocent bystanders in war? Or could an ailing soldier fit that category? The Philadelphia Yearly Meeting called for a universal policy about what it meant to "voluntarily contribut[e] to the support and prosecution of War," lest Friends "become instrumental in the destruction of each other." These Quakers suggested that it was "reasonable to extend some relief" to injured soldiers, and that such actions should be viewed in light of the Friends' "Charitable intention," which "may be fulfilled in a manner consistent with our peaceable principles."[38] The Quaker's intent mattered. A person who aided a rebel so that he might return to wage war on his brother violated the Peace Testimony, but a healer who sought to act as a surrogate for God's will served her faith well.

The logic concerning intent explains why Morris took pains throughout the journal to categorize her actions as those of a Christian broadly speaking, another discursive strategy she uses to claim neutrality during the war. Morris reframes the decision to become involved in the rebels' plight as being

the Christian thing to do, fashioning herself as an agent of God, which is ultimately how the Society of Friends determined it would justify aiding injured
citizens or soldiers. She also is careful to clarify that she was not profiting
directly from the aid that she provided. She writes that the goods the rebels
delivered, which she received for treating their fever, were not from the rebels
themselves but from "our Heavenly Father. . . . May we never forget it." She
explains that she took the food and,

> being now so rich, we thought it our duty to hand out a little to the poor around
> us, who were mourning for want of salt; so we divided the bushel, and gave a
> pint to every poor person that came for it, and had a great plenty for our own
> use. Indeed it seemed as if our little store increased by distributing it, like the
> bread broken by our Saviour to the multitude, which, when he had blessed it,
> was so marvelously multiplied.[39]

Here she likens herself to Jesus in Mark 6:30, when he fed a multitude with
minimal provisions. By framing herself as a disciple of Christ (or Christ himself), rather than a loyalist or rebel, Morris sidesteps any charge that she was
aiding the war effort, describing herself instead as a Christian doing God's
work. She emphasizes the sisters who sent the food, the townspeople who
received the provisions, and the God who inspired Morris to share it. The
rebel who delivered the supplies, and Morris's treatment of the camp fever,
drops from the narrative completely, which erases Morris's tie to the revolution and replaces it with an act of faith.[40] Morris's Quakerism paradoxically
allowed her to script a political persona that was neutral but not pacifist. She
takes refuge in her journal in her identity as a citizen of Zion so that she can
navigate between the moral dilemmas in which living among rebels, Hessians, and British soldiers placed her.

Morris's letter-journal, in sum, offers a problematic example of so-called
loyalist writing. She did not identify herself as a citizen of the British Empire,
although Tory hunters sought her out as a loyalist sympathizer. Rather, she
identified locally with Quakers, other Burlington residents, and people in
the Delaware Valley. Her regionalism made her a global citizen; although she
did not use letters or letter-journals to either affiliate or connect with other
English, transatlantic correspondents (at least through this medium), she did
envision herself as part of an international network of Friends, a connection
that transcended any national affiliation the revolution pressured people to
claim. Morris's journal highlights the complexities that political women faced

during the war. It indicates that she saw herself as both regional and global, neither loyalist nor rebel, and neutral. But it also proves that "neutrality" acted as a blank canvas onto which other people could paint passive loyalties they then sought to control. Although Morris's neutrality may bring into question how well she compares to, for example, Anna Rawle, whose family delivered information for the British, Morris's actions also suggest just how broad the spectrum loyalty and loyalism could span. Her writing exemplifies the idea that when a woman was stripped of the opportunity to craft such definitions for herself, she eschewed the notion of loyalty as a fixed point, choosing instead to script an ideology that allowed her to adapt and survive on the frontlines of war.

CHAPTER FOUR

SCRIPTING LOYALISM

Anna Rawle and Rebecca Shoemaker

Anna Rawle's house, Laurel Hill, still stands tall overlooking the Schuylkill River in Fairmount Park near Philadelphia. I push open its door to see a man dressed in period clothing. He's wearing a vest, a waistcoat, and a cravat, despite the 96-degree heat outside. Reenactors always make me feel like I'm the unwilling participant in a play for which I have neither auditioned nor prepared. He begins to recite some kind of script using an accent, but I say, "I'm here for Anna Rawle." He relaxes his shoulders, abandons his script and accent, and lights up. Two tourists ask, "Who's Anna Rawle?" They're here for the architecture and for Philip Syng Physick, the father of American Surgery, one of the house's other occupants. I see a picture of Joseph Reed hanging near the entryway, not far from portraits of Rawle's mother and stepfather, Rebecca and Samuel Shoemaker. "What's Reed doing here?" I ask the guide. "He took Laurel Hill away from the Shoemakers," he tells me, "after they were marked as traitors." "So, isn't it odd that he's memorialized in the house he stole?" I ask. My guide scratches the side of his face and tilts his head slightly. "Well," he says, "Reed's wife decided it would make a nice summer home." That didn't answer my question. He clips away to tell the tour group about an eighteenth-century highboy in the next room. I think of a story that I read in Rawle's letter-journal. When Reed's wife died, Rawle said, "[She] can never spend another summer at Laurel Hill. She is dead, and of a disorder that made some people whisper . . . 'that she eat too many of Mr. S.[hoemaker']s peaches.'" Rawle's legacy seems crowded here. I wonder about the decision to group Reed's painting with Rawle's. What does it mean that Rawle's story must also share space with her tormenter's? Then I see a sheet of paper propped against a fireplace near Reed and the Shoemakers:

> S.S.: Samuel Shoemaker
> R.S.: Rebecca Shoemaker

Horatio: William Rawle
Adelaide: Margaret or Peggy Rawle
Fanny: Anna Rawle
Juliet: Sarah/Sally Burge
Grandmammy: Mrs. Edward Warner
Lindore: John Clifford
Lysander: Joseph M. Fox

It's a code! The code, actually the epistolary code that the family adopted to continue writing each other after Reed took their house. After Rebecca and Samuel were exiled to New York. When Anna Rawle and her sister wanted to talk to their fragmented family, dispersed across enemy lines.

FIGURE 4. *British Entering Philadelphia September 26, 1777.*
The Library Company of Philadelphia.

REBECCA SHOEMAKER BECAME a loyalist informant when her husband, Samuel, was exiled from Philadelphia in 1778. Samuel was the mayor of Philadelphia from 1769–70 and served two terms in the Pennsylvania Assembly (with Joseph Galloway, who also owned property adjacent to the Shoemakers) in 1771 and 1772. Shoemaker worked as a dry-goods merchant, and he, like many loyalists, supported the colonies' grievances against England's import/export tax policies.[1] Samuel Shoemaker and Henry Drinker— Elizabeth Drinker's husband—violated the Nonimportation Agreements in spring 1775 by petitioning Congress for permission to ship their products to Newfoundland. This petition publicly marked Shoemaker as a loyalist sympathizer, and the Pennsylvania Assembly declared him guilty of treason on March 6, 1778, which meant that all of his property was forfeited to the state.[2] He fled with his nineteen-year-old stepson, William Rawle, to New York on June 17, 1778, just a few days before the British troops left Philadelphia.[3]

After Samuel Shoemaker was exiled, Rebecca Shoemaker and her daughters hoped that they would be allowed to keep the family property, particularly the house "Laurel Hill," because it belonged to Rebecca Shoemaker's first husband, Francis Rawle, who had died years earlier. Under the law, Samuel Shoemaker was a "tenant by the curtesy" at Laurel Hill, which meant that it should have been immune from confiscation because he did not technically own that property. "In [his] patriotic zeal," William Brooke Rawle explains, Joseph Reed, acting as Supreme Executive Council of Pennsylvania, "disregarded the principle of law that the sale of such a life estate had no other effect than to free a wife's houses and lands from all of her husband's estate when he had been attainted for high treason, and to vest the title in her to as full an effect as if he had died."[4] Reed ordered all of the Shoemaker's properties—including that which Rebecca Shoemaker inherited from her former husband—sold on April 12, 1779.[5] Reed then moved his family into Laurel Hill, using it as a summer home.

Rebecca Shoemaker remained in Philadelphia until the Supreme Executive Council intercepted one of her letter-journals in March 1780 and used it to determine that she was helping loyalists pass from Philadelphia into New York. The council then ordered her to join her husband in exile, where, disconnected from her regular informants, she would pose less of a threat. She arrived on June 20, 1780, but her daughters, Anna and Peggy Rawle, remained in Philadelphia, living with their grandmother and brother.[6] The

Rawle-Shoemakers wrote each other frequently during their period of separation, their letters passing in and out of enemy lines, dodging interception and censorship.

When the Revolutionary War dismantled the postal system and as families separated, people went to great lengths to deliver information covertly. Not only did they write in code, as Anna Rawle's family did, but they also hid their missives in quills, shoes, or hollow bullets. Treason laws banned loyalist informants from contacting the British military. These laws, however, did not initially include women, who were "presumed to be harmless—irrelevant to the public world of politics and war."[7] This political invisibility meant that both they and their letters could traverse enemy lines that men could not. One of the most outrageous examples of women who took advantage of such liberties was someone named Kate. She was enslaved to Stephen Heard, who would eventually become the governor of Georgia, and when she learned that Heard had been taken by loyalists, she went to the prison where he was being held. She told the soldiers that she was there to tend to the camp's laundry, indicating a large basket she had balanced just for that purpose, and they let her pass. She then stuffed Heard into the basket and marched out with him on her head.[8] This story is problematic for a number of reasons. It is not only impractical but unlikely that a woman subjected to the system of slavery would go to such lengths to extract her master from imprisonment, only so he could reestablish himself as her own jailer. Nonetheless, this story, however implausible, underscores a key point where women and the dissemination of information is concerned: despite its best efforts, the government could not regulate the country's most essential network of communication. Women responded to these shifting strictures by manufacturing paper bodies that could go where their corporeal bodies could not. Lydia Darragh hid missives about rebel troop movement under the button covers on her coat.[9] Patience Lovell Wright transferred information by hiding her correspondence in wax sculptures that she sent across the country.[10] Elizabeth Murray, for instance, delivered information to a political prisoner in Boston by securing letters to the bottom of rum barrels and nestling them in hair powder.[11] Because these letters (and sometimes the women's bodies) could be folded, concealed, and coded, they transgressed the boundaries that attempted to keep the women who wrote them out.

People like Rawle, Murray, and Darragh found themselves in a paper war with state legislatures who, in an effort to regulate such transgressions, passed new treason acts that broadened both the definition of treason and who could be found guilty of it. Before 1777, British law defined treason as betrayal of the king of England—a definition that would have imprisoned or executed the entire Continental Army—and assumed only men could be guilty of it. After that watershed year, however, places such as Philadelphia passed laws that broadened treason to include granting supplies to the British, providing intelligence to loyalists, or writing letters, all crimes for which women could be prosecuted. Coverture laws up to this point in the war had made trying women difficult for the courts, but the revised treason acts exposed them.

Despite these treason acts, Rawle's family continuously defied edicts that they desist writing each other information "in the political line." Rebecca Shoemaker continued writing her family but in code, while her daughter Anna Rawle eschewed the code, flaunting her brazenness in front of the soldiers that patrolled the borders between rebel- and loyalist-occupied territories. Their family passed letters through Joseph Scott, an elder; the soldiers would not search him due to his advanced age (whether out of respect or for fear of harming him, they did not say).[12]

I have examined thus far competing definitions of loyalty, pacifism, neutrality, and disaffection as these concepts developed in the moments leading up to 1777. I focus in this chapter on how letter-writers and diary-keepers operated after the revised treason acts obliged them to adapt their epistolary performances to evade detection. Anna Rawle and Rebecca Shoemaker, my case studies, cloaked their missives in code, hid their letters as journals, and obscured their critiques of the rebels following that watershed year. Furthermore, they scripted a new writing form that materially reflected and deflected shifting legal strictures that sought to regulate the letter-writers themselves. This collection of letters demonstrates that the more specific codes and strictures became, the more evasive both form and content became, in turn.

The Rawle-Shoemaker Letter-Journals

The genre that the Shoemakers adopted to keep in touch with each other is challenging to define, though I suggest it most closely resembles a letter-journal. Rebecca and her daughters began their period of separation in June 1780 by writing each other traditional epistles, or singular letters with a salutation addressing a named reader that concludes with the author's signature, sealed and delivered to the intended recipient. But as money and paper became scarce, and as letters began to be more strictly regulated, Rebecca Shoemaker suggested to her daughters that they should all "write on the same sheet of paper," adding, "& let it be a whole sheet." "Perhaps," she continues, "there may be a vacancy for me to add a few lines on the same, for every piece of paper, if ever so small, is considered as a letter, & pays as much postage as a whole."[13] Her daughters complied. Anna writes, "And here my dear Mammy I resign the pen to Peggy for some time between us. We will carry on a journal since tis thy request."[14] "Carrying on a journal" meant turning two or three sheets of paper horizontally and folding them in half, forming a small booklet or fascicle. The daughters wrote entries until they filled the booklet, and then they sent it to their mother, who either wrote a response in the booklet or started afresh. This familial letter-journal retains a visual representation of the modifications the family made, as the handwriting shifts between the three women and their voices vie for space as each attempted to negotiate the new epistolary arrangement. Even when Anna Rawle was writing her own missives to her mother, when she chose not to include Peggy as a collective author, she wrote letters that were divided by diurnal markers, each entry divided by "1st day," "2nd day," "3rd day," and so on until she had filled the front and back of every page.[15]

Shoemaker's vigilance was inspired by her own exile, but it was also a response to the newly passed treason acts. These acts are particularly important for this project because they legally uncovered women previously protected by coverture. Accordingly, loyalists-by-association became loyalists in their own right, even if they were women who could not vote, fight, or legislate. Treason laws formed the basis of some of the most crucial legislation responsible for reifying the dividing lines that did not ideologically exist between people during the American Revolution. Congress created the Committees of Safety to patrol the streets looking for traitors, but as discussed in chapter 2 about the Virginia Exile Crisis, identifying and prosecuting detainees turned out to be an enormous challenge. Congress initially instructed committees to ask the people they interrogated a series of questions: "Did he regard all acts of Parliament binding on America? Were the Coercive Acts unjustifiable? Should the acts be obeyed either voluntarily or under coercion? Did he think the British regarded him as a supporter of royal authority? Would he 'adhere' to the recommendations of the Continental and provincial Congresses?" The gendered language of the questions excluded the possibility that women like Rebecca Shoemaker and Anna Rawle could be interrogated using this line of questioning. The goal here was to establish some kind of uniform definition of loyalty—among men. People who attempted to give more than one-word answers were cut short. People who asked for a "pass" to remain neutral were told, "This will not be a satisfactory answer."[16] As the war progressed, Congress used these questions to develop a more inclusive definition of treason to accompany its early draft of resolves rendering treason a capital offense, and it was under this redefinition that Rebecca Shoemaker found herself shunned from her home in Philadelphia and relocated to New York.

Congress began the process of redefining treason in 1776, before Shoemaker began delivering correspondence to the British. No longer did it apply to people who betrayed the king; after the Declaration of Independence, it applied to anyone "offering aid or comfort to the King of Great Britain or other enemies of America" and was punishable by death. Local officials throughout the colonies hesitated to apply the new definition to its citizens, arguing it violated basic human rights. State assemblies countered by writing their own treason acts; one of the most visible and contested was the Treason Act of 1777 in Pennsylvania. Both men and women under this legislation could be prosecuted for accepting commissions, enlisting in the British Army, granting supplies to the British, providing intelligence to loyalists, or "carrying on a traitorous correspondence with the enemy."[17] Letters were so dangerous that they were given their own subcategory.[18] There was even talk of banning all correspondence, regardless of content. Anna Rawle wrote that she read in the newspapers about a congressional resolve "preventing all correspondence between here and N. York. . . . Sure[ly] no honest person would wish to impose laws on another which interfered with the first of all human consideration's, duty to one's parents—and abstaining from writing would be a great failure of what is owing to them."[19] She and many other loyalists faced a difficult decision following these changes: stop writing or evade detection.

Shoemaker and Rawle chose evading detection. The family created the code names, the cipher of which now rests next to Joseph Reed's portrait, which they adapted primarily from Shakespearean plays. Anna was "Fanny"; her brother William, "Horatio"; and her sister Peggy, "Adelaide."[20] Rawle did not adopt a code for her parents, whom she called S.S. and R.S., which represents her often halfhearted attempt at concealment. Perhaps because she resented the need to evade detection, she often did a poor job of it. She once asked a friend to smuggle letters to her family in New York and promised that the letters were written in a discreet language that no one could crack, but her companion refused. She "laughed and said, 'Why your S.S.'s are known thro' all Jersey.'"[21] Rawle's family chided both sisters for their carelessness. "My dear Girls," their aunt Elizabeth Warren Shoemaker warned, "be *very* cautious in mentioning names; let the mode of Conveyance appear ever so certain. . . . Take your Beloved Mother for a Guide, who you may observe is *never* off her guard, nor ever uses even a second alphabet letter where one is sufficient. . . . Do be attentive—. . . . Mention *no names*."[22] Rawle repeatedly defied these orders, despite her family's insistence that Rawle and her sister conceal the letters that linked the women together.

Rawle coded her letters so poorly, in fact, that her family asked her to stop writing for a time, a request she refused to grant, despite knowing that strangers were reading her correspondence.[23] She once grumbled, "This public manner of writing restrains my pen and is very disagreeable," but she continued to communicate with her family.[24] "I fancy Joseph would think me a very bold person did he know how often I have transgressed in writing to New York," she tells her mother, "when he has so positively forbid its being done by any one, without examination—however I . . . hope it does not extend to imprisoning us during the war if discovered."[25] Rawle justifies her action by saying that it represents her small way of standing up to the rebels at a time when all of her agency had been taken from her. "No fears of what may happen shall make me forego an amusement I was ever fond of," she explains, "which now has a thousand charms while thus unbosoming myself to my dear Mother."[26] Rawle did temper her letters, but only after she learned that the rebels were scanning all correspondence that crossed enemy territory. "I am determined to . . . be content to write stupid and uninteresting letters," she claims, rather than avoiding writing altogether. Her content was vapid, but she preferred dullness to complete silence. At least this way, she possessed the satisfaction of forcing the rebels to intercept and open each missive, despite the fact that the letters contained nothing of interest to them.[27]

Rawle serves as an exception. Most women responded to the Pennsylvania Treason Act of 1777 by doing all that they could to protect their legal and epistolary bodies. Writers bent the letter-writing genre by reshaping it— writing letters as diaries and in the margins of newspapers, for example— and coding the language therein as part of this circumvention. The letters of Shoemaker and Rawle demonstrate that elided words and pseudonymized names reflect and defy the changing legal status of women in revolutionary

America. Coverture rendered women politically invisible, as shown through Grace Growden Galloway, a process that stripped women of their legal rights, but it also (ostensibly) protected them from being prosecuted in court. These post-1777 letters, then, are simultaneously artifacts of agency and regression. As they exemplify the loyalist woman's ability to play an active role in war, so they also represent a desire to avoid the consequences for such activities— which they could only have done if they were able to maintain the dependent status that the treason acts threatened to erode.

Read with such context in mind, even the most mundane letters that passed between Rawle and Shoemaker register dissent. Rawle's letters are brazen. They name names, denounce the rebels, and criticize the revolution at a time when legislators demanded she cover up. The new treason laws insisted that all letter-writers tailor the words they used to support the revolution or suffer the consequences. Rawle acknowledged this threat, yet she chose to continue writing her mother, indifferent to both these strictures and the code her family devised to sidestep them. Her letters represent the new tension that female loyalists felt at this juncture in the war. She took steps to evade detection and wove her letters into a letter-journal to mask the form, but she still *wrote* and did so fairly openly. Once united in New York with her mother, she even smuggled letters from other loyalist wives—such as Grace Growden Galloway—from Philadelphia into New York, folding their paper bodies inside of her own to facilitate their successful delivery.[28] Rawle, like Galloway, eventually lost her inheritance, home, and security, but she refused to lose the thread that connected her to her exiled family. She refused to stop writing, and she refused to allow the rebels to dictate what she could and could not say in those letters.

LADIES GOING ABOUT FOR MONEY

Rawle's epistolary form and eschewal of her family's rhetorical coding represent only part of her rebellion. The other involves her letters' subject matter— what she decided to discuss even though she knew that she was under surveillance. The Rawle-Shoemaker correspondence offers an excellent example of the discursive calisthenics loyalists had to perform if they wanted to continue critiquing the rebellion. The missives that best exemplify this deftness are those that, ironically for a family of female informants, categorized political women as "unsexed." Rawle associated these women with prostitutes and refers to them as "ladies going about for money."

Anna Rawle received a knock on her grandmother's door, where she was living while her parents were exiled to New York, in the summer of 1780. When she opened it, a representative from the Ladies Association of Philadelphia stood with her hand outstretched to receive Rawle's donations for the Continental Army, which needed supplies and uniforms.[29] When the volunteer saw it was Rawle who answered the door, she turned her back on Rawle and snubbed her, saying "she did not chuse to face Mrs. S[hoemaker] or her daughters" because they were loyalists.[30] The Ladies Association had come about after Esther DeBerdt Reed read a letter that George Washington wrote to Congress about the rebels' low morale and poor health, exacerbated by a clothing shortage. Reed created her organization to address those needs. Her group and others like it encouraged women to get involved in the war effort without sacrificing their femininity. Reed was the first lady of Philadelphia, married to Joseph Reed, president of the Pennsylvania Assembly, the man who issued the property confiscation orders for Grace Growden Galloway, Samuel Shoemaker, and Elizabeth Fergusson. Reed operated from Anna Rawle's confiscated house. Here stood one of Reed's volunteers, knocking on Rawle's grandmother's door, where Rawle now lived because she no longer possessed a home of her own as her parents had been exiled to New York when Joseph Reed ordered that they go.

As Rawle saw it, Reed's greed was matched only by her minions' vulgarity, an opinion she formed shortly after her confrontation with the Ladies Association. The association's rejection of Rawle was a political performance too. The Ladies Association likely knew full well who lived in that house. Of "all absurdities, the Ladies going about for money exceeded everything," Rawle concludes. When Rawle writes her mother of this encounter, she dismisses it by diminishing the woman who humiliated her, whom she characterizes as a harlot suffering from corrupt femininity. She particularly despised the organization's fundraising methodology. Members went door to door soliciting funds, and if they met a man who would not donate, they would flirt or scorn to achieve the desired outcome. Their purpose "carried to such an excess of meanness as the nobleness of no cause whatsoever could excuse," Rawle writes.[31] The association's treatment of her neighbors and friends disgusted Rawle. When Bob Wharton either would or could not give to the cause, the ladies "reminded him of the extreme rudeness of refusing anything to the fair sex; but he was inexorable and pleaded want of money, and the heavy taxes, so at length they left him, after threatening to hand his name down to posterity with infamy." Historian Emily J. Arendt has noted that the association often relied on "hyperfeminized forms of behavior—flirting, and failing that, scolding—to induce support from those who for economic or political reasons would otherwise not donate," which Rawle reads not as patriotic but as licentious.[32] Their cause unsexed these women because they sold their dignity for supplies, according to Rawle. She critiqued the association as she herself and other loyalist women had been critiqued. She appropriated rebel rhetoric in order to deflect their rejection of her and justify her own family's entrance into politics. Rawle's mother's decision to act as an informant was virtuous and defensible, while the Ladies Association's decision to raise funds for the rebels was gross and immoral. The "us" versus "them" rhetoric that developed during this period, Rawle's letters suggest, cut both ways.

Rawle's account of the association and its treatment of Wharton ran contrary to the association's view of itself—as an organization of Roman matrons guarding the republic's virtue. Esther Reed laid out this vision in a broadside, "The Sentiments of an American Woman."[33] "Animated by the purest patriotism more than barren wishes for the success of so glorious a Revolution," Reed writes, "the Women of America . . . aspire to render themselves . . . really useful." They would, if they could, "march to glory by the same path as the Men," but public opinion constrains them. They must take their cues from other historical female figures—biblical heroines such as Esther, Deborah, and Judith—women who, "forgetting the weakness of their sex," "buil[t] new walls, [dug] trenches with their feeble hands; furnish[ed] arms to their defends," and "hasten[ed] the deliverance of their country."[34] Reed recognizes that others might censure her involvement in the war (and she was right), but she says that she must take that risk for the good of her nation and family. She concludes by reminding her readers that if women involved themselves in the war effort temporarily, the war would end and women would resume their duties as mothers and wives—standard Republican motherhood rhetoric.[35]

Reed believes all actions are justified in the name of restoring the family unity, for which all decorum must be sacrificed:

> We know that at a distance from the theatre of war, if we enjoy any tranquility, it is the fruit of your watchings, your labours, your dangers. If I live happy in the midst of my family; if my husband cultivates his field, and reaps his harvest in peace; if, surrounded with my children, I myself nourish the youngest, and

press it to my bosom, without being affraid of seeing myself separated from it, by a ferocious enemy; if the house in which we dwell; if our barns, our orchards are *safe* at the present time from the hands of those incendiaries, it is to you that we owe it. . . . Let us not lose a moment; let us be engaged to offer the homage of our gratitude at the alter of military valour.

Her apology for writing the pamphlet matches the length of her plan of action, which serves as a useful reminder about the intricacies of the performance women had to undergo if they wanted to print their political opinions. That plan of action called all women to give what they could: time, money, resources, or all three. They should then organize small groups, establish officers, and transmit what they gathered to George Washington, "the first Soldier of the Republic," or his wife, Martha. General Washington broadcasted the names of the volunteers, "if they so desire[d] it."[36] Despite being on different sides of the war, both Rawle and Reed were using letters to engage in political discourse, justify their engagement, and defy strictures against bluestockings. Both also saw their engagement as part of a familial duty. Rawle believed she needed to keep sending correspondence across enemy lines to maintain communication with her family, and Reed believed raising money for the rebels would allow women to reunite with their families. Their filial and connubial demands trumped any concerns that they may have been overstepping their bounds. Reed's apology, then, suggests that loyalist women were not the only ones engaging in discursive exercises to carve out an epistolary space that would serve as a forum for amplifying their political beliefs.

Given the patriotism in Reed's pamphlet, it might be surprising to learn that its author initially identified as a loyalist and may have been using jingoism to broadcast her own revised loyalties. Reed maintained what historians have called a "deep personal attachment to London." When her husband, Joseph, moved from London to America, she hesitated before joining him, feeling the move would make her a "traitor to her homeland," England. She eventually made the transatlantic journey. Joseph pledged his support for Massachusetts, militarily and financially, after the Battles of Lexington and Concord in October 1775. He then became president of the Pennsylvania Assembly and took charge of ordering the confiscation of loyalist properties, which is when Esther realized that his affiliation with the rebel cause meant that she would not be returning home to England anytime soon. The mother of three children, fearing for her family's safety, she quickly switched sides.[37] The Ladies Association could be read as overcompensation for her newfound loyalties. The group was a way to make her affinity for America public by taking it door to door, solidifying her patriotism by branding those who refused to give donations as traitors.[38] These searches for contributions, Linda K. Kerber points out in *Women of the Republic,* ostensibly sought to boost morale and garner funds, but they also identified people for and against independence, serving a purpose much like the treason acts written at the same time as the association's inception.[39] Little divided Reed from Rawle except audience and medium. Rawle noted her dissent in a journal to a small group of readers—her immediate family and possibly a selection of sympathetic friends—while Reed galvanized a number of communities across the colonies. The Ladies Association allowed her to evangelize her loyalties to others, her zeal transforming her into a patriotic icon. Rawle, by comparison, enjoyed only a small circulation to a group of people who, by their own admission, wished to operate quietly and secretively.

These two publications exemplify how rapidly ideological shifts could develop over the course of the war. Both Rawle and Reed at one point claimed fealty to the king of England. And both women believed they possessed a right to engage in civic discourse about the war, though they understood that they had to do so from the confines of their gender. Rawle knew she should (though she did not always choose to) encode and conceal her letters, and Reed knew she could not sign her pamphlet and had to offer her own supporters anonymity if they desired it. Despite recognizing that entering into the political fray might "unsex" them, both did it anyway. And Rawle and Reed, ironically, each condemned other women for engaging in the war in ways they did not deem appropriate. Rawle disapproved of "ladies going about for money," and the association scorned Rawle because her parents were loyalists. Their chosen media signals perhaps the clearest distinction between these two writers. Rawle wrote manuscripts; Reed published an essay. Rawle had to hide her doctrine, while Reed broadcast hers. Reed's form of publicity galvanized her reputation as a converted patriot, while Rawle's endangered her life.

THE LUSTS OF WAR

Although Rebecca Shoemaker was permitted to reunite occasionally with her daughters from 1782 to 1784, she split much of her time between Philadelphia and New York.[40] Anna and Peggy Rawle continued living with their grandmother on Mulberry (now Arch) Street in Philadelphia and with their stepbrother on High (now Market) Street and would write their mother during the months she was away.

On October 19, 1781, during a period of separation for the Rawle-Shoemakers, General Charles Cornwallis surrendered to General George Washington at the Battle of Yorktown. Crowds across America surged into the streets—including in Philadelphia, where Anna Rawle lived—to both celebrate with neighbors and punish those who refused to join them in their revelry. This crowd action involved looting, property destruction, violence, and, as suggested by Rawle's letter-journal about the event, rape and/or assault. Rawle may have broadcast her loyalties for her family, eschewing their suggested code to talk politics, but she was careful about the way she discussed what happened during these events. She describes crowd actions and soldiers so deftly that, at times, her depictions of rebels seem the same as her contemporaries' letters and journal-entries. Yet the way in which she depicts the crowd after the Battle of Yorktown suggests a particular kind of critique of the rebels that paints them as rapists, at worst, and sadists, at best. I suggest that by discussing-without-disclosing exactly what happened during those attacks, Rawle protects her own reputation and social status while exposing what she sees as the corruption of the rebel militia and its cause. She also inverts the discourse that rebels used against loyalists when she paints the rebels as greedy, lustful, and chaotic.

Printed reports documenting key events during the American Revolution insisted on "vagueness" and "intentional obscurity" concerning what happened in the streets on the nights significant crowd actions took place. One report reads, "Every thing was conducted with the greatest order and decorum, and the face of joy and gladness was universal." "The overwhelming intent of these rites," historian David Waldstreicher has noted in his study of the politics of celebration, "was unity. As a result, the achievement of sameness in these rites ... proved that national unity existed."[41] One place the rhetoric of such unity would not have been regulated was in letters and journals. Those who celebrated Cornwallis's defeat lit a candle in the window to signal their approval and were spared punishment. Both dissenters and pacifists refused to light such candles. Quakers kept theirs dark because (as they saw it) a lit wick implied support for bloodshed and violence. On that night in 1781, Anna Rawle's window remained dark.

Rawle tells her mother that, to punish her dissent, a "mob . . . broke the shutters and the glass of the windows, and were coming in," though "none but forlorn women" lived inside. Rawle emphasizes that, though the people threatened her, she never lit that candle, instead huddling "in fear and trembling till, finding them grow more louder and violent, not knowing what to do, . . . ran into the yard." She, her servants, and her family "had not been there many minutes before we were drove back by the sight of two men climbing the fence." For a moment, Rawle and her family believed the crowd had breached the gates. Then the light illuminated the face of two neighbors who had arrived to help beat back the crowds. Just as the crowd began to wreak havoc—smashing windows, tearing doors off of hinges, and shouting epithets—the neighbors struck the match and lit the wick. The crowd, seeing the darkened window ablaze, drew up short. The rioters then gave "three huzzas" and moved on to the next dark house.[42]

The candle-lighting presents an interpretation problem. If the candle represented active participation in the revolution, the lighting of which symbolized a willingness to engage in that war, then how do we understand what happened at Rawle's house? On one level, this scene in Rawle's letter-journal suggests that inaction often weighed as heavily as action. Galloway resisted evacuating her home, Drinker refused to move from her doorway, Fisher failed to hand over supplies, Morris denied access to Odell's hiding place, and Rawle refused to light the wick. All of these women, intentionally or inadvertently, were forming allegiances. We might read the space between the moment when Rawle decides not to light the candle and the moment when two men light it for her as representative of the gulf that divided the privileges men and women could claim during the war. If read this way, I think readers risk missing these women's agency when they are unable to read beyond the loyalists' victimization. Rawle's letters were marked as treasonous, and her missives were being watched. She was not, in fact, inactive. Rawle was speaking out against the revolution and its supporters merely by writing about the incident to critique it. She both refused to light that wick and refused to be silent about her decision (or indecision) when threatened with an attack. I argue that both actions registered her dissent and that she intended her reading audience to interpret her actions as such.

THE POLITICAL RHETORIC OF RAPE

This passage is further complicated by the fact that she seems to imply this crowd action involved sexual assault or rape, though she is unclear whether they hurt her or other townspeople (or both). She writes that she and some friends "nailed boards up at the broken panels," since it "would not have been *safe* to have gone to bed." "Men," she recounts, had broken into neighbors' houses to find that "all of the sons were out"; they then "acted as they pleased"—another phrase that implies (though is perhaps deliberately unspecific about) sexual violence. "In short," she writes, "it was the most alarming scene I ever remember."[43] By stripping her house of its windows, the crowd has stripped her of security. The gaping holes meant anyone could and would come inside—the house or the bodies in it. We can never be completely sure about what happened there, but surety is not the point. Rawle purposefully obscures these details. This vagueness is precisely the kind of rhetoric to which readers must attend. When we read what Rawle prints on the page, we gain information about the facts of the Cornwallis riots; when we read what she leaves out, we gain information about gendered restrictions on rape rhetoric and the ways in which women manipulated such restrictions to couch their own critique of the war without indemnifying themselves in the process.

Rawle certainly worried about whether the crowd would return to damage her home further, but she also feared that the crowd might return to harm her family. Rawle takes pains to clarify for her mother that the men did not return that night, as she feared they would, thanks to the diligence of her neighbors. She assures Shoemaker that she had successfully defended against any would-be rapists. "As we had not the pleasure of seeing any of the *gentlemen* in the house, nor the furniture cut up, and goods stolen, nor been beat, nor pistols pointed at our breasts," she writes, "we may count our sufferings slight compared to many others."[44]

The letter emphasizes that the men left empty-handed—a passage that bears a striking resemblance to Sarah Logan Fisher's letter quoted in chapter 2: "Tho there was a Carpet on every floor, & a Blanket on every Bed, [the soldiers] came down & in a complisant manner told me they had had the pleasure of viewing my Rooms, but saw nothing that suited them."[45] The men in Rawle's house, like the men in Fisher's, also left empty-handed. Rawle apologizes for recounting any part of the incident, although she was left unscathed, and explains, "Was I not sure, my dearest Mother, that you would have very exaggerated accounts of this affair from others, and would probably be uneasy for the fate of our friends, I would be entirely silent about it, but as you will hear it from some one or another, not mentioning it will seem as if we had suffered exceedingly, and I hope I may depend on the *safety* of this opportunity."[46] It is important for us to notice that Rawle refers twice to the issue of safety—once to refer to sexual assault and again to refer to her letter's interception—because her coded rhetoric couches a critique of the rebels as rapists. Her use of coded wording ("safety" rather than "rape") was a means of self-preservation. Rawle connects her paper body with her physical one. Although she assures her mother that her body remained unmolested, she could not make the same assurances about her letters, as indicated by the conditionals "hope" and "may." Her earlier correspondence expresses Rawle's dissent through its defiant form and a subtle critique of rebel supporters, while her later letters do so through denial and accusation—specifically through saying without saying what happened to loyalist households (and their correspondence) throughout Philadelphia.

Why would Rawle eschew using a code to discuss loyalism but embrace it to discuss sexual assault? It seems logical that a sympathetic family made up of a group of active loyalists would receive word of their daughter's devotion to the king better than they would receive news that she had been sexually assaulted. Perhaps she talks around the subject because she fears upsetting her parents. Perhaps she does so because she wants to focus on the rebels' wrongdoing, rather than any culpability her society would have placed on her for her own attack. Voicing rape then, like voicing rape now, was complicated by the fact that victims who named their accusers risked ruining their own reputations if the courts ruled their attackers as innocent.[47] People in the eighteenth century assumed rape victims invited sex. Although today, laws in the United States do not distinguish between the two categories "by force" and "against her will," early American colonists did distinguish them. Passion could cause someone to be violent during sex, but that violence did not necessarily imply a lack of consent; "consensual sex could be physically forceful, and rape could originate in consensual sexual relations."[48] In fact, it was assumed that all women, to some extent, had to be coerced into sex even when they desired physical intimacy, forced to play coy due to society's constraints on their behavior. As such, sex with women was often described in militaristic terms: the female body was something that must be conquered by the male victor. This concept of sex assumed that sex was war, and that women secretly wanted to lose. Rawle, then, may have felt compelled to share her story and the stories of her neighbors in such a way that would mitigate blame. The ways in which she tells the story of crowd action points away from her body and toward the rebels; she focuses more on the perpetrators and less on the victims. The result is that the critique remains firmly fixed on the people in the crowd, perhaps so that the people's actions cannot be placed onto Rawle or her friends.

Rawle spends most of her time discussing what happened in other people's houses, rather than lingering on what happened inside of her own. She writes that after the crowd left her house, it then attacked her uncle's home with "pick axes and iron bars," with an aim to raze it. His window was eventually illuminated just as Anna's was, which again satisfied the crowd, who moved on to the home of the merchant Benjamin Gibbs nearby. "Mr. Gibbs was obliged to make his escape over a fence," Rawle recounts, "and while his wife was endeavouring to shield him from the rage of one of the men, she received a violent bruise in the breast, and a low blow in the face which made her nose bleed." Gibbs's spouse took the hit for her husband's loyalties on her body as he fled the townspeople. The townsfolk struck her chest to strike his. After lingering on Hannah Gibbs as a proxy for Benjamin, Rawle then recounts the property damage done to Elizabeth Drinker and other neighbors, who also refused to illuminate their homes and suffered for it.[49] Rawle writes, "In short it was the most alarming scene I ever remember. For two hours we had the disagreeable noise of stones banging about, glass crashing, and the tumultuous voices of a large body of men, as they were a long time at the different houses in the neighbourhood. At last they were victorious, and it was one general illumination throughout the town."[50] Rawle's entries about this attack highlight the irony of a group of people celebrating liberty by smashing, pillaging, and raping dissenters. Her recollection of this incident fashions the Americans as reckless, violent terrorists. To her, these Sons of Liberty exacted their version of justice by frightening a household of unarmed women who committed no crime, other than failing to strike a match.

Notice that Rawle omits the reason for the riots and focuses instead on the aftermath of the chaos. By denying the crowds an explanation or much of a context, she deflects the accusations their attacks implied. People rarely smashed and burned houses spontaneously; rather, they carefully selected their targets, usually identifying people who supported, implemented, or enforced what they saw to be unfair policies created by the Crown. They tended to target large or ostentatious homes, such as Trevose. This "ritual pillaging" allowed men and women from all ranks and classes to "disrobe," or strip, the house to symbolize stripping the occupants inside of it. The candles in the window, which would protect a house from being "disrobed," served as an important symbol as well. Crowds used large fires, such as bonfires, to signal the start of a march or riot, and small flames, such as candles, to mark houses, because flames of all sizes possessed providential significance. Fire, for mobs, was a "symbol of judgment, punishment, and cleansing, apocalyptic deliverance." Burning a house not only punished the occupants and warned anyone else thinking of siding with the loyalists but also purified what rebels viewed as a scourge on the city. Loyalists were likened to an epidemic that must be contained. Crowds saw fire as a way to stem the "disease."[51] Rawle gives us none of these explanations. To have explained why the crowd targeted certain members of the community would have given these actions justification or credence, something Rawle understandably refused to do. This elision gave her the ability to write the revolution as she saw it—not as an ordered cause for liberty, or the scourge of all symbols of a corrupt monarchy, but a chaotic plunge into an experiment doomed to fail. Rawle strips the rebels' reason for rioting in order to reframe herself not as a loyalist informant or as a loyalist's daughter, but as a vulnerable, single *woman*. Such recasting countered the label that others (such as the Ladies Association) attempted to affix to her family; what she wrote requests the reader's (or readers') sympathy. In order to explore how women were able to script their own political identities when the possibility of doing so had been taken from them, when doing so even threatened their ability to communicate or travel freely, we must return to the earlier question: what (political) purpose might rape rhetoric serve?

In order to answer that question, we need to understand the ways in which loyalty could be tied to sexuality and how crowd action sought to regulate anyone who offered an alternative definition of patriotism or stepped outside of their prescribed gender roles. Many of the letters and diaries featured in this period mention crowds either wearing blackface or marching a woman in blackface through the streets. Blackness here symbolized not race but filth (or race and filth). This image implied a warning about the political women who strayed from "proper" (passive) expressions of femininity. "To be 'dirty' was to imply a perverse sexuality," Susan Klepp explains in her study of crowd action, "so the dirty woman in the street impugned the targeted fashionable elite for their failure to uphold community standards of unspotted morality and undefiled femininity. The dirt was intended to bring shame and humiliation on the offender, besmirching reputations."[52] Extralegal bodies particularly targeted women who entertained unpopular political views, such as

Anna Rawle. The logic was circular. These women were political because they were whores and whores because they were political. The blackened face in these riots symbolized the licentious commingling of sexual with political virtue. Men often raped these so-called dirty women to teach them and onlookers to know their place and to stay in it.

It is perhaps ironic, then, that leaders of the revolution affiliated unchecked sexuality with the British—particularly British and Hessian soldiers—whom they said were incapable of controlling their sexual appetites, so when patriots raped and publicly humiliated loyalist women, they sent a complicated message. These acts suggested that women who could not control their political bodies—or, more precisely, who refused to align with popular definitions of a "regulated" body—would be forced to comply. The female form became an extension of the battlefield on which the revolution played out. This act, Susan Brownmiller affirms, "is a message passed between men—vivid proof of victory for one and loss and defeat for the other."[53] Rape rhetoric—especially the appeal of the threat of rape—has historically been used to keep women subjugated.[54] Just as anti-abolitionists and pro-segregationists capitalized on the fear of rape to fuel their causes in the mid-nineteenth and twentieth centuries, so the rebels used a similar tactic as propaganda during the American Revolution. They suggested that people should join the American cause to protect their wives, sisters, and daughters, and they linked the virtue of the female body with the virtue of the republic; both must be protected at all costs. In the sermons, broadsides, newspaper articles, and other publications that promoted this propaganda, women's agency in these violations had to be removed so that the perpetrators, rather than the victims, could emerge the clear villains. Rebel propaganda sought to achieve this goal by targeting men, rather than women, appealing to their desire to protect their property (and they of course left out any suggestion that rebels raped people during war just as loyalists did). Men recounted tales of their wives and daughters being violated by Hessians or British soldiers to create "a national community of aggrieved American citizens. . . . Such stories were particularly useful against the British because rape illuminated their perversion of power and their betrayal of patriarchal protection."[55] These crowds sought to regulate sexuality with rape, thereby casting the aspersions on themselves that they sought to criticize in their enemies.

Rawle's letter takes on a few different meanings in light of this contextualization. By depicting the men, rather than the women, as responsible for these disruptive, violent, and invasive acts, Rawle displaced the women's "passions" to the patriarchs. This rhetorical shift implies a political critique. If a well-ordered society was predicated on the control of emotions and the rule of reason, as many revolutionary supporters assumed it did, and if this society was unable to control itself, then this republic was doomed before it began. Rawle highlights the flaws in these practices and in the rhetoric these men used to justify their actions. The revelers in the Cornwallis riots supported British defeat, so when Rawle tells this story, she rewrites the crowd's message so that patriot men, not loyalist women, were dirty and unregulated. By breeching these "lone women's" domestic spaces, they made these houses unsafe and unclean when they physically, economically, and emotionally damaged the families that they attacked. Rawle's depiction of the Cornwallis rioters as violent, chaotic rapists creates a counter-narrative to the story that crowds typically aimed to tell about loyalists. The rebels, as she tells it, are not defenders but defilers.

Rawle was both able to accuse and decry the crowd of licentious acts against her neighbors and friends broadly speaking (that is, without identifying female victims by name), which further allowed her to transform the crowd's actions into a political critique while simultaneously deflecting blame from its victims. She was also restricted by the publicity of the writing form if she wanted to tell her mother that the crowd harmed her. Rawle did not manipulate this particular letter's physical form. She did not, for example, tape it to the bottom of a rum barrel or roll it up to deliver it inside a hollow bullet. Nevertheless, she manipulated her words so that she could maintain intimate communication with her family despite the prying eyes of those who might intercept her missives and judge their content.

As I emphasize broadly in this book, letters and letter-journals allowed the people who wrote them a means by which they might resist and perhaps engage in their own form of coercion. Margaret Morris resisted categorization as either rebel or loyalist by creating a "neutral island" in her letter-journal, and Sarah Fisher and Elizabeth Drinker engaged in their own form of coercion by discrediting the impetus for revolution and resisting quartering and requisitions. Rebecca Shoemaker, like these other women, would not be stymied by the rebels' directives. She was told that she could not live in Philadelphia or continue communicating with friends and fellow sympathizers because she was a spy, so she coded her missives so that she might fight those strictures. She veiled her letters as diaries to evade detection and control costs so that she could continue writing her daughters in Philadelphia. Crowds demanded the loyalists light candles; Congress, state assemblies, and confiscation committees required that they take oaths; soldiers commanded that they grant requisitions. All these demands meant that loyalists were often defined by people and mandates they did not recognize as authoritative. These legal and extralegal bodies, mostly controlled by (if not composed solely of) men, vied to determine who would have jurisdiction over women's bodies during the war. And they possessed the privilege to do so. Their gender allowed them to script those definitions via laws, letters, pamphlets, and essays, and circulate them in a way that reified their authority. Women could not. Political engagement came with a price. Letters provided a viable, though still contested, outlet. They allowed writers to travel on paper where they could not in person, providing women with a medium through which they might craft and broadcast their own political voice.

Staying ahead of the rebels proved exceptionally difficult for Rawle and Shoemaker, despite their epistolary deftness. Soldiers for a time allowed what Shoemaker calls "domestic" correspondence to pass, which allowed for the delivery of what some might call familiar letters about life at home, such as the crowd action Rawle described on the night that Cornwallis surrendered. The rebels eventually became wise to the fact that women were manipulating this system. In response, they doubled their diligence and intercepted all of the Shoemaker correspondence that they could, regardless of content. "There are no letters for Your Fr[ien]ds Polly & Betsy F[.] I find upon a further enquiry that every one that did not contain some interesting information in the Political line was destroyed," Shoemaker writes to her daughter.[56] Even innocuous missives did not make it past rebel guards, who kept any letters that they suspected conveyed intelligence and threw out all the others, just to be safe.

The Rawle-Shoemakers were able to cease these epistolary acrobatics when Rebecca was reunited with her daughters in Philadelphia after her husband, Samuel, and son, Edward, sailed for England on November 7, 1783, days before the British evacuated New York. After a complicated legal battle, she was able to begin leasing Laurel Hill, their former home, on February 27, 1784. Anne-César, the Chevalier de Luzerne, minister of France, owned the home but promised to return Laurel Hill to the Rawle family at the end of his lease in 1787.[57] Samuel returned from England on May 27, 1786, and eventually returned to Laurel Hill in Philadelphia to live with his family.[58]

The paper war during the family's separation suggests that it was difficult for rebels or loyalists to regulate intelligence. State legislatures sought to regulate loyalty by passing and publishing broader treason acts, which also allowed them to justify intercepting and interrupting correspondence, so the women who relied on letters as a lifeline continued to shift the genre to meet their purposes. Soldiers scanned for letters, so the women wrote journals instead. Officials forbade political correspondence, so the writers coded what they said. Rebels intercepted all missives regardless of content, so the loyalists hid them in buttons and bullets. These shifts in form and content provide material evidence of loyalist women's attempts to defy the new laws that restricted them but that no one asked them to help create. A new genre was born out of ingenuity and desperation that represents the frustrations and determinations of a disenfranchised group of people who refused to accept the narrow definitions of loyalty that were imposed on them.

CHAPTER FIVE

SCRIPTING PATRIOTISM

Elizabeth Graeme Fergusson

"It's a doll house," the guide says to me as he rotates the model of Elizabeth Graeme Fergusson's house, Graeme Park, so that I can get a better view of it. The fingernail-sized shingles match the ones outside. The windows' trim is painted a robin's egg blue, the same color as the house in which I'm standing. Each tiny wood floor has a red rug with frayed edges. The table is set for dinner, and period dresses swing from a rod in the bedroom the size of a paper clip. The likeness is remarkable. The house is large and takes up a corner of the bedroom. How fitting, I think, yet how completely inappropriate that this immense replica should take up so much of Fergusson's space.

Graeme Park in many ways is metonymic of Fergusson's art. It was here she convened her salon before the war, making friends with some of the greatest minds in the region (if not the colonies). This house, with its gardens and its rural peacefulness, inspired her poetry, weaving its way into her verse. But this house too was her albatross. It made Fergusson literally and figuratively an outlier. Socially well-connected yet geographically isolated, she was simultaneously protected and disadvantaged by Graeme Park's remove from Philadelphia. This estate, unlike Grace Growden Galloway's house Trevose, lacked a river-based route. It was undesirable real estate to anyone but the family, a fact that both protected it as an asset and meant that Fergusson could not use it as collateral in the event that she needed money. And then, of course, there's the fact that it belonged to her husband, Henry, who left town with the British and cast aspersions on the family name. Once he left Graeme Park, he was unable (or unwilling) to return again. When my docent finishes showing me the doll's house, he looks over my shoulder and checks that we're still alone. Apprehensively, he whispers, "Do you think that Elizabeth Graeme Fergusson was a loyalist?"

THE ANSWER TO my guide's question is complicated. Elizabeth Graeme Fergusson and Grace Growden Galloway possess eerily similar life stories, until you compare their conclusions. Both were wealthy women who inherited their father's property when they married their husbands. Fergusson inherited Graeme Park, twenty-nine miles outside of Philadelphia, as Galloway inherited Trevose and her other properties nineteen miles from the center. And both married men who, ultimately, betrayed and abandoned them. Galloway married Joseph, a Philadelphia assemblyman and loyalist sympathizer, who left her when the war began; he never returned. Elizabeth Graeme married Henry Fergusson, who marched with the British during the revolution and never came home. Shortly after Henry left Graeme Park, a friend's servant, Jane (called Jenny), announced that she was pregnant and named Henry as the father.[1] Grace Growden Galloway and Elizabeth Fergusson were assumed to be loyalists-by-association, though both also drew attention to themselves as loyalist sympathizers in their own right. Both had their homes stripped from them by confiscation committees, despite the fact that neither of the wives lived with the husbands whom the committees claimed they were punishing. And only after they lost their properties did both women learn that their estranged husbands had legally manipulated the property documents to deprive their wives of the lands that their fathers willed to them.[2] Both wrote petitions and letters to protest their confiscations, but Galloway lost everything and Fergusson did not. The difference lies in the medium they chose to script their own political personae. Galloway wrote a journal for her daughter and a petition to the Supreme Executive Council, but Fergusson launched a wider-reaching publicity campaign that helped regain her property. She also hoped to further solidify her patriotism in the court of public opinion by writing a 788-line, four-part poem called "Il Penseroso: The Deserted Wife," which she began in 1780 and sent ten years later to her friend Annis Boudinot Stockton, requesting that she share it with friends.[3]

Fergusson's relationship with print—embracing, as she did, poetry, petitions, letters, and newspapers to clear her name—positions her as a generic outlier in many ways when compared to her contemporaries, Galloway, Rawle, Fisher, Drinker, and Morris. None of the traditional missives Fergusson wrote appear to be collectively authored or intended for a broader reading public, which makes her different from Fisher, Morris, and Rawle. She was, at times, more furtive in her epistolary declarations than Rawle or Galloway, particularly when she was trying to avoid treason. Yet when she did go public with loyalties, she filed petitions with the state assembly and sent letters to the newspaper that were then published and republished across the colonies. When Fergusson decided it was time to speak out, she wanted as many people as possible to hear her. Fergusson combined these tactics with writing poetry, which she wrapped in a newspaper and addressed to a friend; the poem's many parts are subdivided by letters to the dedicatee. Fergusson's print culture thus forms a matrix of genres. This matrix, however, is not unique. Galloway petitioned for the right to Trevose while she was keeping her journal for Betsy. Fisher and Drinker petitioned for the Virginia Exiles' release, via the collective missive they signed to Washington. But none of these other writers seemed as invested in the equitable diversification of these generic forms. And none used these genres to convince the public that they sympathized with the rebels, which is what Fergusson eventually did with her letter-poem, "Il Penseroso."

The overarching theme of "Il Penseroso" is Fergusson's abandonment, isolation, and betrayal, which has led critics to read it as proof of her misery and lack of agency during the war. Such a reading of this poem initially makes sense. "Il Penseroso" expresses an earnest desire to discover that the rumors about her husband are falsehoods and drives home the corrosive effects of betrayal on the Fergussons' marriage. The verses move quickly through the stages of grief, vacillating between anger with Jenny, denial about Henry, and bargaining with God. This poem rambles, as Rodney Mader characterizes it. He argues that if Fergusson meant to use the poem to indict her husband or get him to confess his guilt, "it would have certainly failed."[4] I suggest that Henry's confession was not Elizabeth's primary goal; instead, she implemented "Il Penseroso" as the third part of an extensive publicity campaign—primarily involving familiar letters and letters to newspapers—to salvage her own reputation as a traitor.

Fergusson aided and abetted not one but two loyalist informants during the war, yet despite her role in these scandals, she escaped eviction, imprisonment, and confiscation. Fergusson, like Grace Growden Galloway, married a wealthy, high-profile loyalist, and, like Rebecca Shoemaker, was accused of delivering treasonous correspondence. But Fergusson escaped the other women's fates. How did she do that?

Fergusson's work illustrates that to understand how loyalist women writers—particularly those whom their families abandoned—used writing to assert their political agency, one must comprehend how they scripted patriotism without nationalism. The writers I have discussed thus far have all handled this conundrum slightly differently. Galloway used a journal to declare herself disaffected, while Fisher, Drinker, and Morris argued for their exclusion from the loyalist/patriot binary on the grounds of their membership in the Society of Friends. Rawle questioned the morality of the nationalist imperative and the people who supported it. Fergusson's tactic was to revise herself from loyalist-by-association to patriot. The etymology of the term "patriot" suggests that people who adopted that moniker considered themselves "fellow countrym[e]n . . . of [their] fathers."[5] But what of women, like Fergusson, who lacked both country with which to identify and a father/husband/king? Fergusson's letters suggest that people who found themselves in such a situation grafted new loyalties, if not onto figureheads (such as congressmen, generals, or local officials), then at least onto the notion of nation. And since Fergusson achieved this revision of self via a variety of genres, she also demonstrates how missives served as the interstitial tissue that bridged the divide between multiple writing forms. The genres she embraced allowed her to move herself from being known as "more dangerous to the American cause than any other woman" to being remembered as a beloved, admired literary figure, "the most learned woman in America."[6]

THE WASHINGTON-DUCHÉ SCANDAL

Elizabeth Fergusson wrote her way out of property confiscation and social isolation with letters, but her letter-writing initiated many of her troubles in the first place. Jacob Duché, an Anglican minister for Christ Church and St. Peter's Church in Philadelphia, approached Fergusson in 1777 to deliver a message to George Washington. Duché was desperate because he had recently undergone a spiritual and political crisis. The minister felt conflicted about the revolution, a fact that later became crucial in discerning what, if any, culpability Fergusson had in delivering his missive. The first Continental Congress had asked Duché during the Stamp Act Crisis to use his role as an Anglican priest to convince people to support protesting unfair taxation. He acquiesced and gave two sermons arguing that Great Britain's corruption warranted retribution. As a leader of one of the most powerful churches in Philadelphia during a time when people sought religious justification for separating from England, Duché assumed an influential role. He became chaplain of the Continental Congress, which further broadened his influence. But by 1776, he had changed his mind about the war. Pennsylvania's new legislature created loyalty oaths, supported mob rule, arrested prominent members of the community, and stripped the Anglican liturgy of prayers for the king, all decisions that violated Duché's moral code. When the British invaded Philadelphia in 1777, they arrested Duché for being a patriot (unaware of his growing reserve), and he spent a night in jail.[7] He blamed not the loyalists who arrested him but the rebels who initiated the war. He vowed after that night that he would no longer support the rebellion.

He wrote a letter to George Washington one week later to beg him to intervene. Duché pleads, "May heaven inspire you with this glorious resolution of exerting your strength at this crisis, and immortalizing yourself as friend and guardian to your country. . . . Recommend, and you have an undoubted right to recommend, an immediate cessation of hostilities."[8] The letter asks Washington to betray the rebels and calls for a truce with the loyalists. Duché struggled to find a way to deliver this message to Washington's encampment. No one without a pass could cross enemy lines, and Duché lacked one. But he knew someone who might acquire that pass: Elizabeth Fergusson. Washington and Fergusson

FIGURE 5. *Drafting the Letter,* by Edward Lamson Henry (ca. 1871). The painting depicts Fergusson with the Duché letter. Courtesy of the Athenaeum.

had been involved in negotiations to secure permission to allow Henry to return to Graeme Park after he traveled with Lord Howe from New York to Philadelphia. In other words, Fergusson had Washington's ear. When Duché approached her and asked to use her as a courier, Fergusson agreed (fig. 5).

Washington compared the experience of opening and reading Duché's letter to becoming aware that an infectious disease had contaminated him. He was sure that Duché's suggestion would implicate him in a treason scandal were anyone else to read it and that the ripple effect would harm anyone connected to him. The general decided that the only way to stem the "outbreak" was to send the letter to Congress, along with his own note descrying Duché's suggestion. "To this ridiculous, illiberal performance," Washington writes Congress, "I made a short reply, by desiring the bearer of it [Fergusson], she should hereafter, by any accident, meet Mr. Duche, to tell him I should have returned it unopened, if I had any idea of the contents." Washington knew that if he lost the war—which, at the time, seemed a distinct possibility—and was found with Duché's missive, Congress would assume he had purposefully lost his campaigns so that he could adhere to the minister's request. "I thought this a duty," he explains, "which I owed to myself; for had any accident happened to the army entrusted to my command, and it had ever afterwards appeared, that such a letter had been written to and received by me, might it not have been said, that I betrayed my country? And would not such a correspondence, if kept a secret, have given good grounds for the suspicion?" Washington feared looking like a traitor. He then publicly shamed the courier, whom he accused of aiding the disease's spread. He says he "highly disapproved the intercourse she seemed to have been carrying on, and expected it would be discontinued."[9] Although this tactic proved effective, as Congress did not charge him with treason, Washington essentially sacrificed Fergusson's reputation to save his own. He justified his actions by reasoning that he preferred to control the epistolary exchange rather than be controlled by it. Such control hinged on whether all parties involved in the scandal possessed the privilege and platform to get ahead of the story. Fergusson possessed neither.

Congress read Duché's letter and Washington's reply on October 20, 1777, and printed both in its meeting minutes, which meant the missives became publicly available to anyone who wanted to read them. Newspapers then copied and distributed Duché's note, Washington's reply, and Congress's minutes throughout the colonies.[10] The *Pennsylvania Evening Post* responded to this news by questioning neither Washington's nor Duché's but Fergusson's moral values. "We should have despised and banished from social intercourse every character, male or female, which should be so lost to virtue, decency and humanity, as to revel with the murderers and plunderers of their countrymen," one article proclaims, concluding, "Behold the consequence."[11] This article casts the spotlight on Fergusson. How much did she know when she delivered Duché's letter? He had, until a week prior, identified as a patriot as far as his community knew. Had she known of his change of heart? Did her willingness to deliver the missive mean that she agreed with his suggestion? Or had she merely served as courier with no knowledge of the epistle's contents? If she had not opened it, then she could claim innocence and unfortunate timing. If she had opened it, the courts could find her guilty of misprision of treason and fine or imprison her. Fergusson was the only one involved in the affair who did not publicly have her say.

Although it might appear beneficial to analyze the letters that Fergusson writes to address the Washington-Duché debacle, this correspondence does not exist in the archives. Fergusson's letters may not have been saved, or she was not given or did not take the opportunity to speak for herself—at least not yet. Her silence suggests a different type of rhetoric that we should also analyze because silence too can be a political act. The epistolary spaces that Washington and Duché utilized contained more restrictions for Fergusson than they did for the other writers. Both statesmen were backed by their respective governments to whom they owed allegiance, and as such, a political space existed in which they either could be tried or exonerated. These congressional/parliamentary spaces at least allowed Washington and Duché a forum, regardless of the outcome of such a trial or hearing. Fergusson technically could—and eventually did—address these governing bodies, but she hesitated to enter these spheres because doing so would earn her a stigma. Fergusson later explains, "I am sensible . . . that the political opinions of women are ridiculed among the generality of men," and she finds it "hard, very hard . . . to be held out to the public as a tool." Writing a letter to Congress exposed her in a way that it did not expose the men involved in this affair. Taking her grievances to a legislative body not only broadcast her treason but reminded the public of Henry's betrayal, which meant she risked giving the confiscation committee an opportunity to publicly shame her in order to use her as propaganda. She also knew that political women were often accused of having questionable morals (a concept to which Anna Rawle returned frequently). "As a female perhaps to enlarge on [political matters]," Fergusson reflects, "might be deemed an affectation of masculine virtue."[12] She did not want to unsex herself. Her initial reticence to write about the Washington-Duché affair thus further underscores the gendered nature of certain political/epistolary spaces. The consequences of entering those spaces did not always outweigh the costs for women. This reality provides a plausible explanation concerning why she hesitated to enter the fray. But these events initiated the beginning of a series of catastrophes about which Fergusson would not keep quiet. The Washington-Duché scandal marked her as suspicious, but the Johnstone-Reed affair threatened to complete her ruin.

THE JOHNSTONE-REED AFFAIR

In 1778, within one year of the previous scandal, Fergusson made the newspapers again. This scandal, even more so than the one prior, illustrates the ways in which women could act as political agents in the war through letter-writing and letter-delivery, while simultaneously illustrating the dangers these forms of activism held for women. It was after this story broke that Fergusson picked up her pen and began to write letters to clear her name. George Johnstone, an Englishman whom King George III had sent to negotiate peace with the colonies, wanted to send a missive to Joseph Reed, the president of Pennsylvania's Supreme Executive Council.[13] In that letter, Johnstone attempted to bribe Reed. The Englishman said that if Reed called an end to the hostilities, the crown would offer him a prestigious political position and remuneration for his trouble.[14] But Johnstone could not get Reed to grant him an audience. Like Duché, Johnstone quickly realized that one of the most well-connected women in the area could go where he could not. Johnstone then asked Elizabeth Fergusson to take the message to Reed on his behalf, a request she granted—a decision that is somewhat surprising, given her recent trouble with Pennsylvania's government.[15]

Reed, like Washington, treated Johnstone's letter as infected. His worries mirrored the general's: if the colonies lost the war, and the statesmen found him with Johnstone's missive, the rebels would assume he had engineered the loss to curry favor with the king. Reed acted to preserve his reputation using the same methodology as Washington. He forwarded Johnstone's bribe and his own refusal of it to the assembly, who published it in the meeting minutes, where newspapers thereafter copied and distributed the story—again naming Fergusson as the accomplice.[16] Here is another important example of private missives moving rapidly through various public spaces with such dizzying speed that not everyone involved in the correspondence possessed the time to react. Fergusson must have felt a terrible sense of déjà-vu, but this action signaled only the beginning of her troubles. One month after the Johnstone-Reed scandal broke, the Supreme Executive Council found Henry Fergusson guilty of treason and confiscated their family home, Graeme Park.[17] The timing was not coincidental. Elizabeth Fergusson's involvement in both the Duché and Johnstone affairs confirmed suspicions that the entire family sought to undermine the revolution. This time, however, Fergusson did not remain silent.

FERGUSSON RESPONDS

After the Supreme Executive Council confiscated her property—and Graeme Park belonged to her, not to Henry, since her father had willed it to her—Fergusson filed a petition in 1779, penned as a letter to the council, asking to keep it.[18] This letter-petition marked the beginning of Fergusson's public transformation from treasonous loyalist informant to patriotic abandoned wife, a process that she completed with her poem "Il Penseroso." Fergusson adopted the discursive strategy to first clear Henry's name so that she could later, in a different publication, clear her own. Fergusson opens the letter by explaining why Henry no longer lived at home, in part, because he fled to England after the assembly found him guilty. She writes, "although your Memorialist, being well persuaded that her said husband never entertained the least inimical intention towards these American States, nor has ever committed any treasonable act against them, would have been desirous of his return to her, . . . such return was not in his power."[19] He wanted to come home, in other words, but could not.

Fergusson continues this petition by arguing that Henry could never commit treason because he was not born in America, and the definition of treason could only apply to natural-born citizens. "Mr. Ferguson was a native of Britain," she writes, "never resided long in America, and before the declaration of Independence . . . sailed in a Merchant Ship for Bristol, on business merely domestic, to settle some affairs with a brother in North-Britain." Fergusson insists that Henry just happened to set sail for Great Britain on the eve of the revolution. His absence (like her decision to deliver a letter for

Jacob Duché) constituted bad timing, not an admission of guilt. "The public commotions" that then followed in 1776 so frightened her that "altho' known to be as warmly attached to the American cause *as belongs to the sphere of a woman,* [she] wrote to him from time to time to protract his stay" until the war was over. She concludes, "It therefore became natural for a woman, not exempted from the timidity of her sex, to wish her husband as long as possible absent from such a distressing scene."[20] She tacks on the phrase "as belongs to the sphere of a woman" to remind the assembly that she did not identify as a bluestocking. Sentiment compelled her—as it compelled the Virginia Exiles' wives—to discuss her strong attachment to America, but she did not involve herself in its politics and policies to such a degree that she would overstep her boundaries. This was quite an odd argument to make, given her role in delivering those two letters. Nonetheless, this petition ultimately said less about Henry than it did about Fergusson. She was a patriot. She contained an appropriate amount of feminine feeling for her country. She felt responsible for keeping her husband abroad. In other words, none of them could have committed treason if all of them acted out of family feeling.

Fergusson then addresses the fact that Henry had returned to the colonies and marched with British troops. Although his absence alone would have damned him, since flight implied guilt, he exacerbated his situation by coming back with a loyalist army. She explains this decision by writing that in March 1777, "he embarked from Britain to Jamaica, and from thence took the only opportunity he could obtain of coming to Pennsylvania, or its neighbourhood, which was in a ship for New-York." He found Lord Howe's fleet sitting in Chesapeake Bay and thought they could take him home, based on "the advice of some of his friends in New-York." He welcomed any such information at this point, Fergusson explains, "after so long and distressing an absence" from his family. He traveled with them not as a soldier but as a camp follower—nothing more. "As the rout[e] of the British army was the direct way of his family," she writes, again reminding the reader of his obligation as a husband, "and he could not be permitted to leave them for fear of carrying intelligence, he accompanied them as a private man, without taking any part, directly or indirectly in their service." Henry did not flee to England; rather, he waited to sail home. Elizabeth Fergusson adopts a passive strategy in this petition. Perhaps the assembly would dismiss the allegations against them both if it determined that neither she nor Henry purposefully adopted any particular doctrine.[21]

Fergusson next addresses the accusations that Henry tortured American prisoners of war, which she initially denied happened at all and then contextualized by saying that frustrated men (perhaps sexually frustrated men) kept away from the company of their wives often go insane. This particular rhetorical move casts the blame on the rebels who refused him a pass to return to Graeme Park, making them the traitors and Henry the victim. "In November 1777, finding himself *claimed as a British subject*, and refused the privilege of going to his family to assist your Memorialist either in *relieving his own or her wants*, he was prevailed upon, by the advice of some Gentlemen well affected to America, and touched with the distresses of the American prisoners at that time, to accept some part in the care and management of them." What the rebels defined as "torture," Fergusson reframes as "care." Henry merely wanted to "alleviate their sufferings by every means in his power." She offers an alternative explanation for Henry's role in the British Army: maybe the rebels detained him as a political prisoner. The loyalists, she theorizes, "by written authority under their Generals," may have *forced* him to torture the rebels to punish Henry for his ardent patriotism. Surely the government would not punish him (and her) for acting "out of necessity, to the command of the enemy."[22] This part of the letter seems tenuous, which perhaps explains why she did not linger on it, choosing instead to remind the rebels that if they had allowed Henry to return to his wife, none of this would have happened.

Fergusson concludes by clarifying what she wants from the assembly: Henry's name cleared, not for Henry's sake, but for her own—so that she could keep her home. "Your Memorialist," she writes,

> in *hopes of saving her personal estate* . . . now earnestly prays, That the Honourable House of Assembly would take her case into their most serious and compassionate consideration; and, . . . restore her to the use and absolute possession of her patrimony, which she has never forfeited by any act of her own, and which she is advised, and humbly conceives, cannot be affected by any thing alledged to be done by her dear husband.[23]

The close of her letter makes it clear: Pennsylvania must absolve Henry to absolve Elizabeth so that she can regain the rights to Graeme Park. The Supreme Executive Council deliberated about her case and issued its decision: *denied.*[24]

Part of the reason the assembly denied Fergusson's request is that it had recently granted bills of relief to two men—Albertson Walton and Reynold

Keen—though these men had failed to report to the Court of Oyer and Ter-
miner after being accused of treason. "A Whig Citizen" took the legislators
to task in the *Pennsylvania Packet* for what they saw as dangerous laxity.[25]
When Fergusson then presented her petition, the assembly could not grant
her Graeme Park and save face. The assemblymen would have had trouble
explaining this pardon, given her public role in the Duché and Johnstone
controversies. Even if they could have explained away her role, Joseph Reed
was president of that council, and the scandal that expedited the confiscation
of Graeme Park implicated him. Reed resented the aspersions the situation
cast on him and blamed Fergusson for dragging him into it. Rejecting her
petition for Graeme Park provided Reed not one but two prime opportunities: he could recover his own reputation while also punishing Fergusson for
her role in the affair.[26] Graeme Park and most of Fergusson's belongings were
sold at auction on February 15, 1778. Suffering through a similar situation
with the same legislative body just one year prior, Grace Growden Galloway
locked herself in her friend's house and refused to move after a long, public,
humiliating battle that mirrored Fergusson's. Surprisingly, Fergusson ultimately avoided this same fate by regaining what was stripped from her. Her
petition's rejection did not conclude her story but, instead, launched Fergusson into a new beginning.

"To the Public"

Fergusson's petition to the Supreme Executive Council relegated her public
profession of patriotism to a closed circuit of biased readers. Unlike George
Washington's letter to the state assembly, Fergusson's missive did not circulate
from the council to the newspapers. Her primary reading audience consisted
of Joseph Reed and his colleagues, all of whom had something to lose by pro-
nouncing either Henry or Elizabeth Fergusson innocent. Both the audience
and the genre—the letter-as-petition—lacked the power to repair the social
damage that this scandal caused Fergusson. All of her authority stemmed
from her wealth and connections, and she had lost those. Perhaps she realized
that she had to manipulate her social standing if she were going to successfully exert pressure on Reed to reverse his decision. "To the Public," a letter
Fergusson sent to the *Pennsylvania Packet* in 1779, provided her that forum
for redress. Other papers throughout the colonies redistributed this missive, and it was widely read.[27] She uses three different tactics in this petition

that she had not employed in her letter to the Supreme Executive Council. She addresses the public instead of the legislators. She writes an open letter instead of a petition. And she exonerates herself instead of Henry. This shift in genre, audience, and strategy ultimately assisted Fergusson when she sought a second time to recover her property and reputation.

Fergusson's assembly petition addresses Henry's role (or lack of one) in the revolution, but "To the Public" concerns Fergusson's part in the Johnstone-Reed affair. It opens by focusing on her role as messenger, addressing the unanswered questions concerning just how much Fergusson knew when she delivered Johnstone's message. The way Fergusson tells it, Johnstone pestered her "three times," and each time, "he expressed great desire to have been admitted to have passed [enemy] lines." Johnstone insisted that he was "a friend to America, who wished some person would step forth and act a mediatorial part, and suggest something to stop the effusion of blood which was like to ensue, if the war was carried on in its full vigour." He wanted to stop the war. He asked her to courier for him because he categorized Henry as a loyalist and assumed Elizabeth shared his sympathies, which meant he made the same assumptions about Fergusson's covered status that soldiers and legislators made about other so-called loyalist women. Fergusson uses a different discursive strategy than her contemporaries, however; she backpedals. As Reed and Washington immediately regretted opening their treasonous correspondence, so Fergusson says she regretted granting Johnstone an audience. He suggested to her that the American people did not support the revolution but that a small group of violent men had frightened others into acquiescing. "I uniformly told him," Fergusson writes, "that I thought he cherished a delusive idea. . . . I am sure I can say, speaking within bounds, I repeated half a dozen times to him, that I believed, if the votes of the people were or could be impartially taken, they would give the decision in favour of independency; but this sentiment he never coincided in."[28] Fergusson's letter denies entertaining Johnstone's ideas *six times*. She remained as committed to the American cause, she insists, as Johnstone was determined to undermine it.

Fergusson then addresses the most outrageous part of her story: why did she, an ardent patriot, knowingly deliver a bribe to a statesman? This question was crucial. Unlike Reed and Washington, Fergusson had *not* taken Johnstone's missive to the Supreme Executive Council to absolve herself of any guilt. She answers this by explaining that she was distracted and, even though Johnstone may have frequently visited her, she had not familiarized herself with his plan. She writes, "Governor Johnstone sent me a manuscript book, to read the morning he went off, but in so hasty a way, that he asked three or four times for it, before it was possible to have read it a quarter through." Johnstone rushed her, in other words, so she skimmed his proposal. "The general vein that prevailed in it was, pointing out the many advantages arising from a reunion with Britain, and a commercial intercourse, and several good things I believe were in it, but I thought it much too prolix to be of general utility."[29] The parts she did read carefully did not offend her. Everyone wanted the war to end as quickly as possible, and indeed, many thought it would conclude much sooner than it did. She did not have the time to read the treasonous parts carefully. Johnstone snatched the paper from her before she could give the entire document due consideration. The rest of his writing proved too wordy to digest; its verbosity rendered it harmless. No one, Fergusson suggests, should hold her accountable for passing along something she did not read well or understand completely.

The most persuasive part of Fergusson's letter comes at its conclusion, when she explains that she told Johnstone not to communicate with Reed but that nothing would deter him. This strategy removed Fergusson from the incident altogether; if she had not delivered the message to Reed, she implies, someone else would have done so in her stead. Her narrative takes a turn when she arrives at the part of her story where she might have detailed the thought process that convinced her to act as Johnstone's accessory. After Johnstone told Fergusson that he thought Reed and Washington communicated often, Fergusson concedes, "'I believe, sir, . . . that General Reed stands very well with General Washington,' (for I always made it a point to give our officers their titles, immediately when any of the British gentlemen omitted them)."[30] She does not dwell on her own culpability but rather offers the readers a red herring by noting Johnstone's irreverence—and her admiration—for the two generals. She was restoring the titles that he had stripped from them. This detail neither addresses nor concerns why Fergusson delivered Johnstone's letter despite her reservations, but it does underscore her commitment to the rebel cause by rhetorically aligning herself with its leaders.

Johnstone ignored the correction and delivered the proposition that would eventually damn Fergusson and Reed, she continues. He tells her,

> If this affair should be settled in the way *we* wish, *we* shall have many pretty things in our power, and if Mr. Reed, after well considering the nature of the dispute, can, conformable to his conscience and view of things, exert his

influence to settle the contest, he may command ten thousand guineas and the best post in the government, and if you should see him, I could wish you would convey that idea to him.

Fergusson here implies that Johnstone was bribing her along with Reed. "I own I felt hurt and shocked," she professes, "for I regarded the hint as indelicate, and from that moment Mr. Johnstone appeared to me in a different mode of light." She then repeats how she tried to predict for Johnstone the humiliation that this plan would cause him:

> [FERGUSSON] Do you not think, Sir, that Mr. Reed will look upon such a mode of obtaining his influence as a bribe? (I really made use of that plain term.)
> [JOHNSTONE] Do you think so, Madam?
> [FERGUSSON] I really, Sir, should apprehend so.
> [JOHNSTONE] By no means, Madam.
> [FERGUSSON] This method of proceeding is customary in all negotiations, returned I, but this appears to me, that if it is Mr. Reed's judgment that America should give up the point of independence, he will say so, if he has any influence in her counsels, without fee or reward; and if he is of a different opinion, no pecuniary emolument should lead him to give a contrary vote.[31]

She tells the readers that the meeting ended when she insisted Johnstone abandon his plan to bribe Reed, but he would not listen and he left.

The final strategy Fergusson uses in this open letter is to convince her reading audience that her gender made committing treason impossible. She concludes her letter:

> Much could I say with truth of my love to my country, but will here be silent . . . ; as a female perhaps to enlarge on that subject might be deemed an affectation of masculine virtue. . . . Let this appeal to the public be taken in what light it may, I offer it with dissidence; but feel myself much more easy in my mind, now I have given it, than I ever have done since I had that unlucky conversation with Governor Johnstone.[32]

I love America, Fergusson insists, while also noting that someone who might be misconstrued as treasonous would insist the same thing. But she possesses no ability to label herself a loyalist or patriot because to do so, she would have to claim some sort of political identity, which would mean to affect "masculine virtue," a privilege granted to men. She uses her gender to point away from herself—redirecting the attention back onto Reed and Johnstone, who, she argues, deserve the greatest scrutiny. By stripping herself of any agency in the war, emphasizing to readers that she believes war is a "masculine" endeavor, she also removes herself of any culpability. The public should view her as the victim, not the perpetrator. Blame the writers, not the messenger.

"To the Public" suggests that Fergusson learned a few things from her prior experiences with humiliating scandals. Reed and Washington had cleared their names with the Supreme Executive Council because they did not hesitate to turn over the incriminating letters in the name of full disclosure. Fergusson's case, however, was too far gone; on the defensive, she could not claim complete transparency immediately after the fact. She instead attempted to exonerate herself in the court of public opinion, which required a much broader reading public. She also learned that, to save herself, she must sacrifice others. Washington knew that he might ruin Fergusson's reputation if he named her in the affair, but when the assembly pushed him, he did so anyway. The same happened with Reed. When Fergusson published her own story, she too named names in an effort to point away from herself. This strategy shined a spotlight, once again, on Joseph Reed, who then had to address the scandal a second time—not to the assembly, with whom he had already reconciled, but with anyone reading the newspapers. Fergusson's strategy worked. Reed replied, not with one missive but with a book of them, which he published on September 8, 1779, in an attempt to clear his name.[33]

Fergusson recovered Graeme Park after she published this letter to the papers. Other factors abetted her property's return. Graeme Park had been difficult to sell for profit for a few reasons, which made it undesirable real estate. First, if Elizabeth died, her heirs, not Henry's, would inherit it. Any buyer who purchased the property after its confiscation would have to relinquish it to them.[34] Dower law also forbade anyone purchasing this property from "committing waste," which meant forbidding any potential new owner from developing or profiting from the estate.[35] These unattractive disclosures accompanied the advertisement for Graeme Park. A regime change in October 1779 further assisted Fergusson. The citizens of Philadelphia questioned the city's ability to maintain order after a group of militiamen, the "Committee of Privates," began "tak[ing] up all Tories & Quakers." These men took it upon themselves to exile all wives and children left behind by loyalist men who had fled their homes. This extralegal organization raided several houses of suspected loyalists and, in the melee, shot a man who had not been charged with or convicted of treason. Philadelphians registered their dissent at the ballot box. The new government they elected opened the door for Fergusson to make a second appeal for her property. She succeeded and recovered Graeme Park.[36]

Although Fergusson's biographer rightly suggests it was largely her sphere of influence and persistence that caused her to regain her property and convince the Philadelphia Assembly that she was not, in fact, the most dangerous woman in America, I suggest that Fergusson's decision to directly address the public provided the lynchpin she needed to transform her reputation in the court of public opinion. Later reprints of Fergusson's letter "To the Public" include commentary that suggests her audience did accept her rebranding. "Accident flung her into the same house appropriated to the use of Governor Johnstone," one article reiterates in a reflection on Fergusson's epistle. The piece supports Fergusson's decision to deliver Johnstone's missive to Reed, arguing that she merely "seemed very desirous of settling matters upon some amicable footing."[37] If the prior assembly had refused to grant Fergusson her property so that it could in part deflect accusations of favoritism and leniency, then this letter clarifying her political status made it easier for the new assembly to reverse its decision. Fergusson, unlike Galloway, realized that writing private missives to select, powerful men gained her little traction because the intimacy of that writing form did not pressure them to act. She relocated her protest to the public sphere and thereby diverted the story away from her own culpability—placing it back onto Reed—and inspired the public's sympathy as a hapless, abandoned wife.

Once Fergusson regained her property, she implemented the last step in her public transformation: rhetorically divorcing Henry Fergusson, whom she blamed for all of her miseries. Having her house back signified a great victory, but she had been disconnected from her friends along the way. Her family's loyalties had indeed infected her, and no one wanted to be implicated in her fall. Her poem seems an attempt to convince the public and/or herself that she had severed all of her ties to treasonous people, including Jacob Duché, George Johnstone, and Henry Fergusson. Her husband by this point had permanently relocated to England and given her the ultimatum that she join him or consider herself renounced. She could flee her home and be remembered as a traitor, or she could stay and risk further hardship and isolation. As with Morris's assertion of neutrality, discussed in chapter 3, Fergusson knew how to position herself in the way that would be most advantageous. As it did with

Morris, such a performance required flexibility, adaptability, and revisionism before her audience would accept that she did not intend to obstruct the republic imperative.

"IL PENSEROSO: THE DESERTED WIFE"

Fergusson wrote letters and petitions to rewrite her involvement in various scandals so that she might regain her property. Her poem "Il Penseroso" continues those revisions to her public persona. As she distanced herself from treason in the letters she wrote in the 1770s, so she distanced herself from her husband in the poetry she wrote in the 1780s. She sent this poem to her friend Annis Stockton in 1793, ten years after the Treaty of Paris that marked the end of the American Revolution. People no longer thought of themselves as loyalists or patriots by this period—as historian Rebecca Brannon has noted, this was a period of reconciliation as people sought to reconvene for social and economic reasons.[38] It is all the more curious, then, that Fergusson would send her poem to Stockton at this time, indicating that she had yet to rectify the wrongs her husband had done. Others had moved on, but she had not. Perhaps she was trying to convince herself of the transformation as well. Her rhetoric indicates that she wanted a complete separation from anything that would taint her efforts to rewrite herself from traitor to abandoned wife.

Fergusson's "Il Penseroso" breaks generic boundaries as a poem, in part because of the way that the author packaged and delivered her verse. Fergusson wrote part of the poem on blank paper, but the other part she wrote in the margins of a newspaper, which she also used to wrap the verse for her friend Annis Boudinot Stockton, though she likely assumed that Stockton's circle of friends would read it too. Stockton conducted a salon at Morven in Princeton, New Jersey, formed at the same time as Fergusson's, both of which were most active in the 1760s. Fergusson's and Stockton's salons, when in operation, exchanged information with each other. Among Stockton's members were Hannah Griffitts (the loyalist poet featured in Patty Moore's book), Esther Edwards Burr, Mary Read, Anna Young Smith, Rebecca Moore Smith, Elizabeth Norris, and Susanna Wright.[39] "Il Penseroso" also may have been intended for anyone who once formed Fergusson's social circle before she became alienated.[40] The newspaper in which Fergusson wrapped "Il Penseroso" is an extension of the poem itself, as historian Rodney Mader clarifies in his transcription of Fergusson's verse. Fergusson inscribes this epigraph onto her copy of the Philadelphia *General Advertiser*, dated March 27, 1793 (fig. 6):

Il Penseroso
A Poem
Written at different times
To Mrs Stocton

Below that, she writes a letter:

Mrs Stocton is desir'd to show this only to such of her
Friends as have heard

the Cause of my Separation with Mr F[ergusso]n and have Delicacy, Sensibility and Candor to make allowances
April 21, 1793[41]

She thus blurs the lines that might otherwise distinguish these genres—letter, editorial, poem—from one another. The topics that the newspaper addresses correlate with "Il Penseroso's" themes; each column in the edition that she chose features a revolution of one sort or another. The first article, which concerns an uprising in Bridgetown, Barbados, states that on that day, "Many inhabitants . . . assembled, & had the effigy of Thomas Paine with his 'Rights of Man' carried about the town: and afterwards burnt him on the parade, in the green, just above the Cage, while the band played God save the King." The article claims that the protest was signaling a revolution about to erupt in Barbados and warns people to keep their patriotism "confined to our bosoms, and not blaze into a fire that might consume our dwellings," given what the colonies on the mainland had learned about the violence and damage a revolution could cause. The next article featured in the newspaper also laments the American Revolution's aftershocks, but this one focuses on the war's transatlantic effects. This commentary claims, "Not only in England, but in Ireland and Scotland, the basest, slowest arts have been practiced to alienate the minds of the people from the present government, . . . to inflame them to sedition." Graffiti, the writer says, has been chalked onto the "corners of the streets, on the walls of the houses, effigies of the King, . . . with the inscription, 'George the third and last!'" The *General Advertiser* then predicts that these international revolutions would circle back to North America, causing a revolutionary ripple effect that

FIGURE 6. "Il Penseroso," dedication on a copy of the Philadelphia *General Advertiser*. The Library Company of Philadelphia.

would lead to a populist overthrow of the government.[42] Although Fergusson finished the poem in 1783, she clearly amended it when she sent it to Stockton ten years later to incorporate the news of these rebellions into footnotes and passing references.[43] Fergusson's editorial/letter/poem forms a genre as rebellious as its author. Just as she refused to be defined by her loyalist husband, the laws of coverture, or Pennsylvania's definitions of treason, so too her poetry rioted against eighteenth-century conventions. While the world in which she lived was concerned with both the concept and aftereffects of revolution, "Il Penseroso" attempts to contextualize and absolve Fergusson's own role in the war. The poem addresses these concerns in four parts: "Hope," "Doubt," "Solitude," and "Adversity."

Hope

The first part of the poem, written between 1780 and 1781, addresses Fergusson's lack of that titular subject. She emphasizes her abandonment and sadness, emotionally distancing herself from Henry and the rest of her friends following the accusations that he betrayed both his country and his wife—two charges that, in this poem, intermingle. "Hope" opens by lamenting that Fergusson was "on the Brink of Sad *Dispair!* / Remote all Comfort every Succor far, / Far, far removd!"[44] Fergusson wonders throughout part one why she is being tested. She compares herself to Abraham when God asked him to sacrifice his son Isaac to test his faith. In particular, she prays that at any moment, God will snatch her from her tortuous situation just as he "snatc[h]'d young Isaac from the opening grave." Although Morris reflected that her times of stripping led to a revelation of God's providence—a baptism of faith by fire—Fergusson did not frame her suffering in this way. She writes, instead, that her trials inspired gnawing doubt, endless isolation, and overwhelming sadness. She concludes,

> But what alas for wretched me remains;
> But Cutting anguish and corroding pains
> Slow pining Melancholy wasting Woe!
> And Shame deep Blushing in my Path below!
> Distrust, and darkness, and a Spirit vext,
> With Wavering thoughts and Clashing views perplex'd
> These Sad associates for my Future Life!
> Bewildering Guides for a Deserted-Wife.[45]

In these final lines of "Hope," she accuses not just Henry but everyone of abandoning her. God had turned his face from her, and her friends had left her too because they tired of her endless examination of Henry's alleged infidelities and because she had become a political and social pariah. She feared what others would think, not of Henry but of *her*.

While the first part of "Il Penseroso" might register as more personal than political, such themes—of isolation, abandonment, doubt, and betrayal—repeat themselves time and again in other loyalist letters of this era. Rebecca Shoemaker's and Anna Rawle's letters indicate that people hesitated to write to them, given that the Shoemaker family's loyalties might implicate them too. Grace Growden Galloway writes, "I am fled from as a pestilence. . . . I have no friends." Fergusson may have felt her own social isolation deeply while writing this poem in 1780 and 1781, but such a strategy would have benefited her reputation. She lived in a world where the company she kept determined her loyalties, so divorcing herself from people who considered themselves loyalists meant separating herself from their loyalties as well. This separation provided her with a blank slate onto which she could inscribe her own, as she continues to do in part 2, "Doubt."

Doubt

Fergusson separated part 1, "Hope," from part 2, "Doubt," dated 1782, with a letter to Annis Stockton. This 1793 letter, penned long after the poem's completion, serves as a preface introducing the next section of poetry. It explains the inspiration for the poem's tensions. She wanted to believe that Henry was innocent on all accounts, but she was experiencing the crushing weight of losing hope. She doubted that the servant Jenny was telling the truth about her affair with Henry, but Elizabeth also doubted Henry's feeble attempts to reassure her that he was innocent. She elaborates, "This seeming contradiction arises from Circumstances arising in the Course of my Investigation of painful Facts; for and against the Character who is the subject of my affection." Fergusson then directs Stockton to share this letter and the poem that follows with sympathetic readers only: "When it falls in your hand . . . I would wish the perusal of it could be limited to Such few of your Friends; as have feeling delicate Hearts and consider it as a proof of a warm Heart, than the production of a Cool Head."[46] This letter-preface to the poem participates in Fergusson's generic experiment, one that shows her adeptness at moving between various epistolary forms. Neither her private letters to Joseph Reed nor her public epistle to the Philadelphia Assembly had been able to assure her control over her own narrative, but when Elizabeth divided "Il Penseroso" with letters informing Stockton and her friends of how they should read Elizabeth's work, she was wresting control of her epistolary self. By demanding that Stockton share what she wrote only with people who might be open to viewing Fergusson sympathetically, she was cultivating what today we might call an echo chamber or a particular audience who would be receptive to her revised identity—ostensibly other women and wives who might feel sympathy for her situation.

"Doubt" then proceeds to solidify Fergusson's emotional release of Henry, which allows Fergusson to distance herself from all of his transgressions against his country and herself. The poet's doubt comes in two phases. The speaker initially doubts his guilt, but then she grows to doubt Henry himself. Part 2, like part 1, calls out to God, requesting that God prove Elizabeth's suspicions wrong and scrub Henry's reputation in the wake of the scandal with Jenny. She pleads,

> Restore my Henry to a spotless name,
> And teach me how to clear his slander'd Fame
> If he is guiltless may he guiltless shine
> Or if prov'd faulty teach me to resign.[47]

Fergusson could never be certain that he was, in fact, guiltless, so the poem changes tactics. As Grace Growden Galloway shifted her diary's audience to address her daughter when she wanted to rhetorically divorce herself from Joseph, so Fergusson shifts her audience to God so that she can rhetorically divorce herself from Henry. She signals this transformation with a textual indicator. Instead of naming herself a "Deserted Wife," she writes, "Deserted = Wife." Although some have suggested that this could be an eighteenth-century hyphen, my own experience with manuscripts suggests otherwise. Fergusson consistently implements this symbol throughout the poem, suggesting that her new identity has erased any other with which she may have been affiliated (fig. 7).

She claims that her doubts about God and her husband have haunted her and turned her bitter. She demands that her heart release her lack of spiritual and connubial faith:

FIGURE 7. "Deserted = Wife," from Elizabeth Fergusson's "Il Penseroso." The Library Company of Philadelphia.

> Squint Eyed Suspence be gone, with *Janus* look
> Thou double monster by [white] Peace forsook:
> Thou bitter Dasher of serene Repose;
> From thy dark veins a venom'd passion flows.[48]

Her doubt has poisoned her and disrupted her serenity. The dark "venom" then consumes her, and she begins a quest for Henry's innocence that leads her down dark paths indeed. The poem recalls how Fergusson tracked down Jenny, her husband's alleged mistress, so that she could see the child to discern if it favored Henry. Seeing the offspring failed to reassure Elizabeth, however. She sought out the woman's midwife and asked her to verify that Jenny's body bore evidence that she was a whore (which the midwife would not do). Fergusson thought that if the midwife could help her call into question Jenny's reputation, such information might also call into question the child's paternity, thereby opening the possibility for Henry's innocence.[49] Her trip proved fruitless, and Henry refused to discuss the matter any further. His silence further implied his guilt, and, as the poem suggests, she could no longer doubt the accusations against him.

Fergusson then broadens the audience her poem addresses. She moves from talking to Stockton to God to Henry to speaking directly to all other abandoned wives that the war made widows (either because their husbands fled or died). She writes,

> Tears for my Country Sighs for my own Fate
> And Ills unnumber'd in this Bleeding State
> The Sword and Fire was Ravaging around,
> And dearest Friends felt then the general wound![50]

America betrayed its women as Henry betrayed Elizabeth. The revolution separated husbands from wives and children from parents, disrupting families and tearing them apart. She thus displaces some of Henry's blame by transferring it to the rebellion. She gestures to a collective sense of suffering in order to elicit sympathy from those readers. This move was rhetorically complex. Since the government called into question Henry's fidelities when it confiscated his property and ruled his exile an admission of guilt, and when it stuck by that ruling even when it learned that the property was Elizabeth's, it reaffirmed what coverture already implied: Elizabeth's political body extended from Henry's. "Il Penseroso," however, reverses that ruling.

Her sympathies and thus her *loyalties* lay with the wives—the apolitical, victimized, abandoned women who were guilty of nothing more than marrying men who resisted the revolution. Allied with them, she seems as innocent as they. In short, Fergusson rewrites how women might be defined in war when she displaces Henry's culpability by writing it into the fabric of the revolution itself. Her poem suggests that homosocial relationships could define women, just as marriage, oaths, or family could. This suggestion deconstructs the characteristics that legislators, confiscation committees, and her own community tried to use in order to bring political identity into sharp relief, so that they could then discipline and punish as they saw fit.

Fergusson is trying to convince the reader to render her innocent of her husband's crimes, political or domestic, when she returns repeatedly to the notion that she counted herself among the abandoned wives. She calls herself, "Least of the least an unconnected Thing!" Not *disconnected* but *unconnected,* her wordplay aptly summarizes her conundrum. Her husband lived, but he abandoned her; they were married, but his infidelities severed their ties. And here, finally, she addresses her own scandals with Johnstone and Reed, using a pun: "The Reed she lean'd on provd a pointed Spear / To peirce her Soul with agency severe." The men in her life who were supposed to act on her behalf—in these lines, Henry Fergusson and Joseph Reed—have injured her instead. The poem suggests that all of these events must be understood as interconnected. She had not married a loyalist traitor and then become a traitor herself; rather, her husband betrayed both her and her country, so she turned to other men she trusted in his absence, and they betrayed her too. She was a victim, not an agent. She was a courier, not a spy. She writes of her disentanglement from all of these men as a tree that has

> shrunk back to which adhered the Vine
> No Prop it met, its Foliage to entwine,
> No fostering shelter for its Branches found
> [It] Died it wither'd trampled to the Ground!

Henry and Reed may have abandoned her, but here *Fergusson* abandons *them.* While she clearly lamented losing her connections, this loss also benefited her. Reed's name was tarnished, as was Henry's. Absolving her ties to them absolves her too, which the poem recognizes in the final lines of part 1: "Love, pride, and Virtue, Him shall know no Strife / [Each] Tye Disolv'd of the *Deserted-Wife.*"[51]

Solitude

Fergusson separates part 3 of "Il Penseroso," "Solitude," also written in 1782, from the rest of the poem by yet another letter—or, more precisely, two of them: one from Henry to Elizabeth, and another from Elizabeth to Annis Stockton. I read these paratexts as evidence that Fergusson had, at this point in the poem, solidified her "Doubt." She completes her transformation into "widowhood" and patriotism, ultimately forming a new political identity that allowed her to reenter into society. The first letter extracts a missive that Henry wrote to Fergusson when he denied that he had impregnated Jenny; in this text, Henry's denial damns him. Fergusson cut ties with him because he refused to accept culpability for what she suspected he had done. Henry writes, "I can with [the] clearest Conscience asure you, in the most Solemn appeal to every power that has Influence on Society and by the Strongest Ties that Contribute to the happiness of the Human Race that I never [had] Conexion with that woman of a nature to render her pregnant." He tells Fergusson that he did talk to Jenny about her plans to run away with an officer's servant, and that he "diswaded her from it and told her that he would probably leave her, and that such people in the army Seldom made steady good Husbands." But after admonishing her, he "heard no more of the affair." Henry closes his letter by consoling Fergusson in her grief, admitting that such "slander" must have caused her to feel "shorn to the quick," but he swears that "no woman has ever had reason to Shed a tear on my account for any Injury Done to her Virtue or Honor."[52]

Fergusson's second missive indicates that she has refused to believe Henry's profession of innocence. Although wounded by what she considers his lies, she absolves herself of the affair and begins thinking of her situation with "peace and tranquility." "I owe not any one," she writes to Annis Stockton, adding, "I live like a hermit with no maid in this great House."[53] Much like Grace Growden Galloway, who became a recluse in the final years of her life, Fergusson appeared to favor sitting still when her political scandals had passed. She had paid her debts, "settl'd [her] affairs," and lived the life of a widow, at least in name. The letter claims that she had finally let go of all ties to and grievances with Henry, despite the fact that her 788-line poem suggests otherwise.[54]

"Solitude's" opening verse praises "Lone Solitude" as the only companion on whom she could now rely; Fergusson personifies her abandonment as a "Calm silent pensive maid!" who keeps her company. She welcomes these severed ties. "I woo thy Haunts," she writes, "I woo thy solemn Shade / Time hath inur'd me to thy Solemn Scenes / Thy nodding Umbrage and thy darkened Greens!" "Solitude" in particular broadens the scope of her abandonment to include not just her husband but her mother and father. "Death quick tore those kindred ties away / And mixd my Parents with their native Clay," leaving her "alone of ten and last my mother Bore." No relative can assuage her sadness. She concludes by referring to herself as a "widow," which completes her isolation.[55]

Adversity

The poem closes with a sarcastic paean to "Adversity," which she finished in 1783. Fergusson says adversity has molded her into a puppet, a pawn, and an object, much like the women in popular seduction novels of her day. She writes,

> Soft *Eloise* laments in plaintive Strains
> And sweet *Clarissa* every [scene?] Retains
> Great *Clementina* with majestic Grief
> And pious wanderings prays for heavens relief
> Immortal *Richardson* in every Page;
> Draws forth our Pity or provokes our Rage.

These lines suggest that Fergusson saw her own story reflected in Samuel Richardson's *Clarissa* and *Sir Charles Grandison*, Pope's poem "Eloise to Abelard," William Shakespeare's *Romeo and Juliet*, and Nicholas Rowe's play *The Fair Penitent*. She rightly notes that the men rarely suffer in stories like these; rather, the women become ill, mad, and die, poisoned by the abuses of untrustworthy men. She calls for sympathy, for these women and for herself: "Pity for Woman Rage for these vile arts / That man relentless plans for guileless Hearts." She wishes that she could give each woman in each story a proper funeral, but in this rewritten ending, a homosocial network of women assumes care of these lost protagonists. If she could, she says,

> Some Hallowd Tomb I would to thee Erect
> While the Soft Sex thy ashes should protect
> By *Female Hearts* they Eulogy compos'd
> By *Female Hands* thy Spotless marble closd
> By female Brows the Cypress Garland worn
> By Matrons Honour'd, and by Virgins mourn'd!

As Fergusson rewrote the stories of Shakespeare and Richardson, so with this poem she rewrites her own. "Il Penseroso" served as both the elegy and funeral for her former self; she wrote her involvement with Duché, Johnstone, Washington, Reed, and Henry by repeatedly asserting her abandonment and disconnectedness. The poem concludes, "Mark each ascent that fills the Scale of Life, / From the weak Babe to the Deserted Wife."[56] She completes the transformation that she began in her assembly petition and published editorial, "To the Public." She solidifies her identity as a *feme sole* and delivers it to Stockton, whom she asks to pass it along to sympathetic readers. She trusts Stockton would distribute it, and that her homosocial society of women writers and thinkers would once again welcome her and replace Henry as her family.

Fergusson's poem clearly doubles down on the notion that she is a victim of, rather than a participant in, the war. Did it work? To suggest that a poem, in and of itself, reingratiated her with her community is reductive and nearly impossible to discern. Fergusson's biographer Anne Ousterhout notes that friends reached out to Fergusson to encourage her to reestablish connections that had been severed during her ordeal, but she often rejected them. Benjamin Rush invited her to visit his home, but she said no. Elias Boudinot, president of the Continental Congress, likewise asked her to stay with him and his family, but she would not go. Like Grace Growden Galloway, Elizabeth Fergusson lived out much of the remainder of her life as a "semi-recluse." Ousterhout suggests that Fergusson seemed "determined to be unhappy despite all attempts to help her make another life for herself." In the end, she had to sell Graeme Park because it was in such a state of disrepair and her debts were so great that she could not keep it. She moved out in 1793, the same year she sent "Il Penseroso" to Stockton, severing ties simultaneously with both her husband and her homestead.[57]

All of the facts of Fergusson's life story suggest that her fate should have aligned with Galloway's or Rebecca Shoemaker's. Her story could have ended in property confiscation or exile because she made some of the same decisions that those women made and because she occupied a similar socioeconomic status as a wealthy, high-profile loyalist's wife. Yet it did not. Fergusson thus provides us with a unique perspective on loyalism. She was both a passive and active loyalist who convinced the world she was a patriot—or, at least, that she was (to borrow Morris's sticky turn of phrase) *not a traitor.* Fergusson was permitted to stay when other loyalist women in Philadelphia were exiled by decree. She regained her home when others lost theirs. Fergusson remained free when others were imprisoned. She differed from her contemporaries because she manipulated the private-to-public transfer of her epistolary self more successfully than the other writers could, primarily because she seemed to understand that the audience mattered just as much—if not more—than her message did. Fergusson wrote missives she delivered directly to the Pennsylvania Assembly—which published them in the meeting minutes—and to the local newspapers, which disseminated her loyalties for all readers to see, rather than writing a letter-journal meant for just one person or a limited circle of readers. Fergusson's epistolary practices, like Galloway's and Rawle's, both damned and saved her. Although her willingness to write, read, and deliver letters initially embroiled her in these public, political affairs, she used the same form to write her way out. She ultimately scripted herself as an abandoned wife, and because she attended to the nuances of eighteenth-century letter-writing and -reading, she also claimed control over the narrative that Jacob Duché, George Washington, Joseph Reed, George Johnstone, Henry Fergusson, and Pennsylvania society had attempted to write on her behalf.

SCRIPTING ELLIPSES

Deborah Norris Logan

> *The History of our Revolution will be [a] continued Lye from one end to the other. The essence of the whole will be that Dr. Franklins electrical Rod, smote the Earth and out sprung General Washington. That Franklin elec-trified him with his rod—and thence forward these two conducted all the Policy, Negotiations, Legislatures and War.*
>
> —*John Adams, 1790*

Stenton House lies just a few blocks away from where Fisher's Wakefield should have been. It stands a few blocks from where Peale's Belfield is now. Past Fisher, Olney, and Wister Avenues, there's Logan Street, and that's named for the Logan family, including Deborah Norris Logan, Sarah Logan Fisher's sister-in-law. Her house is my final stop. Stenton is run by the Society of Colonial Dames. The Dames have claimed Logan as a patriot, but my research suggests she was a loyalist who refashioned herself a patriot after the fact so that she could publish histories of the American Revolution. It was fashionable to be a patriot after the war. Not so fashionable to be on the losing side.

My guide, Laura, takes me to Logan's room and I behold treasures. I see a double-door press cupboard to the left of the fireplace full of oddities. A lock of Logan's hair. A painting of Logan by Charles Willson Peale. (He's everywhere.) And then: a little round box (fig. 8). It's a present from John F. Watson, the historian that published Logan's work. It's covered in four different woods: the elm of the Treaty Tree, planted to mark a friendship between William Penn and Lenape Chief Tamanend; mahogany from Christopher Columbus's house in Saint-Domingue; gum from William Penn's forest; and oak from the first bridge built over Dock Creek in 1683. Watson calls the gift "Relics of the Olden Time." There's an excerpt from Logan's diary near the relic box, and a Stenton pamphlet suggests that Logan stored her diary on this shelf, near the memoir of her husband, which she also wrote. Diaries, histories, memoirs, relics, and letters all seem to be talking to each other in this space. When Logan placed her book into the cupboard, I learn, she called it "going to press" (fig. 9).

FIGURE 8. Deborah Norris Logan's relic box. Courtesy of the National Society of the Colonial Dames of America in the Commonwealth of Pennsylvania at Stenton, Philadelphia.

STENTON'S PRESS CUPBOARD and its oddities are a fitting display to represent how Deborah Norris Logan used manuscript culture to become a public, published historian. John F. Watson gave Logan a relic because she saw herself as a memory-keeper, her mind its own kind of relic box fashioned from key moments in history. She was an antiquarian. People traveled for miles to access the files in her attic—the papers of William Penn—and stayed to hear her tell stories of statesmen who visited Stenton and of her experiences growing up during the American Revolution.[1] Her ancestor was Penn's secretary, and Logan spent countless hours transcribing the Penn-Logan correspondence. She drafted much of the history that she published elsewhere—in Watson's *Annals* and in her husband's memoir—in her multivolume diary.[2] Her journals possessed prefaces and footnotes. Logan, like the women before her, preferred manuscript culture to publishing through a printing press, though her work did enjoy circulation through private printings by her relatives. She rested her diary in the press cupboard and declared that her work had "gone to press" because, in many ways, it had.

Logan's relic box attests to the fact that she was interested in telling

FIGURE 9. Deborah Norris Logan's press cupboard. Courtesy of the National Society of the Colonial Dames of America in the Commonwealth of Pennsylvania at Stenton, Philadelphia.

histories as she would prefer them to be, not particularly as they were. The Treaty Tree, like the treaty it represented, was likely a myth. Legend had it that William Penn met with the Nanticoke Lenni-Lenape Nation near the Delaware River under an elm tree in 1682 and pledged to coexist peacefully.[3] Artists such as Benjamin West and Thomas Birch depicted the exchange in paintings of the event. When the alleged "Great Elm" that local historians dubbed that famous tree fell during a storm in 1810, people took pieces of it to fashion it into relics (Chief Justice John Marshall claims to have received one of these boxes as well).[4] A monument to the tree was erected in 1827, and one stands there today in Penn Treaty Park in Philadelphia. No one can say for certain that either the Treaty Tree or the treaty it represented actually existed. Certainly, white settlers violated the peace the Treaty Tree was said to represent. If the event between the Lenape and Penn never happened, then Logan's relic box and the story it represents is actually a mystery wrapped up in a legend and shrouded with falsehoods.

Then there is the issue of the wood from Columbus's house. It is said the wood originated from Saint-Domingue, present-day Haiti. This could either refer to some structure Columbus built on La Isabella, which is not Saint-Domingue but the Dominican Republic, or the fort on La Navidad, which is in Haiti; the latter seems more plausible. The problem is that La Navidad was a lost settlement in the nineteenth century. Columbus found it destroyed one year after he left it, and historians and archivists spent hundreds of years searching for its location. They did not unearth what appears to be its foundation until 1977. The fort was likely built out of stone, not wood.[5] As for the other part of the relic, there *was* a bridge built over Dock Creek in 1683.[6] (Incidentally, the waterway the bridge covered was a sewer that one resident described as "a foul place, especially when the tide was out.")[7]Thus, the relic box is made of a pastiche of fabrications, stitched together to represent remarkable moments and monuments in the nation's history, many of which probably never existed. An investigation of Logan's own engagement with history via a diary she kept following the American Revolution suggests that such an object is in fact metonymic of the ways in which she wanted to tell the story of the American Revolution: sliced up, stitched together, and varnished so that she might present it in the best light possible.

LOYALTIES AFTER THE WAR

Some accounts suggest that when the Revolutionary War ended, rebels and loyalists made amends, and dissenters reintegrated into society. Judith Van Buskirk calls the end of the war "anti-climactic" and claims that reconciliation was "a relatively easy and ongoing affair even before the military hostilities ended." She also notes, however, that "national healing did not erase memories of the anxiety and outrage experienced" by the persecuted.[8] Many loyalists felt jaded by the British government after the Treaty of Paris. The Crown did not distribute remuneration equally among the faithful, despite its promises. Great Britain, as historian Maya Jasanoff has noted, "tightened the reins of administration" in British settlements that loyalist exiles had established, believing that "too much liberty, not too little" caused the American colonies to rebel.[9] Some writers documented the tensions in their community after the war just as they documented the tensions in their community during it. Elizabeth Drinker and Anna Rawle noted crowd action and property destruction on nights when they refused to light candles in the window to mark Cornwallis's defeat or other anniversaries commemorating independence. I suggest that the majority of these writers did not reconcile their loyalties; rather, they revised them by eradicating the differences that once divided them from their rebel neighbors so that they might be brought back into the fold. The semantic difference between reconciliation and revision is subtle, but it is an important one.[10] Reconciled loyalists would be people who willingly and of their own accord pledged allegiance to the new nation, believing in the viability of the republic; a revised loyalist, at least for the purposes of the archive that I have studied in this book, is someone who publicly changed her political position so that it might grant her a personal advantage, whether that advantage was reinstatement into her social network, the recovery of her property, or admittance into the group of historians seeking to write the definitive history of the new United States, as Deborah Norris Logan did in 1815. I do not mean to draw lines that did not exist. Someone who revised their loyalties might, eventually, come to buy into those revisions, at which point they would be considered reconciled. What I mean to emphasize here is that these gradients of loyalty often mixed and blurred after the war, just as they did during it.

Logan's proximity to the American Revolution, her intimate connection with important statesmen, and her incredible archive of manuscripts in the attic of her house made her a well-situated historian. Logan's family was prominent in the Philadelphia area; she was John Dickinson's cousin and the great-granddaughter of the lieutenant governor of Pennsylvania Thomas Lloyd, who emigrated with William Penn. Penn corresponded with James Logan, who was Deborah's husband's distant relative. Deborah, then, married into an ancestral archive. As mentioned previously, Stenton housed Penn's papers, which Logan once described as "unintelligible as Egyptian hieroglyphics." Despite their illegibility, she transcribed, edited, introduced, footnoted, and published them as *The Penn-Logan Correspondence*.[11] Logan also wrote biographies. She penned her husband George's life story after he passed away. He possessed access to several prominent political figures because he had served in the Pennsylvania state legislature and Congress from 1801 to 1807. Together, the couple entertained Benjamin Franklin, George and Martha Washington, and Thomas Jefferson at Stenton; the Jeffersons, in turn, entertained the Logans at Monticello.[12] Local historians asked Deborah Logan either to contribute to, proofread, or edit their own books because of her publications about these founding fathers and their families. She wrote parts of John F. Watson's *Annals of Philadelphia* (1830) and went on to publish multiple essays about various historical figures from Pennsylvania.[13] When the Historical Society of Pennsylvania invited her to join their ranks based on her reputation as an historian, she became the first female member to gain admittance.[14]

THE DIARY OF DEBORAH NORRIS LOGAN

Deborah Norris Logan's journey as a public, published historian began with a gift from her husband, George: a blank journal. Logan began this diary in 1815 at age fifty-four and laid down her pen in 1839 at her life's close. Over the course of twenty-four years, she filled seventeen volumes and wrote four thousand pages of material.[15] These diaries not only served as a rough draft for the books she would write (and would help others write) later in her life, but they also facilitated her public revision from loyalist to patriot, which permitted her entry into the nineteenth-century antiquarian movement that sought to mythologize the founding fathers and their cause, creating a version of the American Revolution that John Adams once called "a continued Lye from one end to the other."[16] In many ways, Logan resembled Elizabeth Graeme Fergusson. Logan, like Fergusson, is often described as a patriot.[17] Logan similarly married a politician famous in his lifetime for holding public opinions for which government officials censored him. Both Fergusson and Logan suffered for their husbands' political views. Logan's writing differs from Fergusson's in that, although she did write some letters during the war, she constructed the bulk of her wartime recollections after the revolution concluded.[18] The few letters we do have from that era suggest reticence on her part to support independence; in her recollection of the public reading of the Declaration of Independence, for example, she writes, "It was a time of fearful doubt and great anxiety with the people, many of whom were appalled at the boldness of the measure." She suggests that those who did take to the streets to celebrate the occasion were "neither very numerous nor composed of the most respectable class of citizens."[19] Despite that Logan is now touted as a patriot; her post-revolutionary journal gives no indication of her loyalties in the late eighteenth century. I call these omissions "ellipses." Logan scripted many different kinds of ellipses in her diary. She revised stories of statesmen to mythologize them, she excised material she did not want her audience to read, and she omitted historical events that would have either criticized the rebel cause or aligned her with the loyalists (or both). All of these omissions served to revise and solidify Logan's allegiances with the rebels.

Deborah Norris Logan identified as a devout Quaker and, given the way rebel soldiers treated her family, it is surprising that her journal does not align with other Friends' letters or diaries. Rebels punished her husband's father for his pacifism by forcing him to quarter soldiers.[20] Men tasked with gathering requisitions from Quakers tormented Logan's sister-in-law, Sarah Logan Fisher, despite the fact that she was pregnant and alone. After the revolution, the Pennsylvania Assembly accused George Logan of treason, and he and Deborah were placed under surveillance so that government officials could monitor any suspicious activities.[21] Deborah Logan's journal makes no mention of these events. Instead, her diary implements omissions to affirm her loyalties to the rebels, blacking out in heavy ink any passages that might suggest otherwise (fig. 10). She scrubbed her work free of dissent. Since this text served as a rough draft for other historical accounts and her husband's biography, and since many local historians consulted Logan about her version of the war before writing their own, these edits may have caused an immeasurably vast ripple effect.

The few scholars who have analyzed Logan's diary typically address these blacked-out passages. They are anomalous in an otherwise suspiciously clean manuscript, which I suggest indicates that the extant diary may have been a

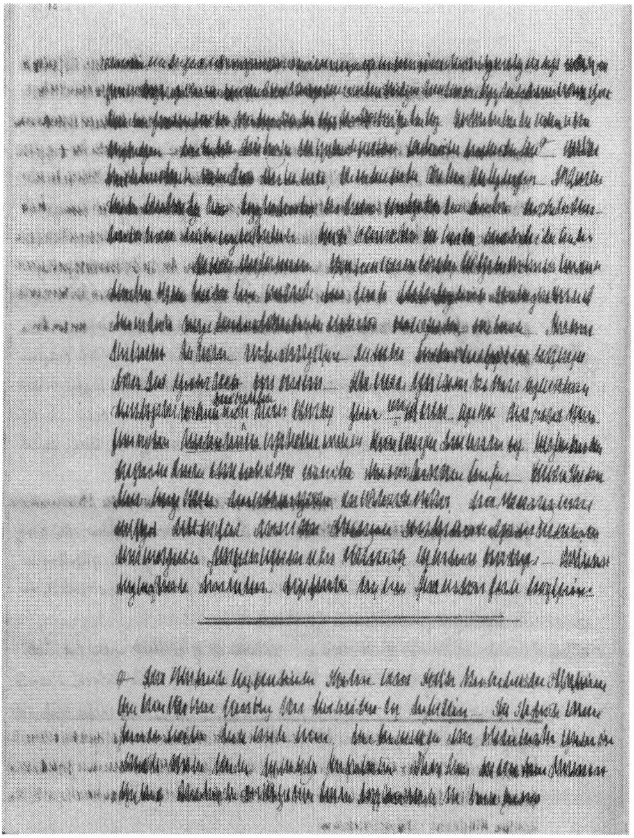

FIGURE 10. Marked-out pages from Deborah Norris Logan's diary. Deborah Norris Logan, Diary, June 2, 1824, to February 24, 1825, vol. 7, 10–11. Deborah Norris Logan Diaries, Historical Society of Pennsylvania.

copy. Frederick B. Tolles posits that the mark-outs suppress unflattering narratives about the founding fathers that Logan later retracted.[22] Sarah Butler Wister speculates that Logan may have changed her mind about including these stories after a friend—a "strict Quakeress"—read her diary and advised her that much of it sounded too worldly and frivolous, and violated "our peaceable testimony." Wister claims that the diarist and her censor "went carefully over the manuscript, erasing with laborious thoroughness all mere chit-chat," so that they might leave behind a version of Logan that aligned with the Friends' primary principles of plainstyle.[23] This critique also implies that Logan was readying her manuscript for circulation, at least among fellow Quakers. Her diary, as such, falls on the public scale of journal-keeping, addressing an audience far broader than Galloway, Drinker, Fisher, or Morris imagined for their texts.

Logan's mark-outs ultimately are as unsatisfactory as Anna Rawle's account of the crowd action at her house; as Rawle refused to specify exactly what happened the night men attacked her, so Logan refused to tell her readers everything she omitted and why. Although I attempted to find some sort of archival x-ray machine—like the one preservationists use to read through layers of paint on canvas—I did not succeed. I am untroubled by the fact that I cannot definitely say what lies under this black ink, however. I am more interested in why Logan left the omissions than I am in what the omissions once said. She was prone to reflect on her mark-outs, even though she did not clarify what caused her to extract information. For example, she writes after a particularly long excision, "The foregoing paragraph was written in a moment of sadness and is not altogether just. . . . The truth in my mind is unhinged and distressed, and as such seasons the most cheerful temper [will] droop.—I must try if possible to find a remedy."[24]

These dark passages form only one small part of a much larger effort to revise or perhaps clarify her political affiliations. What she omitted matters less than the fact that she left a record of these omissions for an audience to "read" and interpret. These silences shout. They serve as a visual representation of an ideology in the process of formation. But why? What benefit could such shaping possibly provide her since the war was long over and any fear of treason just a memory? By themselves, such self-edits would hardly suggest something amiss in a diary, but I suggest that *these* blackouts in *this* text should be recognized as odd because Logan kept an otherwise suspiciously clean journal. Almost every other page is flawless, with only a few inserted words or line edits. Logan marked out entire sections of the diary front-to-back, which means that while she may have wanted to preserve paper, and therefore would have left the edited pages to save the material she wrote on the opposite side, that hypothesis does not fully explain these edits. She could have torn these pages out, and she did elsewhere; the diary evinces ragged edges where the writer has cut out pages (which is even more intriguing if the extant diary *is* a copy).

Did Logan obscure these passages immediately after writing them, or did she return to them later after she had time to reflect? Given evidence elsewhere in the diary, the latter is more likely. Much of Logan's journal features a dark double-line at the bottom of the page, where the author relegated explanatory information or emendations. Some of these footnotes postdate the entries to which Logan appended them, which proves that she did, in fact, revisit and revise her work. One entry that exemplifies this reflective self-editing occurs on a passage dated September 1818, when she wrote that one of the physicians in her town was an "Ignoramus" who almost killed "old neighbor Heaton" with "an overdose of mercury." In that same passage, she similarly blasted "Brownlee," a minister, who "utters from the Pulpit the Blasphemies of Predestination." A footnote amends these characterizations: "This was my impression at the time I wrote, but I have reason since to think things of this sort, in the present Instance are rather Exaggerated—(and upon further Trial, I am told now, in 1822, that [Brownlee's] Congregation, love him, and that he is a pious as well as very learned man.—With what caution ought we to hear injurious reports of others!)."[25] Logan did not date the mark-outs as she did this footnote, but her habit of returning to and revising other passages in her journal suggests that she may in fact have made them after time passed. Logan's excisions signify a meaningful omission. If we believe Tolles's and Wister's theories concerning the content beneath the omissions—and I think we should because they align well with Logan's stated intentions to construct history as she saw necessary—then these deletions provide visible evidence of Logan's revised loyalties. She decided to retain those passages instead of tearing them out altogether, thereby allowing her audience to see her change of heart, but she also made them unreadable. These mark-outs imply, "I have something to say, but I am not telling *you*."

The footnotes and mark-outs exemplify just a few of the paratexts that attest to Logan's diary's intended publicity. She also includes asides and reflective prefaces in each volume, many of which point to an unnamed audience. In one passage, for example, she stops what she is writing to speak to whomever is listening, saying, "My readers could not fail to smile if they were to see how I am sitting to write this paragraph in order to accommodate Lodge [her dog] who desires to be petted. He has placed his head in my lap and unwilling to disturb him, I am leaning over it to the board where my book rests. Lodge, this will not do, I must have room."[26] The diary seems clear that someone—perhaps a relative or friend, even another Quaker—was listening. Logan addresses the unnamed reader through a series of prefaces that introduce each volume of her journal. These prefaces state that she hopes other people will consider her diary a meaningful contribution to history:

> For my own satisfaction I have been induced to begin this Book as a means to preserve fresh in my memory passing events, and because I have frequently reflected on the probability that a great mass of curious and interesting facts and information, are lost to posterity from a want of Record. . . . For myself I write in the first place, and if, hereafter, any thing of mine shall benefit, improve, or inform others, or even innocently amuse them, my end will be obtained.[27]

Logan felt an obligation to record the past, but no obligation to record it exactly as it happened. "The best method of such a record," she decides, "appears to be the habit of noting down as they occur the incidents of the times. To this I shall add whatever I shall hear of Fact or anecdote that shall appear to be worthy of preservation.—and many things perhaps, for my own satisfaction" (fig. 11).[28] Logan's decision to add *either* fact *or* anecdote makes visible her intention to control her life's narrative. To communicate that narrative, she tells historical events as they happened and as she wants us to remember them. This passage echoes the opening lines of Benjamin Franklin's autobiography, where he reflects on how the genre of life-writing allows him to revise his own life story, so that he can frame his life in a favorable light and so that others might learn from his errata. Franklin says he wrote his autobiography so that he "might, besides correcting the faults, change some sinister accidents and events of it for others more favorable. . . . The next thing most like living one's life over again seems to be a recollection of that life, and to make that recollection as durable as possible by putting it down in writing."[29] Life writing allowed both Franklin and Logan to "live their lives over again," to revisit the histories they wished to preserve and revise the memories they wished to forget. Logan read Franklin's writings and may have intended this rhetorical homage.[30] Logan, like Franklin, viewed what she was writing as part of a larger, national endeavor to script the history that she thought America needed. Franklin too utilized narrative ellipses. He demoted the war from a formative event in which he played an integral role to an one-lined inconvenience that disrupted his writing schedule, telling the reader, "The affairs of the Revolution occasion'd the interruption."[31] Just so, Logan's diary contains many well-placed holes: mark-outs, elisions, and revisions to public figures—including her own family. This willingness to write the war favorably

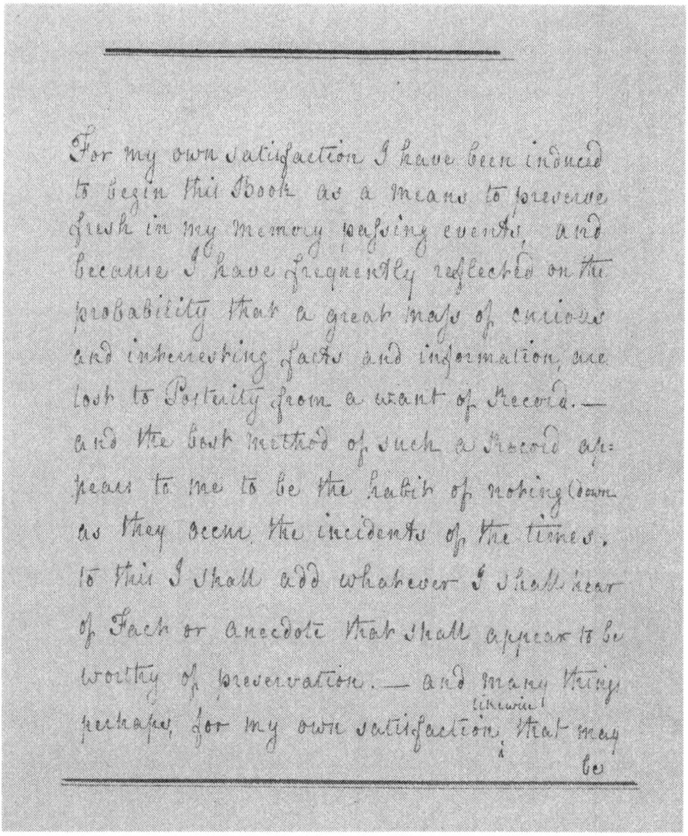

FIGURE 11. Preface to Deborah Norris Logan's diary. Deborah Norris
Logan, Diary, vol. 1, January 1, 1815. Deborah Norris Logan Diaries,
Historical Society of Pennsylvania.

granted Logan entrance into the world of nineteenth-century historians, most
of whom also refused to record history as it happened (whatever that might
mean) but, instead, committed to telling nationalist narratives that corrected
those "faults" and "sinister accidents" which they believed were best left
unrecorded.

Logan's corrections should be read as part of a larger antiquarian movement that swept through America as soon as the war ended. This movement
sought to tell "powerful stories instilling national pride" and marked the rise
of local historical societies, whose objectives involved preserving a nationalist narrative.[32] Loyalists did not serve as the villains in these narratives; rather,

they disappeared from them altogether. Dissent challenged the notion of a unified nation and needed to be eradicated. In the historian Elizabeth Ellet's *Women of the American Revolution* (1848), her conclusion underscores this imperative by addressing and then dismissing the loyalist problem in post-revolutionary America. She tells the story of a loyalist and a rebel who fought on opposite sides of the war, whose relatives inherited the soldiers' swords. These two swords, Ellet writes, now hang "crossed [as] an emblem of peace, in the library of the great American historian [William H. Prescott]— . . . emblematic of the spirit in which our history should be written. Such be the spirit in which we view the loyalists of those days."[33] Ellet points to Prescott's crossed swords to suggest that historians must see the loyalists and rebels as rectified. Once these storytellers eradicated the dissent between these two factions, turning weapons into memorials, the revolution could then become a bloodless, if not peaceable, starting point for a civilized nation. In her call to other historians to reread history as she has, Ellet urges all writers to engage in similar revisionist rhetoric.

Ellet's call was superfluous, however, because the earliest Revolutionary War historians identified as rebels, and they "depicted the war of independence as a struggle by American patriots against British tyranny, personified in King George III. Whig historians infused their accounts with qualities of grandeur, and their hands shaped the American war into an epic, the story of a valiant people struggling for liberty."[34] Given the vehement disagreements between federalists and antifederalists, the polarity and chaos of the election of 1800, and the dire economic straits that plagued America after the revolution, many wondered if the states would be able to form a successful national government. To address these fears, the earliest revolutionary histories "described a Revolution that never happened and never could happen."[35] During this period, Fourth of July celebrations featured tributes to revolutionary heroes, and newly minted patriots showed their unity by lighting fireworks or candles in the windows (both of which Quakers continued to refuse to do just as they had during the war). Historians "lit their candles" by emphasizing American exceptionalism and borrowing from John Winthrop's City on a Hill metaphor to write the revolution as preordained. Part of this exceptionalist narrative involved making heroes of the founding fathers by glorifying them.[36] This imperative to revise the war in this way contextualizes what Deborah Norris Logan did after she penned her diary's prefaces: she made gods of men.

Logan began this deification process by buying into what Barry Schwartz has dubbed "the cult of Washington," which describes the antiquarian movement's collective attempt to lionize America's war hero and first president. Logan writes of herself as Washington's friend, further solidifying her affiliation with the rebel cause and distancing herself from the loyalists.[37] Washington, in Logan's words, "stand[s] Preeminent in the annals of his Country." After he visited Stenton, Logan writes that his "manners were courteous, social and extreamly agreeable. He talkd much on agricultural subjects, caressed my children in the most winning manner, took Albanus [her son] on his knee and kissd him, calling him by the kindest names, and won my heart by his affability as he had before my esteem & veneration, by the splendor of this Character & the greatness of his virtues." This portrait depicts Washington as a *pater patriae* for both her family and the new nation. He kept his word and modeled virtue. She concludes by describing Washington as "Beyond all Greek, beyond all Roman fame."[38] To commemorate the occasion of his visit, she preserved his calling card in her journal (fig. 12).[39]

This ephemera reified her connection to Washington and confirmed that she came into contact with him, thereby verifying her narrative as "true." It also elevated Logan's status as a "patriot" because the card associated her with Washington. By extension, it lent credence to the diary-as-history. Her glorification of the statesman, coupled with proof that he had visited her home, ushered her into the fraternity of other historians who spun such stories. Pro-independence Americans needed a symbol of republican virtue incarnate, and Washington provided that symbol, his mythical status generated by books such as Parson Weems's biography (which created the legend of the cherry tree).[40] Weems claimed that Washington's "private virtues . . . lay the foundation of all human excellence."[41] Logan's flattering depiction of America's first president aligned with the spirit of the age.

Logan's hagiography of Washington may be unsurprising in its historical context, but it seems unusual coming from a Quaker. As noted in chapter 2, the rebels considered Quakers "the most dangerous enemies to the country" because they suspected the Society of Friends of spying on Washington. He bore part of the responsibility for the Virginia Exile Crisis, and one of those exiles was Logan's relative. Yet Logan's diary elides this event and the politics that surrounded the crisis; instead, she writes of her veneration for one of its culprits: "I do not think it easy for one human Being to respect & venerate another, more, than I did George Washington, this truly great man."[42]

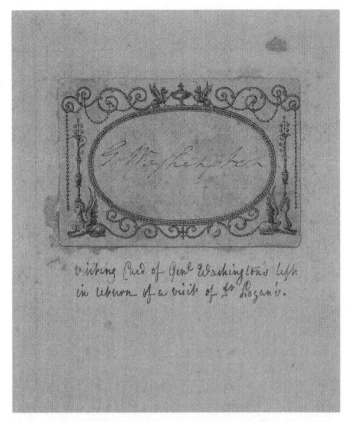

FIGURE 12. "Visiting Card of Genl Washington's left in return of a visit of Dr. Logan's," in Deborah Norris Logan, Diary, vol. 3, 1818. Deborah Norris Logan Diaries, Historical Society of Pennsylvania.

Since her paean to Washington ignores his antagonism with the Quakers and focuses instead on the legendary status he had since acquired, this provides a prime example of one of Logan's ellipses. Despite the Quaker insistence that she resist any outward signs of allegiance or nationalist celebrations, as Anna Rawle did when she sat before her dark window on the night of the Cornwallis riots, Logan lit her candle for the world to see.

Logan similarly spun a biography that she wrote of her cousin John Dickinson, whom she profiled shortly after she wrote about Washington. "My Pen is intirely too inadequate to do justice to his excellent character," she says of Dickinson, "but I will try if I can, to recount the qualities in which he excelled." She goes on to describe him as a gifted rhetorician blessed with "the most commanding & persuasive Eloquence," a man of the utmost "Patriotism & talents . . . a fine Republican, sincerely attached to the free institutions of our Country."[43] While he may have possessed such qualities, Dickinson abstained from voting for independence from Great Britain. He refused to sign the Declaration of Independence. We get none of those details in Logan's version of Dickinson's history; the dissidence we saw in the other loyalist women is missing in Logan.

Perhaps the most severely edited profile in Logan's diary is of Charles Willson Peale. Peale, who had led the Confiscation Committee that evicted Grace Growden Galloway, wrote an autobiography of his life and his role in the war and gave it to Logan, requesting that she assess it. Logan inscribed her review of the book in her diary, calling it a "quite entertaining" text written by a meek and humble artist. This description of Peale vastly underrepresents the Peale we know today and the Peale that Galloway and Logan knew then. While Logan does mention Peale's role as commissioner of confiscated estates, she edits out any reference to the coercion, violence, and aggression he used to carry out his orders. Despite the fact that loyalists in general (and Quakers, specifically) often wrote about him as cold and merciless, leaving women and children screaming and penniless in the snow for a government that sought to auction off their homes to finance the war, Logan omits these details entirely. She says that Peale felt remorse for having mishandled "poor Grace Galloway" in the way that he did and that that incident was a "gloomy day" for him, as it was for Galloway. She waves aside what she deems a small blemish on Peale's character while also insisting that she felt no pity for the loyalists. She writes, "I am not apologizing for the conduct of those who deserted their country, but I believe the confiscated Property never did a dollar's worth of good to the states." In other words, Peale did not cause any irreparable harm because the rebels never profited from the Galloway estate. Logan even concludes her reflection on the commissioner's life story with a joke: "Mrs. Galloway had the reputation of . . . [having] wit and said upon this unpleasant occasion—that others might complain of being *stripped*, but for her part she had been *Pealed!*"[44] Galloway, who was one of the wealthiest people in Bensalem Township at the war's beginning, lost ten thousand acres and her daughter and husband to exile, thanks to Peale. By the end of her life, she was eating off of borrowed plates and living in a friend's spare room. She possessed the reputation of flying into a rage, delivering long speeches against Peale and his ilk at social gatherings. She died a recluse, completely isolated and impoverished. Logan constructs a different narrative that underscores Galloway's tormentor as a prominent politician. This omission allows Logan to displace Peale's culpability onto Galloway; she suggests that Galloway's loyalties, not Peale's corruption, exacerbated an unpleasant situation. As such, Logan sidesteps the murky issues concerning Galloway's disaffection, her husband's exile, and Peale's right to confiscate that family's property—just as Logan passes over Washington's role in the Virginia Exile Crisis and Dickinson's reticence to sign the Declaration.

What if Logan merely thought of the war differently than her family and friends? Or perhaps she experienced a change of heart after the War of 1812 and developed rebel sympathies later in life. Although either is possible, scholarship about post-revolutionary Quakers suggests that such a change would have been highly irregular. Friends did not approve of the nationalist agenda the government pushed after the war, and in response, created separatist communities to attempt to maintain their principles. They constructed "walled garden schools" that reinforced their belief system and taught students about the violence of the revolution because they feared the new rebel regime would attempt to create a "homogenous culture and uncontested allegiance" in the name of nationalism. After the war, Quakers encouraged each other to follow God's law over national law, as they "sought to safeguard [their] holy nation from the encroachment of a geopolitical one." Logan's diary runs antithetical to that objective and marks another type of elision. Instead of maintaining her separation from the new nation with other "walled-garden" Quakers, she self-consciously aligns herself with the patriots.[45]

Logan writes about loyalists, but she makes almost no references to *loyalism*. She features people who fell on both sides of the war, but she whitewashes their history if they favored the British. For example, she often discusses her cousin Hannah Griffitts, one of the most prolific female loyalist poets of her day, but she never mentions the subject of Griffitts's verse.[46] She writes of James Rivington, who ran a loyalist newspaper that Congress considered so dangerous it issued a bounty on his head, yet Logan insists, although Rivington was "accused of Toryism in the extreme," that he was "yet in the American interest." Rather than focus on his loyalist propaganda, she writes that Rivington informed Congress of a "design to Poison General Washington" and saved his life, which was also true. She mentions Samuel Shoemaker, Anna Rawle's stepfather, but she never discusses his status as an exile or his wife,

Rebecca, as an informant.[47] By writing about these figures without registering their dissent, Logan strips them of their political markers. Her diary, in this regard, reads like Elizabeth Ellet's crossed swords: it recognizes that a revolution occurred, but it neutralizes the tensions that existed between rebels and loyalists—and patriotism and loyalism—so that she might minimize the threat those issues posed to the nationalist narrative she hoped to tell (and that she believed her readers wanted to hear).

Logan may have whitewashed these legacies because she needed to whitewash her own, not only because she belonged to the Society of Friends but because the Logans were suspected of treason after the revolution was over. John Adams implemented a trade embargo in 1798, and France held hostage a group of American sailors; war with France seemed imminent. Congress could not broker peace. Exasperated, George Logan sailed to France and met with Charles Maurice de Talleyrand to try to convince him to release the prisoners and relieve the tensions between the two countries. Logan succeeded—America lifted the embargo, and France released the prisoners—but his actions cast aspersions on his family's loyalties. No one had asked him to conduct these negotiations, and that he did so of his own accord suggested his Francophilia.[48]

As the rebel statesmen possessed a with-us-or-against-us mentality during the American Revolution, so did post-revolutionary Americans adopt a similar viewpoint about those who supported the French Revolution. Congress interpreted Logan's intervention as a negotiation with—and thereby support of—the enemy. After George returned home, Deborah tried to clear her husband's name (and her own) by writing a letter to the *Philadelphia Gazette* justifying his decisions and underscoring his loyalties as a true patriot.[49] Some responded to this letter with vitriol and scorn; the paper ran a response saying that George should be "put in the pillory, and his wife with him."[50] Now the Logans possessed two marks on their legacy. They associated with Quakers at a time when the public linked pacifists with traitors, and they associated with the French at a time when the public connected Francophiles with treachery. The Committee of Safety placed Stenton under surveillance to discern if the Logans engaged in any further acts of espionage, and the family was politically and socially ostracized until 1801, when the scandal dissipated and George was elected to the U.S. Senate.[51] Since Deborah Logan was publishing a biography of her husband while also composing a series of histories for which she wanted to secure an audience, she was perhaps stripping narratives in her diary so that she might strip and refinish her own family's narrative as well.

Logan's censorship throughout her diary underscores what the rest of this book highlights about the mercurial nature of loyalty. In the period between 1810 and 1820, as Americans developed a "new sense of the relationship between the present and the past" with the birth of "the fledgling enterprise of antiquarianism," historians sought to paper over the differences that divided loyalists from patriots by eradicating dissent from historical accounts of the American Revolution.[52] Historian Rosemarie Zagarri has noted that it became unpopular for women to discuss politics at this time, even if they had been politically active just a few decades prior. "Women themselves became unwilling to acknowledge the political dimensions of their behavior," she writes, "and disavowed their connection with political parties or partisan causes. It became hard to remember a time when women had openly embraced politics."[53] If Deborah Norris Logan may be read as metonymic of other postrevolutionary perspectives, some writers participated in this erasure. Perhaps they wanted to publish about and participate in the new nationalist narrative, as Logan clearly did. Or maybe they shifted their loyalties because the new government now seemed viable or because they feared retribution after their side lost. Perhaps they felt some combination of all three. Regardless of the impetus for the shift, narratives like Logan's confirm that loyalties after the war, just like loyalties during it, moved and adapted as the writer saw fit, for any number of reasons.

This post-revolutionary posturing—and the reasons for it—can best be summed up via the story about Deborah Norris Logan's portrait, which was ultimately ripped up and tossed into a fire at her directive. Charles Willson Peale—the same commissioner of confiscated estates who received such a glowing review in Logan's diary—began painting her likeness on September 23, 1818, just shy of her fifty-seventh birthday. The artist did not finish this portrait until Logan turned sixty-four. By that time, she loathed to have her visage captured because of her age, so Peale painted a younger-looking version of his subject. Logan hated it. She called it "churlish"—rude, vulgar, common—and hid it for the rest of her life, instructing her descendants to burn it when she died. Her great-granddaughter Maria Dickinson Logan honored that wish after Logan passed away. She cut the portrait into pieces and took it to Stenton, where the Society of Colonial Dames was throwing a party. To warm the old house, the society members lit a roaring fire in the dining room, and Maria crossed in front of them to feed the fragments to the flames while the attendees looked on. When she finished the deed, she "turned towards the Stenton Grave Yard and said 'Deborah Logan, Pax vobiscum.'"[54] Peace with you.

Logan's directive about her portrait grants us some additional insight into her diary's edits. Although she permitted Peale to "revise" the image that would serve as her lasting legacy long after her death, much as she revised Peale's own image through her review of his book, Logan felt dissatisfied with the results because they lacked verisimilitude—an ironic critique, given her own propensity to embellish her art. Just as Logan left her portrait unfinished, and then directed her descendants to dissect and burn it at her command, so her diary was ripped up, marked out, and disseminated according to her instructions. These selective holes provided her a means by which she tried to control her own narrative. If people were going to read the revolution as, to quote John Adams, a "continued Lye from one end to the other," then Logan was going to tell the most favorable "lie" possible. Since that narrative possessed no room for dissent, she rewrote her family's legacy away from loyalists and pacifists to align with the rebels, utilizing the ellipses in her journal to record for posterity this significant shift. Like breadcrumbs along a trail, however, she left a trace of her reticence for anyone who knew how to read it. Her diary provides a fitting metaphor for how most pacifists, neutralists, disaffected, and loyalists felt about the American Revolution. Torn among grief, fear, anger, indignation, betrayal, and the desire to make amends and resume life as usual, people adapted, faked, revised, or suppressed their loyalties as Americans learned what it meant to project a united narrative after a long and painful civil war.

Studying loyalist women writers of the American Revolution illuminates more messy contradictions than it offers neat conclusions about how women constructed political rhetoric in early America. While Sarah Logan Fisher and Elizabeth Drinker wrote letters to George Washington and Congress and reunited with their husbands, neither Grace Growden Galloway nor Elizabeth Graeme Fergusson saw their spouses after the war. The Pennsylvania Assembly denied Joseph Galloway his property and Henry Fergusson a pass to visit his wife (though there exists some doubt as to whether either would have gone home were they given the chance). Although the Shoemaker and Fergusson families regained some of their confiscated properties, Galloway lost everything. Crowds damaged Anna Rawle's family's property, as they did

Elizabeth Drinker's. While Margaret Hill Morris successfully carved out a space in the Delaware Valley for her neutrality, and Deborah Norris Logan convinced historians of her ardent patriotism, the other writers either chose or were pressured to pick a side or suffer the consequences. While recipients of these women's writings might offer them sympathy, agency, or assistance, they could also offer condemnation, punishment, and censure. Letter-writing possessed as many risks as rewards. Despite the variegated outcomes, epistolarity played a crucial role in providing stripped women a space where they might script their allegiances for themselves. These writing forms allowed them to move between public and private spaces, so that they might bypass (or incorporate, in Fergusson's case) more traditional publication methods via the printing press. Because these letter-forms circulated to both intended and unintended reading audiences, their writers shaped and were shaped by their distribution.

Studying the spaces these revolutionary-era letters and letter-journals created allows scholars to resist propagating a homogenous narrative of the American Revolution that privileges only the victors and suggests a myriad of possibilities for the ways in which early Americans interpreted patriotism, loyalty, treason, citizenship, nationalism, and rebellion. Given the partisan divide from which America currently suffers, and the drastic changes communication has undergone today, scrutinizing the moment at which letters and letter-writing helped define and challenge the origins of our contemporary political system gives us the opportunity to contextualize our modern-day arguments concerning surveillance, privacy, patriotism, and safety. Politicians are justifying building walls and burning bridges by echoing the words that rebels used against loyalists to do the same, so the voices and vehicles of eighteenth-century dissenters offer both a model and a warning about the perils and possibilities of the pen. The message is ultimately a hopeful one. Those outside the mainstream continued writing despite efforts at censorship and suppression. Their letters and diaries evince a determination to create a space for that dissent even when the state threatened to eradicate it, a testament to the perseverance of the marginalized, who faced the loss of their civil rights and yet persevered.

NOTES

INTRODUCTION: STRIPPED AND SCRIPT

1. Ann Hulton, *Letters of a Loyalist Lady* (Cambridge, MA: Harvard University Press, 1927), 70, 85–86.
2. Anna Rawle, "A Loyalist's Account of Certain Occurrences in Philadelphia after Cornwallis's Surrender at Yorktown," *Pennsylvania Magazine of History and Biography* 16, no. 1 (1892): 103–7.
3. Elizabeth Sandwith Drinker, *The Diary of Elizabeth Drinker*, ed. Elaine Forman Crane (Boston: Northeastern University Press, 1991).
4. For more on loyalist self-censorship, see Konstantin Dierks, *In My Power: Letter Writing and Communications in Early America* (Philadelphia: University of Pennsylvania Press, 2009), 218–20.
5. Margaret Hill Morris to Milcah Martha Moore, March 1781, Gulielma M. Howland Collection, Haverford Quaker Collection, Haverford, PA.
6. Rebecca Shoemaker to Anna Rawle, September 19, 1781, Pemberton Papers, Historical Society of Pennsylvania, Philadelphia.
7. Dee Andrews and Kathryn Zabelle Derounian, "'A Dear Dear Friend': Six Letters from Deborah Norris to Sarah Wister, 1778–1779," *Pennsylvania Magazine of History and Biography* 108, no. 4 (1984): 503, 502.
8. Tim Compeau, "Dishonoring the Loyalists," Age of Revolutions, February 22, 2016, http://ageofrevolutions.com/2016/02/22/dishonoring-the-loyalists/.
9. Sharon Block, *Rape and Sexual Power in Early America* (Chapel Hill: University of North Carolina Press, 2006).
10. Joan R. Gundersen, "Independence, Citizenship, and the American Revolution," *Signs* 13, no. 1 (1987): 70.
11. W. S. MacNutt, "The Loyalists: A Sympathetic View," *Acadiensis* 6, no. 1 (1976): 9.
12. Ruth H. Bloch, "The Gendered Meanings of Virtue in Revolutionary America," *Signs* 13, no. 1 (1987): 38, 51–52; David Waldstreicher, *In the Midst of Perpetual Fetes: The Making of American Nationalism, 1776–1820* (Chapel Hill: University of North Carolina Press, 1997), 166; Katharina Erhard, "Rape, Republicanism, and Representation: Founding the Nation in Early American Women's Drama and Selected Visual Representations," *Amerikastudien/American Studies* 50, no. 3 (2005): 509; Linda Frost, "The Body Politic in Tabitha Tenney's 'Female Quixotism,'" *Early American*

Literature 32, no. 2 (1997): 114; Michelle Navarre Cleary, "'America Represented by a Woman'—Negotiating Feminine and National Identity in Post-Revolutionary America," *Women's Studies* 28, no. 1 (1998): 59.

13. Janice Potter-MacKinnon, *While the Women Only Wept: Loyalist Refugee Women* (Montreal: McGill-Queen's University Press, 1976), 33.

14. Linda Grant DePauw, *Founding Mothers: Women of America in the Revolutionary Era* (Boston: Houghton Mifflin, 1975), 125.

15. Elizabeth Maddock Dillon, *The Gender of Freedom: Fictions of Liberalism and the Literary Public Sphere* (Stanford, CA: Stanford University Press, 2004), 11–12.

16. Potter-MacKinnon, *While the Women Only Wept*, 47.

17. Judith L. Van Buskirk, *Generous Enemies: Patriots and Loyalists in Revolutionary New York* (Philadelphia: University of Pennsylvania Press, 2004), 51.

18. Carol Berkin, *Revolutionary Mothers: Women in the Struggle for America's Independence* (New York: Vintage, 2006), 97.

19. Linda K. Kerber, "'History Can Do It No Justice': Women and the Reinterpretation of the American Revolution," in *Women in the Age of the American Revolution,* ed. Ronald Hoffman and Peter J. Albert (Charlottesville: University Press of Virginia, 1989), 119.

20. The following texts provide a solid foundation for studying the perspective of those who lost the war: W. G. Shelton, "The United Empire Loyalists: A Reconsideration," *Dalhousie Review* 45, no. 1 (1965): 5–16; Arthur Meier Schlesinger, *The Colonial Merchants and the American Revolution, 1763–1776* (New York: Ungar, 1966); Robert M. Calhoon, *The Loyalists in Revolutionary America* (New York: Harcourt, Brace, Jovanovich, 1973); Wallace Brown, *The King's Friends: The Composition and Motives of the American Loyalist Claimants* (Providence, RI: Brown University Press, 1986); Wallace Brown, "Loyalists and Non-Participants," in *The American Revolution: A Heritage of Change,* ed. John Parker and Carol Umess (Minneapolis: Associates of the James Ford Bell Library, 1975), 120–34; Catherine S. Crary, *The Price of Loyalty: Tory Writings from the Revolutionary Era* (New York: McGraw-Hill, 1973); MacNutt, "The Loyalists," 3–20; Potter-MacKinnon, *While the Women Only Wept*; Esmond Wright, ed., *Red, White and True Blue: The Loyalists in the Revolution* (New York: AMS Press, 1976); Philip Ranlet, "How Many American Loyalists Left the United States?" *Historian* 76, no. 2 (2014): 278–307; and Philip Gould, *Writing the Rebellion: Loyalists and the Literature of Politics in British America* (Oxford: Oxford University Press, 2016).

21. Maya Jasanoff, *Liberty's Exiles: The Loss of America and the Remaking of the British Empire* (London: Harper, 2011), 24, 6.

22. Germinal work on loyalist women and women of the American Revolution includes DePauw, *Founding Mothers*; Joan Hoff Wilson, "The Illusion of Change," in *The American Revolution: Explorations in the History of American Radicalism,* ed. Alfred F. Young (DeKalb: Northern Illinois University Press, 1976), 383–446; Paul Engle, *Women in the American Revolution* (Chicago: Follett, 1976); Van Buskirk, *Generous Enemies*; Berkin, *Revolutionary Mothers*; and Ruma Chopra, *Unnatural Rebellion: Loyalists in New York City during the Revolution* (Charlottesville: University of Virginia Press, 2013).

23. Potter-MacKinnon, *While the Women Only Wept*; Mary Beth Norton, "Eighteenth-Century American Women in Peace and War: The Case of the Loyalists," *William and Mary Quarterly,* 3rd ser., 33, no. 3 (1976): 386–409.

24. DePauw, *Founding Mothers*, 129.

25. Potter-MacKinnon, *While the Women Only Wept*, 12.

26. Gould, *Writing the Rebellion*, 8.

27. My work on loyalism comes from manuscripts composed in the Northeast. For a firsthand account of a female loyalist in Georgia, see Elizabeth Lichtenstein Johnston, *Recollections of a Georgia Loyalist* (New York: M. F. Mansfield, 1901). For research about southern loyalism, see Rebecca Brannon, *From Revolution to Reunion: The Reintegration of the South Carolina Loyalists* (Columbia: University of South Carolina Press, 2016). Thomas Ingersoll provides a useful statistical analysis of loyalism by colony in *The Loyalist Problem in Revolutionary New England* (Cambridge: Cambridge University Press, 2016), 150–56.

28. The *Book of Negroes* can be found via the Inspection Roll of Negroes Book no. 1, 1774–89, Miscellaneous Papers of the Continental Congress, 1765–1821, Record Group 360: Records of the Continental and Confederation Congresses and the Constitutional Convention, 1765–1821, National Archives, Washington, DC. There a few different versions of this book. One can be found at http://novascotia.ca/archives/Africanns/BN.asp, and others at https://research.archives.gov/id/17337716 and https://research.archives.gov/id/5890797. It has also been printed in Graham Russell Hodges, *The Black Loyalist Directory: African Americans in Exile after the American Revolution* (New York: Garland, 1996).

29. For the historical background of black loyalists, see Ira Berlin, *Many Thousands Gone: The First Two Centuries of Slavery in North America* (Cambridge, MA: Harvard University Press, 2003); Thelma W. Foote, *Black and White Manhattan: The History of Racial Formation in Colonial New York City* (New York: Oxford University Press, 2005); John W. Pulis, ed., *Moving On: Black Loyalists in the Afro-Atlantic World* (New York: Garland, 1999); Benjamin Quarles, *The Negro in the American Revolution* (Chapel Hill: University of North Carolina Press, 1996); Jasanoff, *Liberty's Exiles*, 8–13, 73–89; Ingersoll, *The Loyalist Problem*, 225–29; James W. St. G. Walker, *The Black Loyalists: The Search for a Promised Land in Nova Scotia and Sierra Leone, 1783–1870* (London: Dalhousie University Press, 1976); and Cassandra Pybus, "From Epic Journeys of Freedom: Runaway Slaves of the American Revolution and Their Global Quest for Liberty," *Callaloo* 29, no. 1 (2006): 114–30. One should also read Herbert Aptheker's *The American Revolution, 1763–1783* (New York: International, 1977), but do so with the understanding that several of his numbers concerning black loyalists have been adjusted in light of recent scholarship.

30. For the background concerning the creation of the *Book of Negroes*, see Simone Brown, "Everybody's Got a Little Light under the Sun: Black Luminosity and the Visual Culture of Surveillance," *Cultural Studies* 26, no. 4 (2012): 542–64.

31. Francis Smith Foster, "A Narrative of the Interesting Origins and (Somewhat) Surprising Developments of African-American Print Culture," *American Literary History* 17, no. 4 (2005): 714–40; Barbara McCaskill, "Beyond Recovery: A Process Approach to Research on Women in Early African American Print Cultures," *Legacy* 33, no. 1 (2016): 12–18; Lara Langer Cohen and Jordan Alexander Stein, eds., *Early African American Print Culture* (Philadelphia: University of Pennsylvania Press, 2013). A key source for theorizing texts like the *Book of Negroes* is Paul Gilroy's *The Black Atlantic: Modernity and Double Consciousness* (Brooklyn, NY: Verso, 1993).

32. An excellent source that discusses the stories I could not include because of these

limitations is James Sidbury, *Becoming African in America: Race and Nation in the Early Black Atlantic* (New York: Oxford University Press, 2007).

33. Crary, *The Price of Loyalty*, 374. People interested in letters such as this one should look to the Carleton Papers in the British National Archives in Kew and the Haldimand Papers at the British Library in London for others like it.

34. John Marrant, *A Narrative of the Life of John Marrant, of New York, in North America: With an Account of the Conversion of the King of the Cherokees and His Daughter*, ed. W. Aldridge (London: J. Gadsby and R. Groombridge, 1840); Boston King, *The Life of Boston King: Including "Memoirs of the Life of Boston King, Black Preacher Written by Himself, during His Residence at Kingswood School,"* ed. Ruth Holmes Whitehead and Carmelita Robertson (Halifax: Nimbus Publishers and the Nova Scotia Museum, 2003). Primary documents for Ball, Leonard, George, Wilkinson, Perkins, and Limerick can be found on "Black Loyalists," Canada's Digital Collections, blackloyalist.com, and Todd Braisted, "The On-Line Institute for Advanced Loyalist Studies," royalprovincial.com/military/black/black.htm. See also Mary Louise Clifford, *From Slavery to Freetown: Black Loyalists after the American Revolution* (Jefferson, NC: McFarland, 1999), and Christopher Fyfe, *Our Children Free and Happy: Letters from Black Settlers in Africa in the 1790s* (Edinburgh: Edinburgh University Press, 1991).

35. The most well-known exception is Joseph Brant, who served as a negotiator between the Haudenosaunee and the British but was accused of acting as more than an ally in the interest of the Crown. For more on Brant's negotiations and his tensions with other Native representatives, especially Hendrick Aupaumut, see Lisa Tanya Brooks, *The Common Pot: the Recovery of Native Space in the Northeast* (Minneapolis: University of Minnesota Press, 2008), 106–62.

36. Many thanks to the Native American and Indigenous Studies scholars who helped with the consultation for this information, namely Betty Donohue, Kelly Wisecup, Angie Calcaterra, and Caroline Wigginton. For more on fissures between Native American nations concerning their role in the American Revolution, see Kathleen DuVal, *Independence Lost: Lives on the Edge of the American Revolution* (New York: Random House, 2015), particularly "Independence in Creek and Chickasaw Countries," 75–99.

37. Brooks, *The Common Pot*, 106–7.

38. Two useful archives concerning Native, British, and American negotiations are Joseph Brant and Lyman Copeland Draper, Draper Manuscripts: Joseph Brant Papers, 1710–1879, Wisconsin Historical Society, Division of Library, Archives, and Museum Collections, Madison, and Timothy Pickering, Thomas Pickering Papers, 1731–1927, Massachusetts Historical Society, Boston.

39. Lois M. Feister and Bonnie Pulis, "Molly Brant: Her Domestic and Political Roles," in *Northeastern Indian Lives, 1632–1816*, ed. Robert S. Grumet (Boston: University of Massachusetts Press, 1996), 304–5. For two letters attributed to Brant, see Crary, *The Price of Loyalty*, 247–48. Crary notes that these letters are "rare" and "not in Molly Brant's handwriting, as she could only make her mark," 247.

40. Judith Gross, "Molly Brant: Textual Representations of Cultural Midwifery," *American Studies* 40, no. 1 (1999): 26.

41. Maurice Kenny, *Tekonwatonti (Molly Brant): Poems of War* (Fredonia, NY: White Pine Press, 1992).

42. Gross, "Molly Brant," 35.

43. For more on Brant and Native American loyalists, see Jasanoff, *Liberty's Exiles*, 36–66.

44. Ed Larkin, "What Is a Loyalist?" *Common-Place* 8, no. 1 (2007), http://www.common -place-archives.org/vol-08/no-01/larkin/.

45. For the conflicting nature of loyalism, see Gould, *Writing the Rebellion*, 8–19; Jasanoff, *Liberty's Exiles*, 6–17; Shelton, "The United Empire Loyalists," 7–8; Margaret Ells, "Loyalist Attitudes," *Dalhousie Review* 15 (1935): 321; Robert M. Calhoon, "'I Have Deduced Your Rights': Joseph Galloway's Concept of His Role, 1774–1775," *Pennsylvania History: A Journal of Mid-Atlantic Studies* 35, no. 4 (1968): 113; and Chopra, *Unnatural Rebellion*, 2–7. For information about loyalist claims and the claims commission, see L. F. S. Upton, "The Claims: The Mission of John Anstey," in Wright, ed., *Red, White, and True Blue*, 35; Brown, *The King's Friends*, 20; and Eugene R. Fingerhut, "Uses and Abuses of the American Loyalists' Claims: A Critique of Quantitative Analyses," *William and Mary Quarterly*, 3rd ser., 25, no. 2 (1968): 250.

46. Linda K. Kerber, *Women of the Republic: Intellect and Ideology in Revolutionary America* (Chapel Hill: University of North Carolina Press, 1980), 35–36; Jan Lewis, "The Republican Wife: Virtue and Seduction in the Early Republic," *William and Mary Quarterly*, 3rd ser., 44, no. 4 (1987): 699–700.

47. Laurel Thatcher Ulrich, *Good Wives: Image and Reality in the Lives of Women in Northern New England, 1650–1750* (New York: Vintage, 1991).

48. The word "journal" is more gender-neutral than "diary," so I have attempted to use that terminology throughout unless the reader identified her work as a diary. Elizabeth Drinker's text, for example, is often categorized as the latter rather than the former, but I attempt consistency whenever possible. For more on the feminization of the term "diary," see Cinthia Gannett, *Gender and the Journal* (New York: SUNY Press, 1992), 99–100, 188, and Rebecca Steinitz, *Time, Space, and Gender in the Nineteenth-Century British Diary* (New York: Palgrave, 2011), 8.

49. Janet Gurkin Altman, *Epistolarity: Approaches to a Form* (Columbus: Ohio State University Press, 1982), 4.

50. Sarah Logan Fisher, Diaries, 1776–95, Belfield Family Papers, Historical Society of Pennsylvania, Philadelphia.

51. Ronald J. Zboray and Mary Saracino Zboray, "Is It a Diary, Commonplace Book, Scrapbook, or Whatchamacallit? Six Years of Exploration in New England's Manuscript Archives," *Libraries and the Cultural Record* 44, no. 1 (2009): 116.

52. Steven E. Kagle, *Early Nineteenth-Century American Diary Literature* (Boston: Twayne, 1986), 48.

53. Helen M. Buss, "Anna Jameson's *Winter Studies and Summer Rambles in Canada* as Epistolary Dijournal," in *Essays on Life Writing: From Genre to Critical Practice*, ed. Marlene Kadar (Toronto: University of Toronto Press, 1992), 44.

54. William Merrill Decker, "The Epistolary Diary: Henry Adam's Letters from the South Seas," *Interferences litteraires* 9 (2012): 73.

55. Connie Ann Kirk, "Climates of the Creative Process: Dickinson's Epistolary Journal," in *A Companion to Emily Dickinson*, ed. Martha Nell Smith and Mary Loeffelholz (Chichester, West Sussex, UK: Blackwell, 2008), 336, 338. Sharon M. Harris's work also discusses early American women's letter-writing practices. See Sharon M. Harris, "Early American Women's Self-Creating Acts," *Resources for American Literary Study* 19, no. 2 (1993): 223–45, and Sharon M. Harris, "'And Their Words Do Follow

Them'—The Writings of Early American Women," in *American Women Writers to 1800*, ed. Sharon M. Harris (New York: Oxford University Press, 1996), 3–30.

56. My research suggests that loyalists used the letter-journal more often than the rebel women writers did, but it is not a genre that loyalists alone used.

57. Buss, "Anna Jameson's *Winter Studies*," 44.

58. Decker, "The Epistolary Diary," 79.

59. For more on the ways in which the concept of time affects various types of autobiographical manuscripts, especially letters and diaries, see Stuart Sherman, *Telling Time: Clocks, Diaries, and English Diurnal Form, 1660–1785* (Chicago: University of Chicago Press, 1996), 1–28.

60. Jill Lepore, *The Name of War: King Philip's War and the Origins of American Identity* (New York: Vintage Books, 1999), ix–x.

61. Zboray and Zboray, "Is It a Diary," 102.

62. For more about "collective diaries," see Ronald J. Zboray and Mary Saracino Zboray, *Everyday Ideas: Socioliterary Experience among Antebellum New Englanders* (Knoxville: University of Tennessee Press, 2006), and Zboray and Zboray, "Is It a Diary," 103, 116.

63. Amanda Gilroy and W. M. Verhoeven, *Epistolary Histories: Letters, Fictions, Culture* (Charlottesville: University Press of Virginia, 2000), 3; Elizabeth C. Goldsmith, *Writing the Female Voice: Essays on Epistolary Literature* (London: Pinter, 1989), vii, x; Howard Peter Anderson, Philip B. Daghlian, and Irvin Ehrenpreis, *The Familiar Letter in the Eighteenth Century* (Lawrence: University Press of Kansas, 1966), 280.

64. For more on the publicity and privacy of letters, see Gary Schneider, *The Culture of Epistolarity: Vernacular Letters and Letter Writing in Early Modern England, 1500–1700* (Newark: University of Delaware Press, 2005).

65. Dierks, *In My Power*; Sarah M. S. Pearsall, *Atlantic Families: Lives and Letters in the Later Eighteenth Century* (Oxford: Oxford University Press, 2008); Eve Tavor Bannet, *Empire of Letters: Letter Manuals and Transatlantic Correspondence, 1688–1820* (Cambridge: Cambridge University Press, 2005); Theresa Strouth Gaul and Sharon M. Harris, eds., *Letters and Cultural Transformations in the United States, 1760–1860* (Burlington, VT: Ashgate, 2009).

66. William Smith, *The History of the Post Office in British North America, 1639–1870* (New York: Octagon Books, 1973), 2.

67. Whether or not a letter reached its destination depended on the city's network. Boston possessed a fairly well-established hub, but New Netherland and New Amsterdam did not. With the post's more permanent establishment, the colonies began deciding how much they would charge for a letter; each price depended on the letter's weight, an amount that varied from colony to colony. This all changed in 1710, when a post office bill decreed that the English government would regulate costs, basing them on how far the letter traveled and how many pieces of paper were being delivered, which workers determined by holding a candle to sealed epistles. Although postal rates varied during the eighteenth century, generally speaking a single letter—or a letter made of one sheet—cost four pence in America to travel sixty miles. The letter's recipient paid the fee. Smith, *The History of the Post Office*, 19–21.

68. Bannet, *Empire of Letters*, 13.

69. Arthur E. Summerfield, *U.S. Mail: The United States Postal Service, as Told to Charles Hurd* (New York: Holt, Rinehart and Winston, 1960), 16, 31.

70. Bannet, *Empire of Letters*, 252.

71. Rosemarie Zagarri, *A Woman's Dilemma: Mercy Otis Warren and the American Revolution* (Wheeling, IL: Harlan Davidson, 1995), 58–60.

72. L. H. Butterfield, Marc Friedlaender, and Mary-Jo Kline, eds., *The Book of Abigail and John: Selected Letters of the Adams Family, 1762–1784* (Boston: Northeastern University Press, 2002), 106.

73. Bannet, *Empire of Letters*, 9.

74. Patricia A. M. Spacks, *Privacy: Concealing the Eighteenth-Century Self* (Chicago: University of Chicago Press, 2003), 7, 25.

75. Bannet, *Empire of Letters*, 90–91.

76. Spacks, *Privacy*, 194.

77. Steinitz, *Time, Space, and Gender*, 92.

78. Andrew Hassam, "Reading Other People's Diaries," *University of Toronto Quarterly* 56, no. 3 (1987): 435–36.

79. That Habermas's and Warner's definition of the public sphere excluded women is debated and discussed later in this book. For an in-depth discussion of the masculinization and feminization of public spheres and printed forms, see Dillon, *Gender of Freedom*, 11–48.

80. Sydney V. James, "The Impact of the American Revolution on Quakers' Ideas about Their Sect," *William and Mary Quarterly*, 3rd ser., 19, no. 3 (1962): 372.

81. Richard Wilson Renner, "Conscientious Objection and the Federal Government, 1787–1792," *Military Affairs* 38, no. 4 (1974): 142.

82. I am not the first person to consider the possibility of passive loyalism. See also Robert McCluer Calhoon, *The Loyalists in Revolutionary America, 1760–1781* (New York: Harcourt Brace, 1973), 467.

CHAPTER ONE: SCRIPTING DISAFFECTION

1. As I discuss later in this chapter, Grace Growden Galloway consistently signed with both her maiden and married names. I have thus retained her preferred nomenclature.

2. Raymond C. Werner, "Introduction to the Diary of Grace Growden Galloway," *Pennsylvania Magazine of History and Biography* 55, no. 1 (1931): 32; Elizabeth Evans, *Weathering the Storm: Women of the American Revolution* (New York: Scribner, 1975), 185, 187.

3. John E. Ferling, "Joseph Galloway: A Reassessment of the Motivations of a Pennsylvania Loyalist," *Pennsylvania History: A Journal of Mid-Atlantic Studies* 39, no. 2 (1972): 165–66. See also Joseph Galloway, *Cool Thoughts on the Consequences to Great Britain of American Independence* (London: J. Wilkie, 1780).

4. Robert M. Calhoon, "'I Have Deduced Your Rights': Joseph Galloway's Concept of His Role, 1774–1775," *Pennsylvania History: A Journal of Mid-Atlantic Studies* 35, no. 4 (1968): 356–60. His most famous dissenter was Benjamin Franklin. Just why Galloway staunchly held such a position is widely debated; while scholars such as John E. Ferling claim his loyalism stemmed from his identity as a "fervent Anglo-American

nationalist" who "hoped to save the empire," others counter that he sided with Britain for political gain. Ferling, "Joseph Galloway: A Reassessment," 164.

5. Werner, "Introduction to the Diary of Grace Growden Galloway," 34; Evans, *Weathering the Storm,* 188.

6. Werner, "Introduction to the Diary of Grace Growden Galloway," 35.

7. Evans, *Weathering the Storm,* 188.

8. "To Be Sold by Private Sale the Following Capital Estates in Bucks County, in Pennsylvania . . . Apply to Richard Philips, No. 9, Lincoln's Inn," London, 1787, Broadside, Library Company of Philadelphia.

9. Grace Growden Galloway, "Diary of Grace Growden Galloway 1778–1779 no. 1 Photostat" (hereafter Diary Photostat), Historical Society of Pennsylvania, Philadelphia (hereafter HSP), 21. I quote from three different versions of the Galloway journal throughout this chapter because of the state of her manuscripts at the HSP. They are fragile, brittle, and some have disintegrated to such a degree that all that is left is a photocopy of the text that renders the journal difficult to read. Those who handled it in 1931 or 1975 had time on their side and seem to have been able to read the originals; Elizabeth Evans's *Weathering the Storm* has a good transcription of a fragment of the journal, though not the full text, as does the *Pennsylvania Magazine of History and Biography* (*PMHB*) version prepared by Raymond C. Werner. The *PMHB* transcription, while reliable as far as I can discern from what remains, is also incomplete. I quote from all three in an effort to get as complete a picture of Galloway's loyalties as I possibly can.

10. Grace Growden Galloway and Raymond C. Werner, "Diary of Grace Growden Galloway," *Pennsylvania Magazine of History and Biography* 55, no. 1 (1931): 41, 50.

11. Galloway and Werner, "Diary of Grace Growden Galloway," 44.

12. Ibid., 45n25.

13. Galloway, Diary Photostat, HSP, 21.

14. Ibid.

15. It is important to mention here that the Galloways enslaved people to work their orchards, and yet Grace mentions neither their fate nor their existence in this part of the diary. Certainly, the enslaved men and women would have been worried about similar issues concerning the sale of Trevose to the rebel army. Army officers often took enslaved people, alongside other confiscated property, and sold them to finance the war.

16. Frances E. Dolan, "Battered Women, Petty Traitors, and the Legacy of Coverture," *Feminist Studies* 29, no. 2 (2003): 256.

17. G. S. Rowe, "Femes Covert and Criminal Prosecution in Eighteenth-Century Pennsylvania," *American Journal of Legal History* 32, no. 2 (1988): 139, 140–42.

18. Ibid., 150–51.

19. Richard D. Brown, "The Confiscation and Disposition of Loyalists' Estates in Suffolk County, Massachusetts," *William and Mary Quarterly,* 3rd ser., 21, no. 4 (1964): 536, 537–38.

20. Maya Jasanoff, *Liberty's Exiles: The Loss of America and the Remaking of the British Empire* (London: Harper, 2011), 41.

21. Joan R. Gundersen, "Independence, Citizenship, and the American Revolution," *Signs* 13, no. 1 (1987): 71.

22. Grace Growden Galloway, Diary of Grace Growden Galloway, July 1–September 1779, vol. 2, HSP, 15.

23. Ibid., 15.

24. Ibid.

25. For more on black and Native American loyalists, see Jasanoff, *Liberty's Exiles*, 6–29, 38–66 (which concerns Molly Brant), 73–77, as well as the introduction to this book. For the problem with equating the freedom of slaves with the freedom of white women during this period, see Elizabeth Maddock Dillon, *The Gender of Freedom: Fictions of Liberalism and the Literary Public Sphere* (Stanford, CA: Stanford University Press, 2004), 18.

26. Galloway, Letterbook 2, HSP, 15.

27. Other scholars have affirmed that Galloway's ordeal led to both mental and physical suffering. See, for example, Beverley Baxter, "Grace Growden Galloway: Survival of a Loyalist, 1778–79," *Frontiers: A Journal of Women Studies* 3, no. 1 (1978): 64.

28. Galloway, Diary Photostat, HSP, 41.

29. Galloway and Werner, "Diary of Grace Growden Galloway," 63. Galloway addresses her daughter directly in the journal on August 19, 1779: "oh my Dearest Child My heart is ready to break." Galloway vacillates between addressing the diary and her daughter, depending on how much correspondence she has received from Betsy.

30. During the time of her husband's exile, Grace made a bit of money collecting rent from the family's properties located in the country. The government eventually seized those country estates too. See Baxter, "Grace Growden Galloway," 65.

31. Galloway, Diary Photostat, HSP, 25.

32. Mechal Sobel, *Teach Me Dreams: The Search for Self in the Revolutionary Era* (Princeton, NJ: University of Princeton Press, 2000), 3, 14, 51–52, 14.

33. Galloway, Diary Photostat, HSP, 52.

34. Susan Olson, *By Grief Transformed: Dreams and the Mourning Process* (New Orleans: Spring Journal Books, 2010), 25.

35. Ibid., 15, 49, 103; Sobel, *Teach Me Dreams*, 193, 221.

36. Galloway, Diary Photostat, HSP, 52.

37. Ibid., 57–58; emphasis added.

38. Ibid., 73–74.

39. Grace Growden Galloway, Grace Growden Galloway Diaries and Letter Books, 1778–1781, vol. 3, HSP, 16.

40. For more on loyalist compensation and the exiles' response to England's treatment of them, see Jasanoff, *Liberty's Exiles*, 11–13, 79–87.

41. Baxter, "Grace Growden Galloway," 66–67.

42. Galloway, "Diary," in Evans, *Weathering the Storm*, 238.

43. Joseph Galloway to Grace Growden Galloway, March 21, 1777; September 17, 1779; February 4, 1779, Joseph Galloway Papers, Huntington Library, San Marino, CA.

44. Galloway, "Diary," in Evans, *Weathering the Storm*, 239–40, 244.

Chapter Two: Scripting Pacifism

1. Thomas Gilpin, *Exiles in Virginia: With Observations on the Conduct of the Society of Friends during the Revolutionary War: Comprising the Official Papers of the Government Relating to That Period 1777–1778* (Philadelphia: N.p., 1848), 35–37.

2. Robert Oaks suggests that the Virginia Exile Crisis grew out of tensions with Quakers because they refused to support the war generally and because they refused to accept Continental currency specifically. The rebels themselves called the Quakers "notoriously disaffected" in the congressional resolve that justified the arrest. The August 25, 1777, resolve is reprinted in Gilpin, *Exiles in Virginia*, 35. Robert F. Oaks, "Philadelphians in Exile: The Problem of Loyalty during the American Revolution," *Pennsylvania Magazine of History and Biography* 96, no. 3 (1972): 301.

3. Oaks, "Philadelphians in Exile," 303.

4. John Sullivan, *Letters and Papers of Major-General John Sullivan, Continental Army* (Concord: New Hampshire Historical Society, 1930), 433–34.

5. Fifteen of the exiles were Quakers, but thirty total men were arrested and sent to the Masonic Lodge in Philadelphia. Twenty-two of those prisoners were sent to Winchester, Virginia. Two died before the prisoners were released. Wendy Lucas Castro, "'Being Separated from My Dearest Husband, in This Cruel Manner': Elizabeth Drinker and the Seven-Month Exile of Philadelphia Quakers," *Quaker History* 100, no. 1 (2011): 40–63; Sarah Crabtree, *Holy Nation: The Transatlantic Quaker Ministry in an Age of Revolution* (Chicago: University of Chicago Press, 2015), 46. See also Arthur J. Mekeel, *The Quakers and the American Revolution* (York, UK: Sessions Book Trust, 1996), 4–5, and Gilpin, *Exiles in Virginia*, 38, 42.

6. Most scholars have approached the Virginia Exile Crisis from a historical perspective. I approach it from a rhetorical one. For context concerning this watershed moment during the revolution, start with Gilpin's *Exiles in Virginia*. Then see Judith L. Van Buskirk, "They Didn't Join the Band: Disaffected Women in Revolutionary Philadelphia," *Pennsylvania History: A Journal of Mid-Atlantic Studies* 62, no. 3 (1995): 306–29; Kenneth A. Radbill, "The Ordeal of Elizabeth Drinker," *Pennsylvania History: A Journal of Mid-Atlantic Studies* 47, no. 2 (1980): 147–72; Castro, "Being Separated," 40–63; and Oaks, "Philadelphians in Exile," 298–325.

7. In 1778, the pledge was rewritten to be even more specific. Pennsylvanians were supposed to promise, "We, the subscribers, do swear (or affirm) that we renounce and refuse all allegiance to George Third, King of Great Britain, his heirs and successors, and that we will be faithful and bear true allegiance to the Commonwealth of Pennsylvania as a free and independent State, and that we will not at any time do or cause to be done anything that will be prejudicial or injurious to the freedom and independence thereof, as declared by Congress, and also that we will discover and make known to someone Justice of the Peace of the said State all treasons and conspiracies which we now know or hereafter shall know to be formed against this or any of the United States of America." John W. Jordan, *Colonial and Revolutionary Families of Pennsylvania: Genealogical and Personal Memoirs* (Baltimore: Genealogical Publishing, 2004), 73.

8. Mekeel, *The Quakers and the American Revolution*, 2–3.

9. Ethyn Williams Kirby, "The Quakers' Efforts to Secure Civil and Religious Liberty, 1660–96," *Journal of Modern History* 7, no. 4 (1935): 412. Quakers did, however, have the option to affirm instead of swear, but many found this alternative unappealing.

10. Richard Bauman, *Let Your Words Be Few: Symbolism of Speaking and Silence among Seventeenth-Century Quakers* (Cambridge: Cambridge University Press, 1983), 97.

11. Elizabeth Sandwith Drinker, *The Diary of Elizabeth Drinker*, ed. Elaine Forman Crane (Boston: Northeastern University Press, 1991), 60.

12. Sarah Logan Fisher and Nicholas B. Wainwright, "'A Diary of Trifling Occurrences': Philadelphia, 1776–1778," *Pennsylvania Magazine of History and Biography* 82, no. 4 (1958): 411–12.
13. Sarah Logan Fisher, "Sarah Logan Fisher Diaries, 1776–1795," Belfield Family Papers, Historical Society of Pennsylvania, Philadelphia (hereafter Fisher, volume number, year, HSP, page number if available). Fisher asks Tommy not to share it with his fellow prisoners because her work might be judged too harshly by his friends, which was a common enough epistolary practice to warrant a section in many dictaminal manuals. Most eighteenth-century letters opened with a profession of inadequacy, a vestige of the Puritanical insistence on humility. This "ingratio," as Angela Vietto calls it, niether meant the writer believed herself to be truly inadequate nor did it prevent the letter from being shared. Vietto, *Women and Authorship in Revolutionary America* (Aldershot, UK: Ashgate, 2005), 53.
14. Fisher and Wainwright, "A Diary of Trifling Occurrences," 412.
15. Fisher, vol. 15, 1777, HSP, 68.
16. Fisher, vol. 15, HSP. The page is unnumbered and undated, but the dedication to Hannah is on the last page of this volume.
17. Fisher and Wainright, "A Diary of Trifling Occurrences," 413n3.
18. Fisher, vol. 1, 1777, HSP.
19. Harry E. Seyler, "Pennsylvania's First Loyalty Oath," *History of Education Journal* 3, no. 4 (1952): 119.
20. Fisher, vol. 3, 1777, HSP; emphasis added.
21. Gilpin, *Exiles in Virginia*, 38.
22. John Sullivan, "Legislative Acts/Legal Proceedings," *Dunlap's Pennsylvania Packet, or General Advertiser,* September 9, 1777.
23. William Houston, "In Congress, August 28, 1777," *Providence Gazette, and Country Journal,* October 25, 1777.
24. Israel Pemberton, Jr., "The Remonstrance of the Subscribers, Citizens of Philadelphia: An Address to the Inhabitants of Pennsylvania, by Those Freemen, of the City of Philadelphia, Who Are Now Confined in the Mason's Lodge, by Virtue of a General Warrant, Signed in Council by the Vice President of the Council of Pennsylvania," *New-York Gazette, and Weekly Mercury,* September 29, 1777; emphasis added; Henry Drinker, "To the Monthly Meeting for the Northern District, Having Had a Committee Appointed to the Like Service, Produced to That Meeting the Following Report," *Dunlap's Pennsylvania Packet, or General Advertiser,* September 9, 1777.
25. Fisher, vol. 3, 1777, HSP.
26. Dale Spender, "The Politics of Naming," in *Composition of Our "Selves,"* ed. Marcia Smith Curtis (Dubuque, IA: Kendall/Hunt, 2000), 195.
27. Michael V. Bhatia, "Fighting Words: Naming Terrorists, Bandits, Rebels and Other Violent Actors," *Third World Quarterly* 26, no. 1 (2005): 10, 12.
28. Fisher, vol. 3, 1777, HSP.
29. Ibid.
30. Crabtree, *Holy Nation*, 1–28.
31. Ibid., 35.
32. Fisher, vol. 5, 1779, HSP.
33. In addition to the germinal studies on women in the American Revolution, namely Linda K. Kerber, *Women of the Republic: Intellect and Ideology in Revolutionary*

America (Chapel Hill: University of North Carolina Press, 1980), and Jan Lewis, "The Republican Wife: Virtue and Seduction in the Early Republic," *William and Mary Quarterly*, 3rd ser., 44, no. 4 (1987): 689–721, to learn more about how women (particularly loyalist women) were treated during the American Revolution, see Joan Hoff Wilson, "The Illusion of Change," in *The American Revolution: Explorations in the History of American Radicalism*, ed. Alfred F. Young (DeKalb: Northern Illinois University Press, 1976), 383–445; Paul Engle, *Women in the American Revolution* (Chicago: Follett, 1976); Linda K. Kerber, "'History Can Do It No Justice': Women and the Reinterpretation of the American Revolution," in *Women in the Age of the American Revolution*, ed. Ronald Hoffman and Peter J. Albert (Charlottesville: University Press of Virginia, 1989), 3–42; Wallace Brown, *The King's Friends: The Composition and Motives of the American Loyalist Claimants* (Providence, RI: Brown University Press, 1986); Linda Grant DePauw, *Founding Mothers: Women in America in the Revolutionary Era* (Boston: Houghton Mifflin, 1975); Mary Beth Norton, "Eighteenth-Century American Women in Peace and War: The Case of the Loyalists," *William and Mary Quarterly*, 3rd ser., 33, no. 3 (1976): 386–409; Janice Potter-MacKinnon, *While the Women Only Wept: Loyalist Refugee Women* (Montreal: McGill-Queen's University Press, 1976); Judith L. Van Buskirk, *Generous Enemies: Patriots and Loyalists in Revolutionary New York* (Philadelphia: University of Pennsylvania Press, 2004); and Carol Berkin, *Revolutionary Mothers: Women in the Struggle for America's Independence* (New York: Vintage, 2006).

34. Ann Hulton, *Letters of a Loyalist Lady* (Cambridge, MA: Harvard University Press, 1927), 85–86.

35. 2 Corinthians 5:1 (King James Version).

36. 1 Corinthians 6:19 (New International Version).

37. John 14:2 (KJV).

38. Elaine F. Crane, "The World of Elizabeth Drinker," *Pennsylvania Magazine of History and Biography* 107, no. 1 (1983): 5, 4; Radbill, "The Ordeal of Elizabeth Drinker," 148.

39. Radbill, "The Ordeal of Elizabeth Drinker," 148. The children were Sarah (16), Ann (13), William (10), Henry (7), and Mary (3), who was called Molly. Mary Sandwith, Elizabeth's unmarried sister, also lived with them at the time. Castro, "Being Separated," 40. For more on the Drinker household in the 1770s, particularly concerning Mary Sandwith and her care for the children during the Exile Crisis, see Karin Wulf, *Not All Wives: Women of Colonial Philadelphia* (Philadelphia: University of Pennsylvania Press, 2000), 85–117.

40. Richard T. Vann, *The Social Development of English Quakerism, 1655–1755* (Cambridge: Cambridge University Press, 1969), 20.

41. The Drinkers were not "plain" Quakers. Although they lived by most "customs of the Society," they had clothes "from the finest silk, velvet, and cashmere, with only the somberness of its colors (dark greens, grays, and blacks) to compensate for the elegance of the fabric." Their furniture was "carved from the choicest woods," including walnut and mahogany. And they had four vehicles: a wagon, chaise, cart, and carriage. Drinker, *The Diary of Elizabeth Drinker*, xii–xiii.

42. The idea that the early American diary was a semi-public document (and the critical conversation surrounding such a topic) is discussed in detail in the introduction of this book.

43. See Howard H. Brinton, *Quaker Journals: Varieties of Religious Experience among Friends* (Wallingford, PA: Pendle Hill, 1983), and Brinton, *Children of Light: In Honor of Rufus M. Jones* (New York: Macmillan, 1938).

44. Crane, "The World of Elizabeth Drinker," 5.

45. Drinker, *The Diary of Elizabeth Drinker*, 50, 226–27. This is the complete list of the Virginia Exiles' names and their occupations: Edward Pennington: merchant, brewer, sugar refiner; Thomas Coombe: parson; Thomas Affleck: joiner; Thomas Gilpin: inventor; Myers Fisher: lawyer; Phineas Bond: lawyer; Thomas Pike: dancing, fencing, riding master; William Smith: broker; William Drewet Smith: merchant; Owen Jones, Jr.: treasurer; Charles Jervis: hatter; Charles Eddy: merchant; Israel Pemberton: merchant; John Hunt: minister; Samuel Pleasants: merchant, Thomas Fisher: merchant; James Pemberton: merchant; and Samuel Fisher: merchant. Castro, "Being Separated," 40.

46. Drinker, *The Diary of Elizabeth Drinker*, 240–41, 248.

47. Ibid., 251, 258–59, 264; emphasis added.

48. This passage is anomalous when compared to other entries about the Drinkers' relationship with the free and indentured servants in their employ. All accounts suggest that the Drinkers treated their servants humanely, paid them above-average wages, and continued to help those that left for other jobs if they returned to the Drinkers' home seeking money in troubled times. Yet here Drinker writes of Ann the way she might describe a stolen plate. Debra M. O'Neal, "Elizabeth Drinker and Her 'Lone' Women: Domestic Service, Debilities and (In)Dependence through the Eyes of a Philadelphia Gentlewoman," *Pennsylvania History: A Journal of Mid-Atlantic Studies* 68, no. 4 (2001): 435–64.

49. Linda Frost, "The Body Politic in Tabitha Tenney's 'Female Quixotism,'" *Early American Literature* 32, no. 2 (1997): 114.

50. Katharina Erhard, "Rape, Republicanism, and Representation: Founding the Nation in Early American Women's Drama and Selected Visual Representations," *Amerikastudien/American Studies* 50, no. 3 (2005): 509.

51. Drinker, *The Diary of Elizabeth Drinker*, 266–67.

52. Castro, "Being Separated," 46.

53. Radbill, "The Ordeal of Elizabeth Drinker," 150.

54. Ibid., 162–63.

55. Drinker traveled with Mary Pleasants, Susanna Jones, and Phebe Pemberton. Gilpin, *Exiles in Virginia*, 221, 42–45; Radbill, "The Ordeal of Elizabeth Drinker," 165; Mekeel, *The Quakers and the American Revolution*, 208.

56. Gilpin, *Exiles in Virginia*, 222, 223. Wharton was president from March 1777 to May 1778.

57. Castro, "Being Separated," 46.

58. Gilpin, *Exiles in Virginia*, 279.

59. Radbill, "The Ordeal of Elizabeth Drinker," 166; Gilpin, *Exiles in Virginia*, 224.

60. Andrew Burstein, *Sentimental Democracy: The Evolution of America's Romantic Self-Image* (New York: Hill and Wang, 1999), 3, 112.

61. Sarah Knott, *Sensibility and the American Revolution* (Chapel Hill: University of North Carolina, 2009), 10–16.

62. Burstein, *Sentimental Democracy*, 6.

63. Fisher, vol. 5, 1778, HSP. Apparently, the prisoners did not all arrive home together; due to their many infirmities, some arrived later than others.

64. Drinker, *The Diary of Elizabeth Drinker*, 76.

65. Radbill, "The Ordeal of Elizabeth Drinker," 168–69.

66. Mekeel, *The Quakers and the American Revolution*, 216.

Chapter Three: Scripting Neutrality

1. Margaret Hill Morris, *Private Journal Kept during a Portion of the Revolutionary War, for the Amusement of a Sister* (Philadelphia: N.p., 1836), 67. The manuscript is held at Haverford College's Quaker and Special Collections, Haverford, Pennsylvania. Many editions of Morris's letters and journals are excerpted; as a result, I quote from several different editions in an attempt to piece together as complete a version of her text as possible.

2. Richard Hill and Margaret Hill Morris, *Letters of Doctor Richard Hill and His Children; or, The History of a Family, as Told by Themselves. Collected and Arranged by John Jay Smith.* (Philadelphia: N.p., 1854), 210. This admonition's language resembles the letter/poem that Elizabeth Graeme Fergusson sent to her friend Annis Stockton, discussed in chapter 5. Fergusson also writes that her "narrative of Domestic Distress" at times "appear[s] Contradictory." "When it falls in your hand," she asks, "I would wish this perusal of it could be limited to such few of your friends; as have feeling delicate Hearts and consider it as a proof of a warm Heart, [rather] than the production of a Cool Hand." Elizabeth Graeme Fergusson, "Il Penseroso; or, The Deserted Wife," Benjamin Rush Papers XL, Library Company of Philadelphia.

3. Karin Wulf, introduction, in *Milcah Martha Moore's Book: A Commonplace Book from Revolutionary America*, ed. Karin Wulf and Catherine La Courreye Blecki (University Park: Pennsylvania State University Press, 1997). 29. Fergusson's salon was also wide-reaching; it was known as the "Athens of North America" in its day and is discussed in chapter 5.

4. Hannah Griffitts was Milcah Martha Moore and Margaret Morris's cousin. Susanna Wright taught Griffitts to write poetry, and Wright's father and brother served in the Pennsylvania Assembly with Moore's, Morris's, and Griffitts's relatives, Isaac Norris, Jr., and Isaac Norris, Sr. Moore was also close to the Norris family as well; Deborah Norris, later Logan, is the subject of the final chapter of this book. For more on the connection among these women, see Catherine La Courreye Blecki, "Reading Moore's Book: Manuscript vs. Print Culture, and the Development of Early American Literature," in Wulf and Blecki, eds., *Milcah Martha Moore's Book*, 67, and Wulf, introduction, 31–35.

5. Wulf, introduction, 36–37.

6. Morris lived with her sister Sarah Dillwyn and Sarah's husband, George, during the war. Both Morris and Dillwyn write about receiving, enjoying, and sharing Milcah Martha Moore's commonplace book, which featured selections from the writers who participated in her salon. For Sarah Dillwyn's letter about Moore's book, which she calls "a very pleasant companion," see: Hill and Morris, *Letters of Doctor Richard Hill and His Children*, 203. For Morris's discussion of Moore's book—and how she shows it to the children in the house so that they might emulate it—see Morris, *Private Journal Kept*, 239.

7. Wulf, introduction, 38.

8. Richard J. Arneson, "Neutrality and Political Liberalism," in *Political Neutrality: A Re-Evaluation*, ed. Roberto Merrill and Daniel M. Weinstock (New York: Palgrave, 2014), 11.

9. Liam Riordan, "Identity and Revolution: Everyday Life and Crisis in Three Delaware River Towns," *Pennsylvania History: A Journal of Mid-Atlantic Studies* 64, no. 1 (1997): 57.

10. Sung Bok Kim, "The Limits of Politicization in the American Revolution: The Experience of Westchester County, New York," *Journal of American History* 80, no. 3 (1993): 869, 876, 877.

11. Wulf, introduction, 55.

12. Margaret Hill Morris, *Margaret Morris, Her Journal*, ed. John W. Jackson (Philadelphia: G. S. MacManus, 1949), 43, 47.

13. Morris, *Private Journal Kept*, 11.

14. Wulf, introduction, 48; Riordan, "Identity and Revolution," 78–80.

15. Morris, *Private Journal Kept*, 11.

16. Wulf, introduction, 48–49; Cynthia Dubin Edelberg, *Jonathan Odell, Loyalist Poet of the American Revolution* (Durham, NC: Duke University Press, 1987), 147–59.

17. Rodney Atwood, *The Hessians: Mercenaries from Hessen-Kassel in the American Revolution* (Cambridge: Cambridge University Press, 1980), 14.

18. David Hackett Fischer, *Washington's Crossing* (New York: Oxford University Press, 2004), 126, 171–77.

19. An excellent source about the nuances of the Peace Testimony is Meredith Baldwin Weddle, *Walking in the Way of Peace: Quaker Pacifism in the Seventeenth Century* (New York: Oxford University Press, 2001).

20. Ibid., 291, 222.

21. Society of Friends, Minutes, 1775–85, Philadelphia Yearly Meeting (Arch Street) Meeting for Sufferings, Haverford Quaker Special Collections, Haverford, Pennsylvania (hereafter Society of Friends, date, PYM, Haverford, page number).

22. Margaret Morris, "The Revolutionary Journal of Margaret Morris, of Burlington, N.J., December 6, 1776, to June 11, 1778, [vol.] II," *Bulletin of Friends' Historical Society of Philadelphia* 9, no. 1 (1919): 8, 9. Since another part of Morris's journal was published in the *Bulletin of Friends' Historical Society of Philadelphia* with a similar name in 1920, I distinguish abbreviated citations by volume.

23. Samuel Seabury, *Free Thoughts on the Proceedings of the Continental Congress, Held at Philadelphia, Sept. 5, 1774: Wherein Their Errors Are Exhibited, Their Reasonings Confuted, and the Fatal Tendency of Their Non-Importation, Non-Exportation, and Non-Consumption Measure, Are Laid Open to the Plainest Understandings; and the Only Means Pointed Out for Preserving and Securing Our Present Happy Constitution: In a Letter to the Farmers, and Other Inhabitants of North America in General, and to Those of the Province of New-York in Particular* (London: Richardson and Urquhart, 1775).

24. Ibid., 10.

25. Morris and Hill, *Letters of Doctor Richard Hill and His Children*, 221. Morris perhaps meant *Wie Geht's*, pronounced "ve gates" or "veegate," which is a German greeting for "how are you?"

26. Atwood, *The Hessians*, 68, 171.

27. Margaret Morris, "Revolutionary Journal of Margaret Morris of Burlington, New

Jersey. [vol.] III, Conclusion," *Bulletin of Friends' Historical Society of Philadelphia* 9, no. 3 (1920): 104.

28. Morris, "Revolutionary Journal [vol.] II," 67.

29. Morris, "Revolutionary Journal [vol.] III," 103–5.

30. Rufus M. Jones, *The Later Periods of Quakerism* (Westport, CT: Greenwood Press, 1970), 86.

31. Sarah Crabtree, *Holy Nation: The Transatlantic Quaker Ministry in an Age of Revolution* (Chicago: University of Chicago Press, 2015), 2, 92, 174.

32. For more on gundalow boats, see Alan Axelrod, *The Real History of the American Revolution: A New Look at the Past* (New York: Sterling, 2009), 121, and Nancy Coffey Heffernan and Ann Page Stecker, *New Hampshire: Crosscurrents in Its Development* (Hanover, NH: University Press of New England, 2004), 71.

33. Morris, "Revolutionary Journal [vol.] II," 73.

34. The Philadelphia Yearly Meeting minutes confirm that Quakers decided to banish from the society anyone who participated in the war for either side. Although "participation" was up for debate in these minutes, it was decided that anyone who aided either side in any way would be considered for banishment. Participation for the Quakers included requisitions, quartering, correspondence, military action, political office, or participating in crowd action, celebrations, or protests. Society of Friends, "29th day of the 9th Month [September] to the 4th of the Tenth Month [October] 1777," PYM, Haverford.

35. Society of Friends, PYM, Haverford. Morris describes the sickness as "the camp or putrid fever." The men she treated "broke out in blotches," which caused Morris to diagnose it as "itch fever." Epidemic typhus, transmitted by body lice and characterized by a rash and high temperature, was also known as camp, jail, or war fever, since it plagued bodies living in close, unsanitary quarters. Although this seems a likely diagnosis, given that it was and would continue to be one of the top three diseases killing people in encampments even well into the nineteenth century, Morris does not provide enough information to say with complete certainty which disease was ravishing the soldiers. Morris learned to practice medicine from her father, Henry Hill, who was, at least for part of his life, a physician. She made medicines and in 1779 opened an apothecary shop. She was part of a broad network of female physicians, many her kin. For more on Morris as a medical practitioner, see Susan Brandt, "'Getting into a Little Business': Margaret Hill Morris and Women's Medical Entrepreneurship during the American Revolution," *Early American Studies: An Interdisciplinary Journal* 13, no. 4 (2015): 774–807.

36. Morris, "Revolutionary Journal [vol.] III," 109.

37. For Quaker debates about what constituted gray-area engagement, see Society of Friends, PYM, Haverford, 174–83. About the Meeting for Sufferings, see Crabtree, *Holy Nation*, 15.

38. Society of Friends, 9 mo. [September] 1776, PYM, Haverford, 362.

39. Morris, "Revolutionary Journal [vol.] III," 110.

40. Morris was not the only female Quaker healer to create such a compromise with her faith. Ann Cooper Whitall's house served as a military hospital in Red Bank, New Jersey, in 1777, and she treated hundreds of Hessians and rebels and still considered herself a member of the Society of Friends. Abigail Marshall (whose family was counted among the Fighting Quakers, or Quakers who supported or

fought in the revolution) occupied a similar position. Brandt, "'Getting into a Little Business,'" 792.

CHAPTER FOUR: SCRIPTING LOYALISM

1. Craig W. Horle, Joseph S. Foster, and Laurie M. Wolfe, "Samuel Shoemaker," in *Lawmaking and Legislators in Pennsylvania: A Biographical Dictionary*, ed. Craig W. Horle, Joseph S. Foster, and Laurie M. Wolfe (Harrisburg: Commonwealth of Pennsylvania House of Representatives, 2005), 3:1289, 1284–86.

2. In September 1777, in the same raid that arrested the Virginia Exiles, the Supreme Executive Council sent men to Shoemaker's home to arrest him for conduct "hostile to the American cause." Unlike the Virginia Exiles, however, Shoemaker was allowed to remain in his house if he promised not to leave it. He narrowly escaped Henry Drinker's and Tommy Fisher's fate. Horle, Foster, and Wolfe, "Samuel Shoemaker," 3:1291.

3. Rebecca Warner, Anna's mother, married Francis Rawle on December 21, 1756. Together, Rebecca and Francis had three children: Anna, William, and Margaret (Peggy) Rawle. Francis died on June 7, 1761, and Rebecca married Samuel Shoemaker on November 10, 1767. Their only child was Edward. Samuel's previous wife was Hannah Carpenter, whom he married in 1746. Together, Samuel and Hannah had Samuel (d. 1748), Samuel (d. 1750), Isaac (d. 1752), Benjamin, Sarah, Hannah, Mary, Samuel (b. after July 15, 1750), and Isaac. Rebecca Warner Rawle Shoemaker, Anna Rawle, and Margaret Rawle, "Letters and Diaries of a Loyalist Family of Philadelphia. Written between the Years 1780 and 1786 by Rebecca Shoemaker Wife of Samuel Shoemaker and Her Daughters, Anna Rawle, Afterwards the Wife of John Clifford, and Margaret Rawle, Afterwards the Wife of Isaac Wharton," typescript, Letters and Diaries Shoemaker, Historical Society of Pennsylvania (hereafter HSP). See also Horle, Foster, and Wolfe, "Samuel Shoemaker," 3:1757–75.

4. William Brooke Rawle, "Laurel Hill and Some Colonial Dames Who Once Lived There," *Pennsylvania Magazine of History and Biography* 35, no. 4 (1911): 399–400.

5. Ibid., 394. The Shoemakers owned six houses consisting of a 29½-acre country house called Laurel Hill, located on the banks of the Schuylkill River; a three-story home on Water Street (one of the wealthiest neighborhoods in Philadelphia); a house on Market Street that was Rebecca's; a mansion on Mulberry Street, later renamed Arch Street, complete with wharves, a stable, coach house, and offices; and two houses on Fourth Street. The plantation also contained two houses, a barn, and a six-acre orchard. Horle, Foster, and Wolfe, "Samuel Shoemaker," 3:1284–89.

6. Rawle, "Laurel Hill and Some Colonial Dames Who Once Lived There," 395, 397.

7. Konstantin Dierks, *In My Power: Letter Writing and Communications in Early America* (Philadelphia: University of Pennsylvania Press, 2009), 209, 216.

8. Merrill D. Smith, *Women's Roles in Eighteenth-Century America* (Santa Barbara, CA: Greenwood, 2010), 119. Barbara McCaskill calls this story "legend," which it likely was, in "Beyond Recovery: A Process Approach to Research on Women in Early African American Print Culture," *Legacy* 33, no. 1 (2016): 15.

9. Henry Darrach, *Lydia Darragh, One of the Heroines of the Revolution* (Philadelphia: Historical Society of Pennsylvania, 1916), 388.

10. Sharon M. Harris, *American Women Writers to 1800* (New York: Oxford University Press, 1996), 281. Wright was a patriot spy.

11. Archibald Campbell to Elizabeth [Murray] Inman, August 8, 1777, Murray-Robbins Family Papers, Massachusetts Historical Society, Boston.

12. Elizabeth Evans, ed., *Weathering the Storm: Women of the American Revolution* (New York: Scribner, 1975), 287.

13. Rebecca Shoemaker to Anna and Peggy Rawle, September 29, 1781, "Letters and Diaries of a Loyalist Family of Philadelphia," HSP.

14. Anna Rawle and Elizabeth Evans, "Anna Rawle Clifford," in Evans, ed., *Weathering the Storm*, 291. This method of economy—keeping a journal instead of a letter—continued to be a popular practice after the war. Ronald J. Zboray and Mary Saracino Zboray write that in the antebellum period, people sent collective diaries to loved ones to keep costs down: "Paper costs ranged between one and seven cents per sheet, and ink prices varied even more: a bottle might run from four to twelve cents, and if of quality ink, from twenty-five cents to thirty-seven and a half cents. Inkstands and wells, depending upon their materials of construction (for example, freestone or glass), were priced at between ten and thirty-five cents, but cost even more when made of brass or highly ornamented. Quills might be had at four for a penny, steel pens cost about one cent each, and gold pens could fetch two dollars. Envelopes, which could be obviated by skillful folding, averaged about a cent and half each, and sealing wax . . . cost about fifty cents a bottle, with a pack of the wafers that added color and further adhesiveness to the seal at about twelve cents." Ronald J. Zboray and Mary Saracino Zboray, *Everyday Ideas: Socioliterary Experience among Antebellum New Englanders* (Knoxville: University of Tennessee Press, 2006), 19–20.

15. For an example of the ways in which Rawle subdivides her letters into diary-entries, see Anna Rawle to Rebecca Shoemaker, May 18, 1781, "Letters and Diaries of a Loyalist Family," HSP. Rawle also calls her letter a "journal" in this entry, writing, "I shall now close for the present this journal—whatever titles may be bestowed on it[.] I think nobody will call it a sentimental one."

16. Robert M. Calhoon, *The Loyalists in Revolutionary America, 1760–1781* (New York: Harcourt Brace, 1973), 303.

17. Henry J. Young, "Treason and Its Punishment in Revolutionary Pennsylvania," *Pennsylvania Magazine of History and Biography* 90, no. 3 (1966): 290, 294.

18. Under this new law, 118 people were prosecuted for treason and 81 for abetting (misprision) in Pennsylvania. Ibid., 294–95.

19. Anna Rawle to Rebecca Shoemaker, 1787, "Letters and Diaries of a Loyalist Family," HSP.

20. She also names a friend Sally, "Juliet"; her step-uncle John, "Lindore"; and her friend Joseph, "Lysander." Horatio was from *Hamlet*, Juliet from *Romeo and Juliet*, and Lysander from *Midsummer Night's Dream*. The source for the other monikers are unclear.

21. Rebecca Shoemaker to Anna Rawle, October 1781, "Letters and Diaries of a Loyalist Family," HSP.

22. Elizabeth Warren Shoemaker to Anna Rawle, n.d., "Letters and Diaries of a Loyalist Family," HSP.

23. Rebecca Shoemaker to Anna Rawle, September 19, 1781, "Letters and Diaries of a Loyalist Family," HSP.

24. Anna Rawle to Rebecca Shoemaker, June 7, 1780, "Letters and Diaries of a Loyalist Family," HSP.

25. Although she did write to Joseph Fox, who is "Lysander," in the correspondence, I believe here she is talking about Joseph Reed, who by that time had issued a decree that all letters be scanned before entering New York. It would have been irreverent—purposefully so—for Rawle to refer to him by his first name, as she does here.

26. Anna Rawle to Rebecca Shoemaker, September 22, 1780, "Letters and Diaries of a Loyalist Family," HSP.

27. Anna Rawle to Rebecca Shoemaker, December 18, 1781, "Letters and Diaries of a Loyalist Family," HSP.

28. Rawle wrote to her mother that Galloway requested she smuggle any letters from Joseph and Betsy Galloway "under cover" through the Rawle/Shoemaker connection. Anna Rawle to Rebecca Shoemaker, September 7, 1781, "Letters and Diaries of a Loyalist Family," HSP.

29. The representative was Sarah Franklin Bache, Benjamin Franklin's daughter. That is an interesting dynamic as well, given that Sarah Bache's own half-brother, William, was also a loyalist, estranged from his family for refusing to side with the colonies.

30. Rawle, "Laurel Hill and Some Colonial Dames Who Once Lived There," 398.

31. Anna Rawle to Rebecca Shoemaker, June 30, 1780, "Letters and Diaries of a Loyalist Family," HSP.

32. Emily J. Arendt, "'Ladies Going about for Money': Female Voluntary Associations and Civic Consciousness in the American Revolution," *Journal of the Early Republic* 34, no. 2 (2014): 182; Rawle and Evans, "Anna Rawle Clifford," 289.

33. This broadside was anonymous, but Reed is widely accepted to be the author. Lisa L. Moore, Joanna Brooks, and Caroline Wigginton, eds., *Transatlantic Feminisms in the Age of Revolutions* (New York: Oxford University Press, 2012), 173; Dorothy A. Mays, *Women in Early America: Struggle, Survival, and Freedom in a New World* (Santa Barbara, CA: ABC-CLIO, 2004), 447; Sharon M. Harris, "Whose Past Is It? Women Writers in Early America," *Early American Literature* 30, no. 2 (1995): 179.

34. [Esther Reed], "The Sentiments of an American Woman," *Pennsylvania Magazine of History and Biography* 18, no. 3 (1894): 361, 362.

35. This is the same logic in Deborah Sampson Gannett's "Speech Delivered with Applause," where Gannett explains what compelled her to be a crossdressing rebel soldier. Gannett, who earned a pension for her service, escaped the usual punishment for crossdressing (public humiliation), in part because of the closing section of her speech. Like Reed's pamphlet, Gannett's rhetoric couches her service in terms of patriotism and domesticity, rather than a plot to undermine her expected role as wife and mother. Deborah Sampson Gannett, *An Addr[e]ss, Delivered with Applause, at the Federal-Street Theatre, Boston, Four Successive Nights of the Different Plays, Beginning March 22, 1802 and After, at Other Principal Towns, a Number of Nights Successively at Each Place* (Dedham, MA: H. Mann, 1802).

36. [Reed], "The Sentiments of an American Woman," 363, 366.

37. Owen S. Ireland, "Esther DeBerdt Reed and Female Political Subjectivity in Revolutionary Pennsylvania: Identity, Agency, and Alienation in 1775," in *Pennsylvania's Revolution*, ed. William Pencak (University Park: Pennsylvania State University Press, 2010), 169, 173, 179.

38. Arendt, "'Ladies Going about for Money,'" 181.

39. Linda K. Kerber, *Women of the Republic: Intellect and Ideology in Revolutionary America* (Chapel Hill: University of North Carolina Press, 1980), 102.

40. Rebecca Shoemaker remained in New York until April 1782, when she returned to Philadelphia by permission of the Supreme Executive Council. She returned to New York again in April 1783 and remained there until November 1784, when she returned again to Philadelphia. Rawle, "Laurel Hill and Some Colonial Dames Who Once Lived There," 395.

41. Not all rebels supported these types of celebrations. They recognized that a mob that claimed to riot in support of independence ran the risk of making the rebels look wild, cruel, and disorganized. For more on rebel reticence during pro-revolutionary celebrations, see David Waldstreicher, *In the Midst of Perpetual Fetes: The Making of American Nationalism, 1776–1820* (Chapel Hill: University of North Carolina Press, 1997), 17–52, 35.

42. Anna Rawle to Rebecca Shoemaker, October 27, 1781, HSP. She identifies the neighbors as "Coburn and Bob Shewell." Robert Shewell, a member of the Bucks County Committee of Safety, was practically her neighbor. He lived in a house on Second Street, near Anna Rawle's grandmother's estate, the Edward Warner house on Front Street, which is where this incident took place. John W. Jordan, *Colonial and Revolutionary Families of Pennsylvania: Genealogical and Personal Memoirs* (Baltimore: Genealogical Publishing, 2004), 652–53. Although Rawle does not provide enough information to identify "Coburn" with certainty, Thomas Cobourn lived near her house. William Henry Egle, *Pennsylvania in the War of the Revolution: Associated Battalions and Militia, 1775–1783* (Harrisburg, PA: Meyers, 1890), 701.

43. Anna Rawle to Rebecca Shoemaker, October 27, 1781, "Letters and Diaries of a Loyalist Family," HSP; emphasis added.

44. Anna Rawle to Rebecca Shoemaker, October 27 [1781], "Letters and Diaries of a Loyalist Family," HSP.

45. Sarah Logan Fisher, "Sarah Logan Fisher Diaries, 1776–1795," Belfield Family Papers, HSP.

46. Anna Rawle to Rebecca Shoemaker, October 27 [1781], "Letters and Diaries of a Loyalist Family," HSP.

47. Sharon Block, *Rape and Sexual Power in Early America* (Chapel Hill: University of North Carolina Press, 2006), 38.

48. Ibid., 17.

49. Rawle does not identify Benjamin Gibbs's wife, but given that Rawle also mentions Robert Shewell jumping over a fence to light the candle that disperses the mob, it seems logical that the Benjamin Gibbs to which she refers is the Philadelphia merchant that lived nearby; that Gibbs married Hannah Shewell in 1774. "Pennsylvania Marriage Licenses, 1769–1776," *Pennsylvania Magazine of History and Biography* 41 (1917): 351.

50. Anna Rawle to Rebecca Shoemaker, October 27, 1781, "Letters and Diaries of a Loyalist Family," HSP.

51. Robert B. St. George, *Conversing by Signs: Poetics of Implication in Colonial New England Culture* (Chapel Hill: University of North Carolina Press, 1998), 206–7, 231, 243, 247, 249. To be clear, loyalists also burned the houses of rebels when loyalists occupied rebel territory.

52. Susan Klepp, "Rough Music on Independence Day, Philadelphia, 1778," in *Riot and Revelry in Early America*, ed. William Pencak, Matthew Dennis, and Simon P. Newman (University Park: Pennsylvania State University Press, 2002), 165.

53. Susan Brownmiller, *Against Our Will: Men, Women, and Rape* (New York: Bantam, 1975), 31.

54. Sabine Sielke, *Reading Rape: The Rhetoric of Sexual Violence in American Literature and Culture, 1790–1990* (Princeton, NJ: Princeton University Press, 2002), 2.

55. Block, *Rape and Sexual Power in Early America*, 230, 130, 231–32.

56. Rebecca Shoemaker to Anna Rawle, September 19, 1781, "Letters and Diaries of a Loyalist Family," HSP.

57. Rawle, "Laurel Hill and Some Colonial Dames Who Once Lived There," 406.

58. Ibid., 396.

CHAPTER FIVE: SCRIPTING PATRIOTISM

1. Rodney Mader and Elizabeth Graeme Fergusson, "Elizabeth Graeme Fergusson's 'The Deserted Wife,'" *Pennsylvania Magazine of History and Biography* 135, no. 2 (2011): 152. I also consulted the manuscript: Elizabeth Graeme Fergusson, "Il Penseroso; or, The Deserted Wife," Benjamin Rush Papers XL, Historical Society of Pennsylvania, Philadelphia. I quote from Mader's transcription, which is excellent, because it is more widely available.

2. That Joseph changed Grace's name on her land deeds is discussed in chapter 1. For Henry's manipulation of Elizabeth's rights to Graeme Park, see Anne M. Ousterhout, *The Most Learned Woman in America: A Life of Elizabeth Graeme Fergusson* (University Park: Pennsylvania State University Press, 2004), 173.

3. Ibid., 153–54.

4. Mader and Fergusson, "Elizabeth Graeme Fergusson's 'The Deserted Wife,'" 154.

5. *Oxford English Dictionary*, s.v. "Patriot."

6. Both Anne Hollingsworth Wharton and Anne M. Ousterhout have dubbed Fergusson "the most learned woman in America." Ousterhout, *The Most Learned Woman in America*, xiii; Anne Hollingsworth Wharton, *Salons Colonial and Republican* (Philadelphia: J. B. Lippincott, 1900), 13. Henry J. Young called her "more dangerous to the American cause than any other woman, except possibly Susanna Adams and Margaret Arnold." Young, "Treason and Its Punishment in Revolutionary Pennsylvania," *Pennsylvania Magazine of History and Biography* 90, no. 3 (1966): 312.

7. Ousterhout, *The Most Learned Woman*, 297, 293, 295.

8. "Copy of a Letter from the Rev. Mr. Jacob Duche, to General Washington," *Rivington's New-York Loyal Gazette*, November 29, 1777.

9. George Washington and Jacob Duché, *The Washington-Duché Letters [Being Correspondence between George Washington, Jacob Duché and Francis Hopkinson.] Now Printed, for the First Time, from the Original Manuscripts, with an Introductory Note by W. C. Ford. L.P.*, ed. Worthington Chauncey Ford and Francis Hopkinson (Brooklyn, NY: N.p., 1890), 8–9, 28–29.

10. The letters were published in *Rivington's New-York Loyal Gazette*, November 29, 1777;

New-York Gazette, and Weekly Mercury, December 1, 1777; *Pennsylvania Evening Post,* December 13, 1777; and *Pennsylvania Ledger; or, The Philadelphia Market-Day Advertiser,* December 17, 1777.

11. *Pennsylvania Evening Post,* September 30, 1780; reprinted in *Providence Gazette,* October 18, 1780.

12. Joseph Reed, *Remarks on Governor Johnstone's Speech in Parliament; with a Collection of All the Letters and Authentic Papers, Relative to His Proposition to Engage the Interest of One of the Delegates of the State of Pennsylvania, in the Congress of the United States of America, to Promote the Views of the British Commissioners* (Philadelphia: Francis Bailey, 1779), 56–57, 50

13. Reed was also the man who ordered the confiscation of Grace Growden Galloway's house in chapter 1 and Anna Rawle's house in chapter 4.

14. Reed, *Remarks on Governor Johnstone's Speech,* 9–12.

15. Reed confirms receipt of the letter from Fergusson in ibid., 17. Fergusson's letter introducing Johnstone to Reed can be found in the same text on pp. 17–18.

16. Ibid., 12, 21–22. The Pennsylvania Executive Council published the following in response to the case: "Resolved, That the contents of the said paragraphs, and the particulars in the said declaration, in the opinion of Congress, cannot but be considered as direct attempts to corrupt and bribe the Congress of the United States of America. Resolved, That as Congress feel, so they ought to demonstrate, the highest and the most pointed indignation against such daring and atrocious attempts to corrupt their integrity. Resolved, That it is incompatible with the honour of Congress to hold any manner of correspondence or intercourse with the said George Johnstone, Esq., especially to negotiate with him upon affairs in which the cause of liberty is interested." Johnstone then sailed for England in October 1778. William Bradford Reed and Joseph Reed, *Life and Correspondence of Joseph Reed, Military Secretary of Washington, at Cambridge, Adjutant-General of the Continental Army, Member of the United States, and President of the Executive Council of the State of Pennsylvania* (Philadelphia: Lindsay and Blakiston, 1847), 389, 392.

17. Ousterhout, *The Most Learned Woman,* 229.

18. Ibid., 228, 231.

19. Elizabeth Fergusson, "To the Honorable the Representatives of the Freemen of the Commonwealth of Pennsylvania in General Assembly," *Pennsylvania Gazette,* February 24, 1779. The word memorialist can mean "a petitioner" or, more generally, someone who is the author of a letter (*Oxford English Dictionary*).

20. Fergusson, "To the Honorable the Representatives of the Freemen"; emphasis added.

21. Ibid.

22. Ibid.; emphasis added.

23. Ibid.

24. Ousterhout, *The Most Learned Woman in America,* 229–31.

25. "To the Freemen of Pennsylvania," *Pennsylvania Packet,* February 6, 1779.

26. Ousterhout, *The Most Learned Woman in America,* 237–38, 137–38.

27. "To the Public" was printed in the following papers: *Pennsylvania Packet* (Philadelphia), February 20, 1779; *Continental Journal, and Weekly Advertiser* (Boston), March 11, 1779; *Providence Gazette,* March 13, 1779; *Thomas's Massachusetts Spy; or, American Oracle of Liberty* (Worcester), March 18, 1779; and *Norwich Packet*

(Norwich, CT), March 29, 1779. This letter was also reprinted in Reed, *Remarks on Governor Johnstone's Speech,* 39–52.

28. Reed, *Remarks on Governor Johnstone's Speech,* 41, 42.
29. Ibid., 43, 44.
30. Ibid., 45.
31. Ibid., 46, 47.
32. Ibid., 50.
33. Ibid.
34. Ariela R. Dubler, "In the Shadow of Marriage: Single Women and the Legal Construction of the Family and the State," *Yale Law Journal* 112, no. 7 (2003): 1664.
35. Marylynn Salmon, "The Legal Status of Women in Early America: A Reappraisal," *Law and History Review* 1, no. 1 (1983): 140.
36. Ousterhout, *The Most Learned Woman,* 243, 247, 248–50.
37. "To the Public," *Providence Gazette,* March 13, 1779. This article excerpts parts of "To the Public" and intersperses (anonymous, perhaps editorial) commentary on Fergusson's story throughout the reprint of the letter.
38. Rebecca Brannon, *From Revolution to Reunion: The Reintegration of the South Carolina Loyalists* (Columbia: University of South Carolina Press, 2016).
39. Sacvan Bercovitch, *The Cambridge Companion to American Literature* (Cambridge: Cambridge University Press, 1997), 1:339.
40. Rodney Mader assumes the poem was initially written for Henry, "perhaps as an argument or a way of stating her case," but no proof exists that she sent it to Henry or that he ever read it by any other means. Mader and Fergusson, "Elizabeth Graeme Fergusson's 'The Deserted Wife,'" 153.
41. Ibid., 156.
42. Philadelphia *General Advertiser,* March, 27, 1793.
43. Mader and Fergusson, "Elizabeth Graeme Fergusson's 'The Deserted Wife,'" 156.
44. Ibid., 160. lines 65–67.
45. Ibid., 160, lines 68, 75–83.
46. Ibid., 161.
47. Ibid., 162, lines 21–24.
48. Ibid., 163, lines 51–54.
49. Ousterhout, *The Most Learned Woman in America,* 266.
50. Mader and Fergusson, "Elizabeth Graeme Fergusson's 'The Deserted Wife,'" 171, lines 311–14.
51. Ibid., 171–72, lines 335, 337–38, 339–42, 359–60.
52. Ibid., 173.
53. Ibid., 174.
54. This section of "Il Penseroso" actually has three "letters," but the third and final one does not quite fit with the other two and may have been written after the poem was completed in "an effort to use paper efficiently." Her "Note on French Affairs" says, "The Tragedy of France has deeply occupy'd my Mind. . . . I have a decided Idea that poor Lewis XVIth did nothing that merited such a fate. . . . [That the French would] pull [his Crown] off [and] take the Head along with it. . . . These may be unfashionable Sentiments for the times But they are the Dictates of my Mind." Ibid., 175n44.

55. Ibid., 175, lines 1, 2–4; 178, lines 72, 68–69; 179, line 117.

56. Ibid., 179, lines 120–25, 126–27; 180n59; 180, lines 128–33; 182, line 217.

57. Ousterhout, *The Most Learned Woman in America,* 293, 285, 292, 310. She sold the house on April 30, 1791, to Dr. William Smith but did not move out until two years later.

AFTERWORD: SCRIPTING ELLIPSES

1. Barbara Jones, "Deborah Logan" (M.A. thesis, University of Delaware, 1964), 114–36.

2. John F. Watson, *Annals of Philadelphia, and Pennsylvania, in the Olden Time; Being a Collection of Memoirs, Anecdotes, and Incidents of the City and Its Inhabitants, and of the Earliest Settlements of the Inland Part of Pennsylvania,* ed. Willis P. Hazard (Salem, MA: Higginson, 1999); Deborah Norris Logan, *Memoir of Dr. George Logan of Stenton by His Widow Deborah Norris Logan with Selections from His Correspondence,* ed. Frances A. Logan (Philadelphia: Historical Society of Pennsylvania, 1899).

3. Ann Uhry Abrams, "Benjamin West's Documentation of Colonial History: William Penn's Treaty with the Indians," *Art Bulletin* 64, no. 1 (1982): 60.

4. John Marshall to Roberts Vaux, "To Roberts Vaux," October 6, 1831, in *The Papers of John Marshall,* vol. 12, ed. Charles F. Hobson (Chapel Hill: University of North Carolina Press, 2006), 114.

5. Kathleen A. Deagan and Jose Maria Cruxent, *Archaeology at La Isabela: America's First European Town* (New Haven, CT: Yale University Press, 2002), 87; Kathleen A. Deagan and Jose Maria Cruxent, *Columbus's Outpost among the Tainos: Spain and America at La Isabela, 1493–1498* (New Haven, CT: Yale University Press, 2002), 47, 109.

6. Harold E. Gillingham, "The Bridge over the Dock in Walnut Street," *Pennsylvania Magazine of History and Biography* 58, no. 3 (1934): 260.

7. Benjamin Kite, "Recollections of Philadelphia near Seventy Years Ago," *Pennsylvania Magazine of History and Biography* 19, no. 2 (1895): 265.

8. Judith Van Buskirk, "They Didn't Join the Band: Disaffected Women in Revolutionary Philadelphia," *Pennsylvania History: A Journal of Mid-Atlantic Studies* 62, no. 3 (1995): 323, 324.

9. Maya Jasanoff, *Liberty's Exiles: The Loss of America and the Remaking of the British Empire* (London: Harper, 2011), 13.

10. For more on loyalist reconciliation, particularly in the South, see Rebecca Brannon, *From Revolution to Reunion: The Reintegration of the South Carolina Loyalists* (Columbia: University of South Carolina Press, 2016).

11. Sarah Butler Wister, *Worthy Women of Our First Century* (Philadelphia: J. B. Lippincott, 1877), 319. She transcribed this correspondence in 1814. The Historical Society of Pennsylvania (HSP) published it in 1870–72. William Penn and James Logan, *Correspondence between William Penn and James Logan, Secretary of the Province of Pennsylvania, and Others, 1700–1750, from the Original Letters in Possession of the Logan Family,* ed. Deborah Logan and Edward Armstrong (Philadelphia: Historical Society of Pennsylvania, 1872). The HSP requested the right to publish the letters in 1825, but Deborah refused. She wrote, "I dread blame, and I want not praise." Terri L. Premo, "'Like a Being Who Does Not Belong': The Old Age of Deborah Norris Logan," *Pennsylvania Magazine of History and Biography* 107, no. 1 (1983): 108.

12. Wister, *Worthy Women of Our First Century,* 305, 214.

13. Premo, "'Like a Being Who Does Not Belong,'" 106.

14. Ibid., 87–88.

15. Jones, "Deborah Logan," vi.

16. John Adams to Benjamin Rush, April 4, 1790, in Benjamin Rush, *Letters of Benjamin Rush,* ed. L. H. Butterfield (Princeton, NJ: Princeton University Press, 1951), 2:1207.

17. Premo, "Like a Being Who Does Not Belong," 87.

18. Some of these letters are preserved in Dee Andrews and Kathryn Zabelle Derounian, "'A Dear Dear Friend': Six Letters from Deborah Norris to Sarah Wister, 1778–1779," *Pennsylvania Magazine of History and Biography* 108, no. 4 (1984): 487–516.

19. Penn and Logan, *Correspondence between William Penn and James Logan,* xlvi. Logan would often interject her own recollections about various historical events in footnotes of the correspondence she transcribed; she does so in this passage.

20. Sarah Logan Fisher, who lived near Stenton at Wakefield, which was then the home of Sarah's father, William Logan, describes Stenton's occupation during the war. Both Generals Washington and Howe boarded there. Fisher writes that "as the Americans have now possession of Stenton . . . I expect little else but that it will be destroyed, not only because we are generally known to be steady friends to government, but General Howe's having made it his Headquarters will render it more obnoxious to them, & no doubt it will be propagated that we entertained him with open heart and arms, when in reality we knew nothing of his coming till he had possession of the place, & it is more than probable, if they should have an engagement near the city & be defeated, they will endeavor in their retreat to do all the mischief in their power to these person's effects who have befriended the English." They did not destroy the house. Fisher writes that a friend checked on Stenton and "found everything safe." Sarah Logan Fisher and Nicholas B. Wainwright, "'A Diary of Trifling Occurrences': Philadelphia, 1776–1778," *Pennsylvania Magazine of History and Biography* 82, no. 4 (1958): 452, 458.

21. Wister, *Worthy Women of Our First Century,* 305–7.

22. Frederick B. Tolles, "Deborah Norris Logan," in *Notable American Women, 1607–1950: A Biographical Dictionary,* ed. Paul S. Boyer, Edward T. James, and Janet Wilson James (Cambridge, MA: Harvard University Press, 1971), 418–19.

23. Quakers were encouraged to adopt an unadorned lifestyle as part of their spiritual practice. This involved, but was not limited to, speaking without encomiums and titles, dressing simply, and eschewing materialism elsewhere in their lives. Wister, *Worthy Women of Our First Century,* 322.

24. Deborah Norris Logan, Diary, vol. 7, 1824, Logan Family Papers, 1664–1871, Historical Society of Pennsylvania, Philadelphia, 117–18 (hereafter Logan, Diary, volume, date, HSP, page number). The volume numbering is Logan's (not the HSP's). Most of the diary is at the HSP, but some of her papers are at the Library Company of Philadelphia. Some have volume numbers and/or are paginated, but some are unnumbered and/or unpaginated. I attempt to distinguish clearly between the two and provide as much identifying information as the text provides.

25. Logan, Diary, vol. 3, September 1818, HSP, 144.

26. Logan, Diary, vol. 17, December 2, 1837, HSP, n.p.

27. Logan, Diary, vol. 1, January 1, 1815, HSP, 1.

28. Ibid.

29. Benjamin Franklin, *Benjamin Franklin's Autobiography: An Authoritative Text, Backgrounds, Criticism*, ed. Joseph A. Leo Lemay and Paul M. Zall (New York: Norton, 1986), 1.

30. Deborah Norris Logan knew Benjamin Franklin and was familiar with his work. Franklin visited Stenton, as did his son, William. Logan recalled visiting a friend's home that featured rooms of Franklin's books, and Logan writes, "I could spend days there, especially if permitted to open the drawers of the Old Bureaus and Cases and examine the contents of the trunk." George Logan knew Franklin as well. George lived in Paris at the same time as Franklin, who wrote George letters of recommendation when he returned from a stay abroad in 1780. For Logan's remarks on Franklin, see Deborah Norris Logan, *Biographical Sketches of the Life and Character of Doctor George Logan*, 1821, Library Company of Philadelphia, 9–11, and Logan, Diary, vol. 3, 1818, HSP, 93. For George and Franklin's relationship, see Wister, *Worthy Women of Our First Century*, 288, 290, 298, and Jones, "Deborah Logan," 142.

31. Franklin, *Benjamin Franklin's Autobiography*, 57.

32. François Weil, "John Farmer and the Making of American Genealogy," *New England Quarterly* 80, no. 3 (2007): 413.

33. Elizabeth Ellet, *Women of the American Revolution* (1848; reprint, Carlisle, MA: Applewood Books, 2009), 22. Ellet profiles twenty-five women of the American Revolution; three of them were loyalists (four if you count Fergusson, which Ellet did not).

34. Alexander Deconde, "Historians, the War of American Independence, and the Persistence of the Exceptionalist Ideal," *International History Review* 5, no. 3 (1983): 401.

35. Sydney G. Fisher, "The Legendary and Myth-Making Process in Histories of the American Revolution," *Proceedings of the American Philosophical Society* 51, no. 204 (1912): 55–56.

36. Weil, "John Farmer and the Making of American Genealogy," 413, 407.

37. Barry Schwartz, *George Washington: The Making of an American Symbol* (Ithaca, NY: Cornell University Press, 1990), 205.

38. Deborah Norris Logan, "Deborah Norris Logan Diary, 1808–1814," Logan Family Papers, Library Company of Philadelphia, 81, 84, 85–86 (hereafter Logan, Diary, LCP, page number).

39. Logan, Diary, vol. 3, 1818, HSP. This card is pasted to the last page in her diary.

40. Fisher, "The Legendary and Myth-Making Process," 64; Mason L. Weems, *The Life of George Washington* (Philadelphia: Joseph Allen, 1837), 14. Weems first published his biography one year after Washington's death, in 1800. He added the cherry tree myth to the 1806 version of the text.

41. Weems, *The Life of George Washington*, 6.

42. Logan, Diary, LCP, 84.

43. Ibid., 87.

44. Ibid., 35.

45. Sarah Crabtree, *Holy Nation: The Transatlantic Quaker Ministry in an Age of Revolution*, (Chicago: University of Chicago Press, 2015), 104–5, 114, 122.

46. Logan, Diary, LCP, 22.

47. Logan, Diary, vol. 4, October 31, 1819, HSP, 5; Logan, Diary, vol. 9, HSP, 35; Michelle Navarre Cleary, "'America Represented by a Woman'—Negotiating Feminine and National Identity in Post-Revolutionary America," *Women's Studies* 28, no. 1 (1998): 59.

48. Wister, *Worthy Women of Our First Century,* 305–11. His actions inspired the Logan Act, which is still in effect; it forbids private citizens from negotiating with other countries in a dispute with the United States.

49. George Logan and Deborah Norris Logan, "Extract of a Letter from Doctor Logan, dated Bourdeaux, September 9, 1798, to His Wife," *Philadelphia Gazette,* November 9, 1798.

50. The "pillory" quote is Deborah Logan's paraphrase of the article, the source for which is Logan, *Memoir of Dr. George Logan of Stenton,* 80. The original letter she was writing about can be found in William Cobbett, "Logan and Wife," November 10, 1798, in *Porcupine's Works: Containing Various Writings and Selections, Exhibiting a Faithful Picture of the United States of America; of Their Governments, Laws, Politics, and Resources; of the Characters of Their Presidents, Governors, Legislators, Magistrates, and Military Men: And of the Customs, Manners, Morals, Religion, Virtues, and Vices of the People* (London: Cobbett and Morgan, 1801), 10:15–17. A few respondents considered Logan's actions in good faith. For one such letter, see James Wolf et al. "Bourdeaux, Sept. 8, 1798, to Dr. George Logan," Newark, NJ, *Centinel of Freedom,* December 4, 1798. For more on the backlash concerning George Logan's political scandal and the fallout that ensued, see Susan Branson, *These Fiery Frenchified Dames: Women and Political Culture in Early National Philadelphia* (Philadelphia: University of Pennsylvania Press, 2001), 86–99.

51. Wister, *Worthy Women of Our First Century,* 311, 314.

52. Weil, "John Farmer and the Making of American Genealogy," 414–16.

53. Rosemarie Zagarri, *Revolutionary Backlash: Women and Politics in the Early American Republic* (Philadelphia: University of Pennsylvania Press, 2007), 181. The epilogue, "Memory and Forgetting," also addresses other instances of "willful misremembering" or historical "forgetfulness" in context with the budding women's movement of the mid-nineteenth century (181–86).

54. Jones, "Deborah Logan," 55, 23.

INDEX

Page references in *italics* refer to figures.

Kacy Dowd Tillman was born and raised in Linden, Texas. She received her BA and MA in English from Baylor University and her PhD in literature from the University of Mississippi. She is currently an associate professor of English and writing and the codirector of the Honors Program at the University of Tampa, where she teaches classes on gender, cultural studies, and early American literature. She researches loyalism and early American life writing, particularly women's letters and diaries of the American Revolution, a subject about which she has published in *Early American Literature, Tulsa Studies in Women's Literature,* and *Literature of the Early American Republic.* She currently lives in Tampa, Florida, along with her husband, Andrew, and her son, Jackson.